The Political Economy of the Asia Pacific

Editor
Vinod K. Aggarwal, University of California, Berkeley

For other titles published in this series, go to
www.springer.com/series/7840

Min Gyo Koo

Island Disputes and Maritime Regime Building in East Asia

Between a Rock and a Hard Place

 Springer

Min Gyo Koo
Yonsei University
Seoul
Republic of Korea
mgkoo@yonsei.ac.kr

ISSN 1866-6507   e-ISSN 1866-6515
ISBN 978-0-387-89669-4   e-ISBN 978-0-387-89670-0
DOI 10.1007/978-0-387-89670-0
Springer Dordrecht Heidelberg London New York

Library of Congress Control Number: 2009926180

Springer is part of Springer Science+Business Media (www.springer.com)

To my parents, my wife, and my daughters

Acknowledgments

I would like to take this opportunity to express my immense gratitude to my mentors, colleagues, and family without whose support and understanding this book would never have come into being. My first mentors at Seoul National University, Professors Byung-Sun Choi and Young-Kwan Yoon, have served as exemplars of the scholar and the educator, and opened my eyes to the field of International Political Economy.

This book on East Asian island disputes was originally conceived in my dissertation, submitted to the Department of Political Science at the University of California at Berkeley. My deepest and most profound indebtedness goes to my advisors at Berkeley – Vinod K. Aggarwal, Hong Yung Lee, T.J. Pempel, and Steven K. Vogel. This book would not have existed without the wise and selfless mentorship and support of my committee chair, Vinod K. Aggarwal. His work truly set a high standard for mine. It was also my great privilege to work for him as Project Director at the Berkeley APEC Study Center (BASC) during my tenure as a graduate student. I would also like to thank Hong Yung Lee, T.J. Pempel, and Steven K. Vogel for having generously contributed their time to reading a number of earlier versions of this book. They imparted on me many aspects of the best tradition of East Asian studies.

This book also benefited from constructive and insightful comments from my teachers and colleagues on both sides of the Pacific. Beth A. Simmons had helped me to shape this research agenda in its early stage before she left Berkeley for Harvard. Yong-chool Ha of the University of Washington in Seattle and Chung-in Moon of Yonsei University also provided me with their valuable insights into East Asian international relations. John Doces, Ralf Emmers, Stephan Haggard, Chaibong Hahm, Evan Harrje, Takashi Inoguchi, Patrick James, David Kang, Myung-Koo Kang, Saori Katada, Bum-soo Kim, Seungjoo Lee, Kun-chin Lin, Kyung-Hwan Mo, John Ravenhill, Peter Rosendorff, Akihiko Tanaka, and Keiichi Tsunekawa also contributed to their time and energy to this book in various ways.

My more recent colleagues at Yonsei University, including Tae Ho Eom, Yeon-Seob Ha, Yong Suk Jang, Whasun Jho, T. J. Lah, Sam Youl Lee, Yeonho Lee, M. Jae Moon, Yul Sohn, and Jae-jin Yang provided me with intellectual stimulation and much-needed encouragement. The work of graduate research assistants at Yonsei proved crucial during the final stages of this book. I specially thank Eunjin Koo and Yooshik Hong for their excellent assistance.

Generous financial support from various institutions greatly contributed to the completion of this book. I am very grateful to the Institute of East Asian Studies and the Center for Korean Studies at UC Berkeley, both of which generously provided me with research funds during my dissertation's final stages. I also owe my deep gratitude to the Center for International Studies and the Korean Studies Institute at the University of Southern California, where I served as Postdoctoral Research Fellow for two years. In addition, I appreciate the generous financial support from Yonsei University and the Korea Foundation.

During the editorial and production process, I have been particularly fortunate to have the benefit of steadfast support from Niels Peter Thomas and Jon Gurstelle of Springer. I am deeply grateful to Vinod K. Aggarwal for seeing the merit of this book as part in the series entitled *The Political Economy of the Asia Pacific* that he has edited for Springer.

Finally, my parents, my sister, and my brother have earned my deepest gratitude for their unwavering love and faith in me since I decided to pursue a career in academia. Last but not least, I would like to thank, my wife, Eunhee, and my daughters, Yoonji and Sooji, for their utmost patience and affection through my journey to this book.

Seoul, Korea   Min Gyo Koo

Abbreviations

AMF	Asian Monetary Fund
APEC	Asia-Pacific Economic Cooperation
APT	ASEAN Plus Three
ARF	ASEAN Regional Forum
ASEAN	Association of Southeast Asian Nations
ASEM	Asia–Europe Meeting
CCOP	Committee for Coordination of Joint Prospecting for Mineral Resources in Asian Offshore Areas
CCP	Chinese Communist Party
CINC	Composite Index of National Capability
COW	Correlates of War
CPR	Common Pool Resource
EEZ	Exclusive Economic Zone
FTA	Free Trade Agreement
GATT	General Agreement on Tariffs and Trade
ICJ	International Court of Justice
IGO	Intergovernmental Organization
IHO	International Hydrographic Organization
IMF	International Monetary Fund
ITLOS	International Tribunal for the Law of the Sea
JDZ	Joint Development Zone
JFZ	Joint Fishing Zone
KCIA	Korean Central Intelligence Agency
LDP	Liberal Democratic Party
NATO	North Atlantic Treaty Organization
NM	Nautical Mile
ODA	Official Development Assistance
OLS	Ordinary Least Squares
PFT	Peace and Friendship Treaty
PLA	People's Liberation Army
PLAN	People's Liberation Army Navy
PMZ	Provisional Measure Zone
PTA	Preferential Trading Agreement

SCAPIN	Supreme Commander for the Allied Powers Instruction
TAC	Treaty of Amity and Cooperation
TD	Trade Dependence
TZ	Transitional Zone
UN	United Nations
UNCLOS	United Nations Convention on the Law of the Sea
UNECAFE	United Nations Economic Commission for Asia and the Far East
UPU	Universal Postal Union
WTO	World Trade Organization

Contents

List of Figures

List of Tables

List of Maps

Chapter 1
East Asian Island and Maritime Disputes in a World of Globalization

1.1 The Puzzle

East Asia is home to many of the world's most vexing territorial disputes.[1] The territories in dispute need not cover the entire soil of a particular state, as in the cases of the two Chinas and the two Koreas, in order to seriously strain interstate relationships. Even small, barely habitable islands and rocks in semi-enclosed waters like the East Sea/Sea of Japan, the East and the South China Sea can be the most persistent and explosive bone of contention. The danger of conflict escalation looms particularly large during a global shortage of energy and marine resources. All the energy-hungry littoral states in the region eye the high potential of oil and gas deposits in the vicinity of the disputed islands. They also rely on contested offshore areas to provide a large portion of their marine diets. Yet material concerns are hardly the sole drivers of the island disputes in East Asia. Many of the disputed areas raise questions of national identity and pride, thereby feeding territorial nationalism following the end of ideology in contemporary East Asia.

The distinction between territorial disputes and other types of interstate disputes is not always straightforward. At one level, one may regard a significant portion of interstate disputes as having a territorial component. Most obvious are conflicts over the delineation of land borders, as occurred between China and India (1962) and China and the Soviet Union (1969). More problematic are cases involving disputes over resources – for example, the scramble for the numerous islands in the South China Sea – when control over those resources is linked with control over the

---

[1] In East Asia, there are at least thirty-five territorial dyads contiguous on land or within 400 nautical miles (the sum of two hypothetical countries' 200 nautical mile exclusive economic zones) of water between their undisputed land territories. Many of these dyads have outstanding territorial disagreements with each other: China–Taiwan, China–Japan, China–Vietnam, China–Philippines, North Korea–South Korea, South Korea–Japan, Japan–Russia, Philippines–Taiwan, Thailand–Myanmar, Thailand–Cambodia, and Cambodia–Vietnam, among others.

M.G. Koo, *Island Disputes and Maritime Regime Building in East Asia,*
The Political Economy of the Asia Pacific,
DOI 10.1007/978-0-387-89670-0_1, © Springer Science+Business Media, LLC 2009

territory in which they are located. Even more difficult to distinguish are ethnic, religious, or ideological conflicts when such differences are intimately connected to specific territories, such as the Sino–Vietnamese War of 1979 and archipelago-wide secessionist movements and religious violence in Indonesia.

An ideal definition of territorial disputes must distinguish between disputes that are primarily over territory and those that merely have a territorial component. In reality, much of how an analyst views different kinds of territorial disputes is determined by the breadth of one's definition of the phenomenon (Diehl 1999: xii–xiii). Some analysts focus exclusively on one type of territorial dispute: the delineation of an international border, referred to as a "positional" dispute by Kratochwil, Rohrlich, and Mahajan (1985). Kocs (1995) makes the distinction between previously resolved and never-resolved disputes. Even when territorial claims are ongoing and competing, not all of them involve the threat of militarized action or the actual escalation of the conflict beyond the militarized threshold.

In order to capture the wide variance in East Asian island disputes as much as possible, I adopt a relatively broad yet precise definition used by Paul Huth. Huth (1996: 19) defines interstate territorial disputes as cases of governments' disagreement over the location of a border, either land or maritime. Territorial disputes may take place when one government occupies the national territory of another and refuses to relinquish control or withdraw; when one government does not recognize the sovereignty of another over some portion of territory within the border of that government; or when a government does not recognize the independence and sovereignty of another government, and seeks to annex some or all of its territory. Therefore, the secessionist movements between governments and various ethnic and religious groups, particularly in Southeast Asia and in some parts of mainland China, are excluded in this definition.

Overlapping claims to the same territory have historically contributed to violent interstate conflict, persistently causing warfare for over 360 years of the modern nation-state system since the Peace of Westphalia in 1648 (Holsti 1991; Goertz and Diehl 1992; Vasquez 1993; 2001; Kocs 1995; Hensel 1996; Huth 1996; Senese 1996; Diehl 1999; Vasquez and Henehan 2001; Senese and Vasquez 2003). In the wake of superpower confrontation between the U.S. and the Soviet Union, territorial quarrels at the regional level seemed to have been muted significantly. Yet territorial disputes have survived the Cold War and remain an important source of conflict (Kolodziej and Kanet 1996). For example, one study shows that among the 292 international conflicts that took place between 1945 and 1995, 122 involved territorial disputes – by far the largest category (Bercovitch and Jackson 1997).

In this book, I focus on the three most prominent island disputes in East Asia: the dispute in the East Sea/Sea of Japan over a small group of islets known as *Dokdo* in Korea and as *Takeshima* in Japan (hereinafter referred to as the "Dokdo" dispute), the dispute in the East China Sea over a group of rocky outcroppings known as *Senkaku Retto* in Japan and *Diaoyutai* in China (hereinafter referred to as the "Senkaku" dispute), and the dispute in the South China Sea over the Paracel and Spratly archipelago. Coupled with their material values, the centrality of territory in national identity formation suggests that the disputes over these islands are highly contentious and intractable, although their likelihood to spark full-scale militarized conflict and strategic instability are fairly low. By thoroughly analyzing the underlying causes of recurrent disputes, this book aims to offer a contribution to the understanding and further elaboration of the basic principles of East Asian maritime regime building.[2]

The Dokdo issue first emerged in the 1950s when South Korea established its *de facto* control over the islands. In the first half of the 1960s, the island question continued to serve as one of the most contentious bilateral problems, threatening to wreck the conclusion of the South Korea–Japan normalization treaty in its final stage of negotiations. The sovereignty question surfaced again in 1977–78 when the Japanese government proclaimed new exclusive fishing zones in the East Sea/ Sea of Japan. After a relatively calm interlude, the sovereignty question flared up again in 1996–1998 when South Korea and Japan both demonstrated unusually hard line territorial and maritime policies. In 2004–05, the Dokdo dispute seriously strained the relationship between Seoul and Tokyo, as demonstrated by the controversies over South Korea's Dokdo postage stamps and Japan's designation of "Takeshima Day."

The Senkaku dispute has unfolded in five distinct rounds of diplomatic clashes in the postwar period. The Chinese had not clearly challenged the Japanese claim to the islands until 1968 when a high potential of oil and gas deposits were found in the vicinity of the islands. The diplomatic spat over the islands intensified when the U.S. agreed to return them to Japan in 1971 along with the Okinawa Islands. This very first dispute in 1968–1971 was followed by four successive rounds of challenge-the-status-quo in 1978, 1990–91, 1996–97, and 2004–05.

Finally, a number of military and diplomatic skirmishes have marked the South China Sea, but the most important bilateral disputes have taken place between China and Vietnam over the Paracel and Spratly Islands. In the eyes of China and Vietnam, the offshore island disputes have not been an isolated issue from the very beginning. Since its gradual initiation in the 1950s, the Paracel and Spratly dispute has evolved through three violent rounds of clashes in 1974, 1978–79, and 1987–88. In contrast to other East Asian island disputes, military action has been a viable option to resolve the sovereignty issue in the South China Sea.

As summarized above, disputant countries have engaged in varied patterns of diplomatic and military behaviors when dealing with these island disputes. In some cases, one can find examples of the aggressive use of military force and intransigent bargaining strategies, while in others military inaction and accommodative diplomacy are equally evident. When and why do disputants pursue conflictual policies? Conversely, why do they at other times seek the containment, if not the resolution, of territorial disputes by shelving thorny sovereignty issues?

---

[2] Unless otherwise noted, I use the Korean and Japanese names to refer to the disputed islands in the East Sea/Sea of Japan and the East China Sea, respectively, because the two countries exercise *de facto* control over the respective islands.

Within the realist camp, the territorial explanation of conflict and war presented by John Vasquez maintains that territorial disputes have a greater probability of getting into militarized conflict and war than other types of disputes. This approach assumes that "human territoriality" is responsible for the division of the Earth into territorial units, serving as the underlying cause of war between competitive territorial entities (Vasquez 1993: 140–1). The territorial explanation of interstate conflict sees the outbreak of war as a process in which an initial crisis or militarized dispute creates a certain level of hostility that quite often is insufficient to result in war, especially among prudent and powerful actors. As disputes repeat, however, states may learn from their previous interactions with their opponent that war is the best, or perhaps the only, way of handling the situation facing them (Brecher and Wilkenfeld 1997; Senese and Vasquez 2003: 278).

For this reason, it would be expected that when disputes recur, there is a greater probability of a war ensuing. This implies that territory does not immediately produce war, but rather sets off a chain of events that eventually result in war. In other words, territorial issues, while they may increase the risk of war, will only lead to war depending on how they are handled in the practices of power politics. Such practices include the threat, display, and use of force, the making of alliances, and the building up of one's military to increase power (Vasquez 1993; Hensel 1998; Senese and Vasquez 2003: 277–8).

Can territorial explanations of conflict and war hold in a world of globalization? The liberal view of territory poses a challenge to such a realist perspective, both conceptually and empirically. In a liberal rendering, it is plausible that the simple act of communication to sustain interstate relations could possibly pave the way to international cooperation by increasing people's knowledge of others and their ways, customs, practices, and concerns (Deutsch 1953; 1957; 1968; Haas 1958; 1964; 1990; Mitrany 1976; Stein 1993). According to Deutsch (1957), states can be "integrated to the point that they have a sense of community, which in turn creates assurance that they will settle their differences short of war" (quoted in Adler and Barnett 1998: 3). When benign security cultures converge, when interests are interpreted in a similar way, and when cooperative institutions abound, states may form "security communities" or "regional zones of peace" (Katzenstein 1996; Solingen 1998). For liberals, therefore, states can overcome the security dilemma if war becomes an unthinkable possibility (Mueller 1989: 240).

The sociological constructivist variant of liberal vision goes a step further, envisaging a post-statist, cosmopolitical world order in which pacifying forms of political representation are not tied exclusively to territorial statehood (Linklater 1982; 1990; Archibugi and Held 1995; Held 1995; Franceschet 2002).[3] For the adherents of "cosmopolitan democracy" theory, the failings and limitations of classical liberal

---

[3] Several ideational elements inherent in the cosmopolitical world order can be identified: (1) shared identities, values, and meanings (intersubjectivity); (2) interconnectedness among its members; and (3) dense communication networks that help take partners' preferences into account (Risse-Kappen 1995; Adler and Barnett 1998).

views are rooted in the inability of sovereign states and statist intergovernmental institutions to meet the growing demands for global justice and peace.[4] For example, James Rosenau (1997) attacks the state-centered paradigm of international relations theory, promoting the "transnationalization of world politics." From this perspective, the erosion of the state's actual autonomy due to globalization is apparent and significant, and the increased transborder flows of goods, money, and cultural commodities attest to the increased power of nonstate transnational actors. Adler and Haas (1992) and Haas (1992) conceptualize such transnational "epistemic communities" and theorize about the relationship between consensual knowledge and power.

Using a territorial bargaining game approach, this book examines whether or not a greater approximation of complex interdependence would lead to a decrease, if not an end, to territorial politics. Consistent with the conventional wisdom, I find that the combination of resource competition, fluid geopolitics, and unstable domestic power dynamics has invariably brought about the initiation and escalation of island disputes. I find little evidence that supports the mitigating influence of intergovernmental organizations on these disputes. More broadly, there is little systematic evidence that the transnational global society has overtaken the world of territorial states in East Asia. Yet I demonstrate that increasing economic interaction has played a pacific role in containing, if not resolving, intractable territorial disputes in East Asia. Indeed, the pacific influence of economic interdependence has repeatedly prevented the sovereignty disputes from escalating into a full-scale diplomatic and/or military crisis.

This finding concerning the pacific influence of economic interdependence is of great significance both theoretically and practically. In the postwar period, most notably since China adopted its reform policy in 1978, the economic integration of East Asian countries has been truly remarkable, as manifested by soaring intraregional flows of trade, capital, long-term investments, and technology. The rapid economic integration of East Asian countries has led to a burgeoning interest in the "liberal peace" debate about whether or not economic interdependence fosters peaceful relations by giving states an economic incentive to avoid costly disputes. Liberals would argue that maritime disputes in East Asia remain a potential source of conflict, but that their salience has seen a steady decline due to increasing

---

[4] The sociological constructivist approach is predicated on a unique assumption of international anarchy, which is inherently different from its realist and classical liberal counterparts. Wendt (1999) suggests three cultures of anarchy – Hobbesian (realist), Lockean (classical liberal), and Kantian (sociological constructivist): (1) Hobbesian anarchy is the least stable among the three, since it is populated by revisionist states which seek to maximize power by conquering each other's territory. Conflict is therefore the norm rather than the exception; (2) Lockean anarchy is populated by *status quo* states that usually respect each other's sovereignty. The institution of sovereignty makes security less scarce, so *status quo* states are less likely to go to war against each other, unless trapped in a serious security dilemma; and (3) in Kantian anarchy, states share substantial collective identities, which prevent them from worrying about their survival and security. Observation of the rule of law in settling their disputes makes security abundant in a Kantian world, as long as states have internalized the legal principles.

economic interdependence, while realists would remain skeptical about the mitigating influence of economic interdependence (Shirk and Twomey 1996; Harris and Mack 1997; Mochizuki 1998; Wan 2003).

1.2   Conventional Explanations

Despite the present rise of globalization, nowhere is the significance of territorial states more evident than in East Asia. In East Asia, waves of globalization and the rise of the post-Cold War order have not yet eroded practices of the traditional notion of Westphalian sovereignty, broadly defined as immunity from external interference that the state enjoys in its domestic structure of authority. Not surprisingly, the naked pursuit of state sovereignty often results in contestation over territory, over political integrity, and even over international recognition among East Asian countries (Moon and Chun 2003).

The enduring territorial disputes in East Asia can be characterized in various ways, but four features are particularly important: (1) despite the frequent resort to the past to justify their contemporary claims to contested territory, most disputes originated in colonial times during the late nineteenth and early twentieth centuries, often exacerbated by the arbitrary map-making of colonial powers and exploited by postcolonial nationalists; (2) in contrast to other parts of the world, few territorial disputes have been formally resolved, and very few target states, whose territorial claim is challenged by revisionist states, recognize the existence of disputes at all, preventing claimant countries from engaging in negotiations; (3) a periodic pattern exists in the iteration of disputes, repeating between initiation, escalation, and de-escalation, if not termination; and (4) nevertheless, recurring crises have rarely increased the levels of escalation and hostility beyond control.

We can characterize existing explanations for East Asian island disputes in three categories: (1) the first accounts for the disputes' ongoing nature and motivations for dispute escalation; (2) the second examines the factors that account for the mutual restraint that has repeatedly been shown in past disputes; and (3) the third attempts to account for periodic patterns of dispute escalation and de-escalation. It is notable that, despite their partial explanatory utility, none of these traditional accounts fully explain the patterns we see.

1.2.1   Explanations for Continuity and Escalation

In this category of work, some arguments are based directly or indirectly on historical and cultural approaches to international relations. Symbolic attachment of territory to national identity and pride often makes territorial conflicts all the more intractable and difficult to resolve. This can be the case even when pragmatic solutions – for example, setting aside sovereignty claims in favor of shared ownership – may appear applicable in theory. From this perspective, China's growing irredentist tendency, combined with Japan's habit of glossing over its war past, increases the likelihood of territorial conflicts by fueling nationalist sentiments in its neighbors (Suganuma 2000; Suzuki 2007).

Other accounts within this category treat East Asian island disputes as a result of competition for locations of strategic and economic value. At a time of volatile oil prices, this view contends that island disputes have unfolded as an issue of resource nationalism concerning hydrocarbon potential. Another tangible value of disputed areas lies in their potential to be bases for air and naval operations. Given the growing economic and strategic value of disputed maritime areas, this perspective predicts that East Asian countries are likely to pursue maximal territorial demands frequently backed by the threat or use of force (Park 1973; O'Brien 1977; Roy 1994; Valencia 1995; 2000; Calder 1996; 1997; Ahmad 1997; Catley and Keliat 1997; Valencia et al. 1997; Kim 2000; Meconis and Wallace 2000; Mearsheimer 2001; Kenny 2004).

The validity of contending historical evidence – such as government documents and maps – provides a near constant source of turbulence at sea. Differing interpretations of international treaties – ranging from the 1895 Treaty of Shimonoseki to the 1951 San Francisco Peace Treaty – also serve as sources of heated debate (Hara 2001). The global trend to adopt the United Nations Convention on the Law of the Sea (UNCLOS) further complicated the picture in East Asian seas, as most countries in the region ratified it. Negotiations with one another over how to delimit the overlapping claims of their respective 200 nm EEZs near the disputed islands became the hottest area of contention. Yet, none of the claimant countries present conclusive evidence of territorial and maritime boundaries, which in turn becomes a constant source of differences (Park 1973; Cheng 1974; Buzan 1978; Haller-Trost 1990; Charney 1995; Matsui 1997; Valencia et al. 1997; Austin 1998; Djalal and Townsend-Gault 1999; Kim 1999; Kim 2000; Kim 2004; Donaldson and Williams 2005). Whether or not they are ever submitted to international judiciary bodies such as the International Court of Justice (ICJ) and the International Tribunal for the Law of the Sea (ITLOS), or otherwise resolved in accordance with international law, it is inevitable that international legal principles affect the way in which East Asian territorial disputes are argued and dealt with.

In sum, most explanations in this category of work predict that East Asian island disputes would likely continue and escalate, as long as both material and symbolic, as well as legal and historical, issues remain unresolved. However, these claims do not stand up to scrutiny, as all the previous flare-ups have eventually been calmed rather than further escalating out of control.

1.2.2 Explanations for Mutual Restraint

In contrast to the first category of work, structural accounts explain why the tensions surrounding maritime areas have not spun out of control. From this perspective, the island disputes in East Asia almost certainly involve the U.S. as a hegemonic power balancer. Through its alliance and commitment to defend Japan, the U.S. has allowed Japan to avoid direct confrontation with China, thus ensuring that Sino–Japanese disputes (as well as other regional conflicts) take place within certain confines (Blanchard 2000; Hara 2001; Lind 2004).[5] However, U.S. preponderance has not necessarily facilitated a Pax Americana. The pacific role of the U.S. vis-à-vis East Asian island disputes remains inherently limited. The U.S. government has taken a neutral stance over those disputes, claiming that America's involvement could in no way prejudice any underlying claims and that any conflicting claims are a matter for resolution by the parties concerned (Park 1973: 233; Hara 2001: 376–80).

Furthermore, existing structural accounts for mutual restraint do not adequately capture the rise of China as the biggest source of structural uncertainty in contemporary East Asia. Although not all draw worst-case conclusions about a nascent China threat, uncertainty about the ways in which a more capable China would employ its power has made everyone scramble (Friedberg 2005; Goldstein 2005; Christensen 2006). During the Cold War period, the U.S. and the Soviet Union both had geopolitical interests of their own, but not territorial ambitions. In stark contrast, China presents a different landscape for the future of East Asian territorial disputes since it has both geopolitical and territorial ambitions.[6]

1.2.3 Explanations for Repeated Ups and Downs

To better understand the repeated ups and downs of East Asian island disputes, the third category of work opens up the black box of the domestic decision-making process. From this perspective, the timing, and the manner in which dispute escalation has taken place, have been driven by domestic actors, especially state elites and opposition groups, who attempt to defend and enhance domestic legitimacy and public support for their regime or particular policy goals. Many scholars in this camp thus explore how state elites' desire to remain in office allows domestic

---

[5] Most East Asian island disputes have evolved under the so-called San Francisco System, which has served as the backbone of the Cold War system in the region since a peace treaty between the U.S. and Japan was concluded in San Francisco in 1951. The San Francisco Peace Treaty sowed the seeds of many of the sovereignty questions since it did not specify to which country Japan renounced its former colonial territories or define the precise limits of these territories, leaving a web of competing claims across the region (Hara 2001; Calder 2004).

[6] The evidence is mixed on China's territorial ambitions. Alastair Ian Johnston (1998: 1–30) contends that China was more likely to resort to force when disputes involve territory and occur during periods in which the perceived gap between ascribed and desired international status is large or growing. However, M. Taylor Fravel (2005: 46–83) argues that China has been more cooperative and peaceful in its territorial disputes than is commonly believed. He finds that China has participated in twenty-three unique disputes with its neighbors on land and at sea since 1949, of which it has settled seventeen peacefully.

coalitions and/or electoral politics to influence their decisions on conflict behavior (Downs and Saunders 1998/1999; Deans 2000; Bong 2002; Chung 2004; Fravel 2005; Hagström 2005).

At a time of legitimacy deficit, state elites in some East Asian countries have indeed shown a tendency to resort to aggressive territorial policies in order to capitalize on nationalist and irredentist sentiments. For instance, in the early stage of the 1996 flare-up, the Chinese government supported the public who were upset by the landings of Japanese ultranationalists on the disputed islands. In the wake of a series of anti-Japanese protests in China, Vice-Premier Zhu Rongji strongly accused Japan of failing to comprehend China's sensitivity over the islands issue, presumably in order to display his patriotism. In the middle of the 1996 flare-up, Japanese Prime Minister Ryutaro Hashimoto and his party cohorts were not in a position to show a conciliatory attitude either, as they faced a general election on October 20, 1996. Conversely, when political leaders in rival countries enjoy a surplus in political capital or face no major elections, they may take a more pragmatic stance to promote tangible diplomatic and economic gains. During his tenure after 1978, for instance, Deng Xiaoping reiterated China's claim to the islands, but recognized that it was dangerous to press Japan too hard on the territorial front. He believed that cooperation with Japan was critical not only for China's economic development, but also for his own domestic power position. Taken together, these explanations provide important insights. When forced to choose, political leaders in East Asia tend to pursue economic gains at the expense of their nationalist credentials. Yet, what is striking in this category of work is that few studies have been clearly linked to international relations theories that can help generalize such findings.

1.2.4 Summary

The analysis of East Asian territorial disputes bears directly upon the future of peace and stability in the region. Yet a number of existing studies tend to treat each dispute as a discrete and unique event, subject to the dynamics of the bilateral relationship in question alone. They have explored individual disputes in depth, but rarely compare one dispute to another or to the broader international relations literature on territorial disputes. Despite the growing significance of international boundaries, the systematic study of East Asian territorial disputes in general has not received any attention either by area specialists or by broader scholarship in international relations.

As a result, the existing studies of East Asian territorial disputes all share several spatial and thematic limitations. They examine only a portion of East Asian territorial disputes in a particular time and space, thereby making the conclusions tentative and ungeneralizable. For example, the historical and legal issues surrounding the Senkaku dispute in the late 1960s are not compared with those of the Spratly dispute in the 1980s; the limited use of force over the Dokdo Islands in the 1950s is not juxtaposed with the intensive use of force over the Paracel Islands in the 1970s.

In addition, the arguments in these studies have not been integrated either in international relations theory or in more general literature on territorial disputes in other regions. Put in a different way, East Asian territorial disputes have received little attention by broader scholarship in international relations and territorial disputes despite their analytical and practical importance. Also, surprisingly little scholarly attention has been paid to the influence of complex economic interdependence between disputant countries on their enduring territorial disputes. Although there have been some burgeoning interests in the pacific effect of economic interdependence on East Asia's key flashpoints, few studies have been dedicated to territorial disputes as a distinct category of regional conflicts.

In sum, despite their explanatory utility, none of the existing explanations alone presents a coherent account of the dual nature of continuity and mutual restraint in East Asian territorial disputes. Neither realist nor historical/cultural accounts capture the restrained nature, although they may be useful for explaining the continuity. While international legal scholarship provides rich information about the legal aspects of contemporary disputes, it does not attempt to explain the political and economic barriers that prevent East Asian countries from seeking legal settlements. The empirical findings of the domestic power politics perspective vis-à-vis the dual aspect of East Asian territorial disputes are mixed at best. The unsatisfactory nature of existing explanations calls for a more comprehensive approach that can take a broader comparative and international perspective into account.

1.3   Research Strategy

The major challenge in putting together this study is to provide a systematic account of the transition between, and the conclusion of, repeated rounds of maritime disputes in East Asia and to guide actions for the future for scholars and statesmen alike. Using a territorial bargaining game perspective as a guiding conceptual framework, I approach this issue both quantitatively and qualitatively. I first test the hypotheses generated by the territorial bargaining game framework using ordinary least squares (OLS) and binary logistic regression techniques. Then, I explore the three prominent island disputes in an in-depth, qualitative manner. In this section, I sketch out the dependent and independent variables of this book.

1.3.1   The Dependent Variable: Intensity of Dispute

Various international conflicts range from verbal disputes (e.g., diplomatic rebukes) to outright military showdowns and wars. Most scholars agree that there tends to be a temporal sequence between mild rhetorical disputes and intensive wars (Snyder and Diesing 1977; Brecher 1993; Brecher and Wilkenfeld 1997). Put differently, territorial disputes involve various stages and when seen in isolation, each of these phases can be characterized by its own set of traits attributable to the sequence of relationship phases that have preceded the one being looked at presently. Decisions or circumstances that have guided a set of relations in the past may have an important impact on the features associated with present and future events (Senese and Vasquez 2003: 276).

In defining the dependent variable, I focus on the annual variation in the process of the three island disputes between three pairs of countries: South Korea and Japan, Japan and China, and China and Vietnam. Yet the lines between each stage may not always be clearly defined. In terms of operationalizing the outcome variable, the crucial question is where to draw the lines between given dyad-years. That is, what degree of behavior do we classify visible or invisible territorial claims as an act of initiation, escalation, militarized confrontation, or de-escalation? Drawing upon Zeev Maoz's Correlates of War (COW)-revised Dyadic Militarized Interstate Dispute (MID) dataset (DYMID 1.1), supplemented by a comprehensive island dispute chronology that I have collected, I use a five-point scale, categorical measure to code the highest level of hostility reached in a given territorial dyad-year.[7]

According to the coding scheme, cases are coded with a value of 0 if pairs of countries have minimal or no diplomatic/political conflict over a specific territory. This category also includes cases where disputes are being negotiated for a settlement or stalemated with no apparent adverse effect on bilateral relations between dispute dyads.[8] Cases are coded with a value of 1 if the dyad-year experiences the occurrence of a dispute in a challenge-the-status-quo stage, where a challenger country starts actively pressing its claim against a target country through hostile rhetoric and public recriminations, often preceded by some unexpected minor incidents. An escalation of challenge-the-status quo stage may ensue when either challenger or target country seizes civilians in the disputed areas, or uses the threat or show of force to reinforce its territorial claim. In this stage, disputants may use sanctions or restrictions on bilateral diplomatic, economic, or military ties (coded with a value of 2). Cases are coded with a value of 3 if there are mild physical clashes or isolated incidents between police and armed forces. If the circumstances stop escalating, a de-escalation of challenge-the-status-quo stage ensues, followed by either a stalemate stage or diplomatic negotiations to settle territorial differences (coded with a value of 0). If the circumstances continue to escalate, a military escalation may follow with an outbreak of a MID or a full-fledged war (coded with a value of 4).

---

[7] A MID is defined as "a set of interactions between or among states involving threats to use military force, displays of military force, or actual uses of military force" (Gochman and Maoz 1984: 586). The MID dataset permits researchers to measure the occurrence of MIDs, as well as several characteristics of these events.

[8] In terms of underlying intentions, "holding talks" and "doing nothing" may be substantively different from each other: holding talks might signify an attempt to resolve the territorial issue cooperatively, whereas doing nothing implies maintaining one's territorial claim without escalating or compromising. In terms of the visibility and intensity of dispute, however, both concepts can be treated in the same category, since neither involves visibly violent conflict behavior (Huth 1996).

Using this coding scheme, I construct a dataset of the three island disputes since their initiation in the 1950s and 1960s. At the bilateral level, unfortunately, there is no single source that lists the evolutionary process of East Asian territorial disputes other than the COW-revised Dyadic MID dataset, which itself requires substantial updates and enhancements. As a result, I consult a broad range of sources. In classifying different levels and stages of hostility reached in a given dyad-year, I require confirmation of a dispute and its process from at least two different scholarly sources. In general, it is not difficult to identify conflicts when public statements are issued by state leaders that a dispute exists, or when physical conflict takes place. Nevertheless, there will undoubtedly be some debate and questions concerning the coding of specific cases. For example, only limited documentation is available for less publicized periods and disputes between former and current communist regimes – namely China before 1978 and Vietnam before 1986. In such cases, different scores in the coding will be assigned to see if they make any significant difference in the results.

1.3.2 The Independent Variables

Building upon the studies of Aggarwal (1998) and Huth and Allee (2002), I construct a territorial bargaining game approach to more systematically analyze the evolution of the three island disputes and to draw broad policy implications. As Schelling (1980: 89) notes, territory involves "mixed motive games," which can be characterized as having elements of "mutual dependence, and conflict, of partnership and competition." Realists spell out quite well the competitive elements in territory, which may have symbolic, political, economic, historical, or other kinds of significance that make it difficult for states to give it up. By contrast, for many liberals, territory is becoming a less significant obstacle to international cooperation and peace, while some constructivist variants anticipate a "borderless world" as opposed to a system of "territorial states" (Simmons 2003: 11).

As detailed in Chapter 2, I conceptualize a territorial bargaining game process as consisting of several distinct stages as well as explanatory components associated with the development of each stage over time. A territorial bargaining game approach begins by identifying *initial impetus* – either international or domestic – for a territorial change from the prevailing *status quo* over some territorial issue(s). The examples of initial impetuses include post-colonial independence, the UNCLOS, military coups, and ultranationalist activities.

The initial impetus often creates certain types of externalities that affect the value of territory concerned, which can be divided into tangible and intangible dimensions. The initial impetus and subsequent changes in the value of territory often lead to contending territorial nationalism, particularly when disputant countries harbor a perception of enduring rivalry with each other. Yet the rise of territorial nationalism alone falls short of uncovering the causal links behind conflict behaviors. In reality, countries may respond in various ways based on their *individual bargaining situations*, consisting of their (1) complex economic interdependence; (2) geopolitical postures; (3) domestic power dynamics; and (4) regional and global contexts of intergovernmental organizations.

A *challenge-the-status-quo stage* is initiated if a challenger country registers its revisionist claim and a target country responds with a countermeasure. If either country initiates a threat or use of force, then a *military escalation stage* ensues. By contrast, if both countries choose not to risk a large-scale conflict, they may enter into a *negotiations stage*. If either a military or diplomatic settlement is reached, the dispute may end; otherwise, the dispute will continue in a *stalemate stage*, thereby leading to another round of challenge-the-status-quo.

Many of these components of a territorial bargaining game are not novel. Yet the innovation here is that this approach allows us to consider simultaneously both independent and interactive effects of individual components on the different stages of a territorial dispute. Also, economic interdependence is a new, important addition to a bargaining game approach. This general analytical framework is broad enough to incorporate key factors that affect territorial disputes, but narrowly focused enough to generate reasonable explanations and useful predictions on the future direction of maritime disputes in East Asia.

The three island disputes that will be examined in more detail in the following chapters clearly illustrate the repeated process of a territorial bargaining game, while neither reaching peaceful resolutions nor escalating into full-scale militarized conflicts. The evidence presented in this study shows that the combination of growing resource competition, increasingly fluid geopolitics, and the tenacious and pernicious presence of competing nationalisms has had an enduring influence on the initiation and escalation of the recurring rounds of the challenge-the-status-quo stages. More intriguingly, I find that the pacifying influence of economic interdependence has repeatedly mitigated the aggravating circumstances, making it a convenient strategy for most territorial disputant countries to continue to shelve the final resolution of their disputes in favor of improving their bilateral economic relations.

1.4 Plan of the Book

Chapter 2 elucidates the explanatory components of a territorial bargaining game in more detail. The territorial bargaining game approach begins by identifying initial impetuses for a territorial change from the prevailing territorial *status quo*. Initial impetuses affect the provision of certain type of goods, ranging from public to private. Competitive territorial entities respond to such initial impetuses and subsequent changes in the provision of goods in various ways based on their individual bargaining situations, consisting of their (1) complex economic interdependence; (2) geopolitical postures; (3) domestic power dynamics; and (4) institutional context at the regional and global level. The territorial bargaining game approach can capture the dual nature of continuity and mutual restraint in East Asian island disputes in a systematic way.

Chapter 3 examines the three island disputes using regression techniques designed to assess the empirical accuracy and generalizability of the components of the territorial bargaining game. I present two closely related dependent variables. The *intensity of dispute* is a five-point scale, categorical dependent variable that measures the highest level of hostility reached in a given territorial dyad-year. The *initiation of dispute* is a dichotomous dependent variable of whether or not a dispute occurs. I test the intensity and initiation hypotheses using OLS and binary logistic regression techniques, respectively. The OLS regression model tests under what conditions countries choose to *escalate* the territorial dispute, once initiated. The binary logistic regression model tests under what conditions countries are likely to *initiate* a territorial dispute. After describing the hypotheses and operational measures, I present the empirical results of the regression analysis. The findings of this chapter fill a significant gap in the empirical studies of East Asian island disputes. Yet as with any kind of regression analysis with a relatively small N, these statistical findings require cautious interpretation. Also, given the historical complexity surrounding these island disputes, there remain stories to be explained in a qualitative manner. Hence I turn to in-depth, qualitative analyses in the following three chapters.

Chapter 4 analyzes the dispute over the Dokdo Islands between South Korea and Japan. The evidence provided in this chapter shows that the transition between, and the conclusion of, different dispute stages are closely associated with the key components of a territorial bargaining game, particularly the complex economic interdependence between South Korea and Japan. Coupled with unresolved historical animosities, growing resource competition, and pressures from ultranationalist groups, the clash of rival nationalisms has provided fertile ground for the initiation and escalation of the Dokdo dispute. Yet along with the overriding demands of alliance politics between the U.S., South Korea, and Japan, the high priority given to stable economic relationship has motivated both South Korea and Japan to stop pushing for a definitive and final political showdown over the disputed islands.

Chapter 5 explores the recurring patterns of the Senkaku dispute between Japan and China. First, China as a territorial challenger has used the island dispute to mobilize nationalism by fanning anti-Japanese sentiments. For Japan, pushing the island issue beyond a certain threshold has long been a political taboo, but the timing, method, and intensity of its claims have been dictated by ultranationalist groups not fully within the control of the Japanese government. As in the case of the Dokdo dispute, the evidence presented in this chapter indicates that contending nationalisms are potentially capable of spinning the Senkaku dispute out of control, particularly if the costs and benefits of economic interdependence are distributed unequally between the two regional rivals. At the expense of their nationalist credentials, however, both Japanese and Chinese political elites have repeatedly chosen to contain their territorial claims for fear that excessive tensions would damage their otherwise mutually beneficial economic ties.

Chapter 6 investigates the dispute over the Paracel and Spratly Islands between China and Vietnam respectively, which has unfolded in three violent rounds of clashes since its inception in the early 1970s. Among other factors, the shifting strategic environment in Indochina has had the most significant impact on the initiation and escalation of the Paracel and Spratly dispute. Throughout the Cold War period, the Sino–Vietnamese relationship also lacked deterring economic forces, as opposed to the cases of South Korean–Japanese and Sino–Japanese relations. From a liberal peace perspective, it is not surprising that the Paracel and Spratly dispute became one of the most violent island disputes in East Asia. Yet in the post-Cold War period, the Sino–Vietnamese relationship has undergone steady improvement, although it continues to be imbued with mutual suspicion. The process of Sino–Vietnamese territorial rapprochement culminated at the 2002 Association of Southeast Asian Nations (ASEAN) summit where the ten member-states of ASEAN and China signed a Declaration on the Conduct of Parties in the South China Sea, with the aim of preventing conflict and promoting cooperation in the region. To a large extent, this change can be attributed to the growing significance of economic ties between China and Vietnam in recent years.

Chapter 7 begins with an observation that the task of delimiting national boundaries, whether land or maritime, is often time-consuming, requiring strong political will and tireless diplomatic efforts of all neighboring states with conflicting claims. After exploring key legal issues with which East Asian countries are currently grappling, this chapter examines emerging options for the resolution and regulation of maritime boundary disputes with a focus on joint development regimes. Then, it assesses the possibility of a regional maritime regime building, with the littoral states able to pursue their maritime interests and manage their marine resources in accordance with agreed principles of international law.

Chapter 8 summarizes the findings of my quantitative and qualitative analysis. In view of the rising pressure of territorial nationalism and fluid geopolitics in the post-Cold War and post-9-11 era, even the mere containment of these island disputes requires the skillful diplomacy and tireless efforts of political leaders. The best strategy to hedge against potentially disruptive behaviors is to engage more with each other by facilitating greater economic and maritime interdependence. I conclude by noting that the path to deeper and wider economic and maritime integration is likely to be a bumpy one, but that the burgeoning efforts to form regional agreements may help to smooth it.

References

Adler E, Barnett M (1998) Security communities in theoretical perspective. In: Adler E, Barnett M (eds) Security communities. Cambridge University Press, Cambridge

Adler E, Haas PM (1992) Conclusion: Epistemic communities, world order, and the creation of a reflective research program. International Organization 46(1):367–390

Aggarwal VK (1998) Reconciling multiple institutions: Bargaining, linkages, and nesting. In: Aggarwal VK (ed) Institutional designs for a complex world: Bargaining, linkages, and nesting. Cornell University Press, Ithaca

Ahmad H (ed) (1997) The Straits of Malacca: International cooperation in trade, funding, and navigational safety. Pelanduk Publications, Selangor Darul Ehsan

Archibugi D, Held D (eds) (1995) Cosmopolitan democracy: An agenda for a new world order. Polity Press, Cambridge

Austin G (1998) China's ocean frontier: International law, military force and national development. Allen and Unwin, Canberra

Bercovitch J, Jackson R (1997) International conflict: A chronological encyclopedia of conflicts and their management 1945–1995. Congressional Quarterly Books, Washington, DC

Blanchard JM (2000) The U.S. role in the Sino–Japanese dispute over the Diaoyu (Senkaku) island, 1945–1971. China Quarterly 161:95–123

Bong YD (2002) Flashpoints at sea? Legitimization strategy and East Asian island disputes. PhD Dissertation in Political Science, University of Pennsylvania, Philadelphia

Brecher M (1993) Crises in world politics: Theory and reality. Pergamon, Oxford

Brecher M, Wilkenfeld J (1997) A study of crisis. University of Michigan Press, Ann Arbor

Buzan B (1978) A sea of trouble? Sources of dispute in the new ocean regime. Adelphi Paper 143, International Institute for Strategic Studies, London

Calder KE (1996) Pacific defense: Arms, energy, and America's future in Asia. William Morrow, New York

Calder KE (1997) Asia's deadly triangle: How arms, energy and growth threaten to destabilize Asia-Pacific. Nicholas Brealy, London

Calder KE (2004) Securing security through prosperity: The San Francisco system in comparative perspective. The Pacific Review 17(1):135–157

Catley R, Keliat M (1997) Spratlys: The dispute in the South China Sea, Ashgate, Brookfield

Charney JI (1995) Central East Asian maritime boundaries and the law of the sea. The American Journal of International Law 89:724–749

Cheng T (1974) The Sino–Japanese dispute over the Tiao-yu-tai (Senkaku) islands and the law of territorial acquisition. Virginia Journal of International Law 14(2):221–266

Christensen TJ (2006) Fostering stability or creating a monster? The rise of China and U.S. policy toward East Asia. International Security 31(1):81–126

Chung C (2004) Domestic politics, international bargaining and China's territorial disputes. Routledge, New York

Deans P (2000) Contending nationalisms and the Diaoyutai/Senkaku dispute. Security Dialogue 31(1):119–131

Deutsch KW (1953) Nationalism and social communication: An inquiry into the foundations of nationality. MIT Press, Cambridge

Deutsch KW (1957) Political community and the North Atlantic area: International organization in the light of historical experience. Princeton University Press, Princeton

Deutsch KW (1968) The analysis of international relations. Prentice-Hall, Englewood Cliffs

Diehl PF (ed) (1999) A road map to war: Territorial dimensions of international conflict. Vanderbilt University Press, Nashville and London

Djalal H, Townsend-Gault I (1999) Managing potential conflicts in the South China Sea: Informal diplomacy for conflict prevention? In: Crocker CA, Hampson FO, Aall PR (eds) Herding cats: Multiparty mediation in a complex world. United States Institute of Peace Press, Washington, DC

Donaldson J, Williams A (2005) Understanding maritime jurisdictional disputes: The East China Sea and beyond. Journal of International Affairs 59(1):135–156

Downs ES, Saunders PC (1998/1999) Legitimacy and the limits of nationalism: China and the Diaoyu islands. International Security 23(3):114–146

Franceschet A (2002) Kant and liberal internationalism. Palgrave Macmillan, New York

Fravel MT (2003) The long march to peace: Explaining China's settlement of territorial disputes. PhD Dissertation in Political Science, Stanford University, Stanford

Fravel MT (2005) Regime insecurity and international cooperation: explaining China's compromises in territorial disputes. International Security 30(2):46–83

Friedberg A (2005) The future of U.S.–China relations: Is conflict inevitable? International Security 30(2):7–45

Gochman CS, Maoz Z (1984) Militarized interstate disputes, 1816–1976: Procedures, patterns, and insights. Journal of Conflict Resolution 28(4):585–615

Goertz G, Diehl PF (1992) Territorial changes and international conflict. Routledge, London

Goldstein A (2005) Rising to the challenge: China's grand strategy and international security. Stanford University Press, Stanford

Haas EB (1958) The uniting of Europe: Political, social and economic forces, 1950–1957. Stanford University Press, Stanford

Haas EB (1964) Beyond the nation-state: Functionalism and international organization. Stanford University Press, Stanford

Haas EB (1990) When knowledge is power: Three models of change in international organizations. University of California Press, Berkeley

Haas PM (1992) Introduction: Epistemic communities and international policy coordination. International Organization 46(1):1–35

Hagström L (2005) Quiet power: Japan's China policy in regard to the Pinnacle islands. The Pacific Review 18(2):159–188

Haller-Trost R (1990) The Spratly islands: A study on the limitations of international law. Occasional Paper 14. Canterbury: Centre of South-East Asian Studies of University of Kent at Canterbury

Hara K (2001) 50 Years from San Francisco: Re-examining the peace treaty and Japan's territorial problems. Pacific Affairs 74(3):361–382

Harris S, Mack A (eds) (1997) Asia-Pacific security: The economics-politics nexus. Allen & Unwin Australia, St. Leonards

Held D (1995) Democracy and the global order: From the modern state to cosmopolitan governance. Stanford University Press, Stanford

Hensel PR (1996) Charting a course to conflict: Territorial issues and interstate conflict, 1816–1992. Conflict Management and Peace Science 15:43–73

Hensel PR (1998) Interstate rivalry and the study of militarized conflict. In: Harvey F, Mor B (eds) New directions in the study of international conflict, crises, and war. Macmillan, London

Holsti KJ (1991) Peace and war: Armed conflicts and international order, 1649–1989. Cambridge University Press, Cambridge

Huth PK (1996) Standing your ground: Territorial disputes and international conflict. University of Michigan Press, Ann Arbor

Huth PK, Allee TL (2002) The democratic peace and territorial conflict in the 20th century. Cambridge University Press, Cambridge

Johnston AI (1998) China's militarized interstate dispute behavior, 1949–1992: A first cut at the data. China Quarterly 153:1–30

Katzenstein PJ (1996) Introduction: Alternative perspectives on national security. In: Katzenstein PJ (ed) The culture of national security: Norms and identity in world politics. Columbia University Press, New York

Kenny HJ (2004) China and the competition for oil and gas in Asia. Asia Pacific Review 11(2):36–47

Kim D (2000) Naval strategy in Northeast Asia: Geo-strategic goals, policies, and prospects. Frank Cass, London

Kim SP (2004) Maritime delimitation and interim arrangements in Northeast Asia. Martinus Nijhoff Publishers, The Hague/London/New York

Kim Y (1999) Korea and international maritime laws, Hyosung Publisher (in Korean), Seoul, Korea

Kocs S (1995) Territorial disputes and interstate war, 1945–1987. Journal of Politics 57(1):159–175

Kolodziej E, Kanet R (eds) (1996) Coping with conflict after the cold war. Johns Hopkins University Press, Baltimore

Kratochwil F, Rohrilich P, Mahajan H (1985) Peace and disputed sovereignty: Reflections on conflict over territory. University Press of America, Lanham

Lee CM (2004) Rethinking future paths on the Korean peninsula. The Pacific Review 17(2):249–270

Lind JM (2004) Democratization and stability in East Asia. Paper presented at the 2004 Annual Meeting of the American Political Science Association, Chicago, IL

Linklater A (1982) Men and citizens in the theory of international relations. Macmillan, London

Linklater A (1990) Beyond Realism and Marxism: Critical theory and international relations. Macmillan, London

Matsui Y (1997) International law of territorial acquisition and the dispute over the Senkaku (Diaoyu) islands. Japanese Journal of International Law 40:3–31

Mearsheimer J (2001) The tragedy of great power politics. W.W. Norton, New York

Meconis C, Wallace M (2000) East Asian naval weapons acquisitions in the 1990s: Causes, consequences, and responses. Praeger, Westport

Mitrany D (1976) The functional theory of politics. St. Martins Press, New York

Mochizuki MM (1998) Security and economic interdependence in Northeast Asia. Asia/Pacific Research Center Working Paper, Stanford University, Stanford

Moon C, Chun C (2003) Sovereignty: Dominance of the Westphalian concept and implications for regional security. In: Alagappa M (ed) Asian security order: Instrumental and normative features. Stanford University Press, Stanford

Mueller J (1989) Retreat from doomsday: The obsolescence of major war. Basic Books, New York

O'Brien, R (1977) South China Sea oil: Two problems of ownership and development. Occasional Paper, 47, Institute of Southeast Asian Studies, Singapore

Park C (1973) Oil under troubled waters: The Northeast Asia sea-bed controversy. Harvard International Law Journal 14(2):212–260

Risse-Kappen T (1995) Bringing transnational relations back in: Introduction. In: Risse-Kappen T (ed) Bringing transnational relations back in: Non-state actors, domestic structures and international institutions. Cambridge University Press, Cambridge

Rosenau JN (1997) Along the domestic-foreign frontier: Exploring governance in a turbulent world. Cambridge University Press, Cambridge

Roy D (1994) Hegemon on the horizon? China's threat to East Asian security. International Security 19(1):149–168

Schelling TC (1980) The strategy of conflict. Harvard University Press, Cambridge

Senese PD (1996) Geographical proximity and issue salience: Their effect on the escalation of militarized interstate conflict. Conflict Management and Peace Science 15:133–161

Senese PD, Vasquez JA (2003) A unified explanation of territorial conflict: Testing the impact of sampling bias, 1919–1992. International Studies Quarterly 47(2):275–298

Shirk SL, Twomey CP (eds) (1996) Power and prosperity: Economics and security linkages in Asia-Pacific. Transaction Publishers, New Brunswick

Simmons BA (2003) Trade and territorial conflict: International borders as institutions. Paper presented at the annual meeting of the American Political Science Association. Philadelphia, PA

Snyder G, Diesing PA (1977) Conflict among nations: Bargaining, decision making, and system structure in international crises. Princeton University Press, Princeton

Solingen E (1998) Regional orders at century's dawn: Global and domestic influences on grand strategy. Princeton University Press, Princeton

Stein A (1993) Governments, economic interdependence, and international cooperation. In: Tetlock P, Husbands J, Jervis R, Stern PC, Tilly C (eds) Behavior, society and international conflict. Oxford University Press, New York

Suganuma U (2000) Sovereign rights and territorial space in Sino-Japanese relations: Irredentism and the Diaoyu/Senkaku islands. University of Hawaii Press, Honolulu

Suzuki S (2007) The importance of 'othering' in China's national identity: Sino-Japanese relations as a stage of identity conflicts. The Pacific Review 20(1):23–47

Valencia MJ (1995) China and the South China Sea disputes: Conflicting claims and potential solutions in the South China Sea. Adelphi Paper 298, The International Institute for Strategic Studies, London

Valencia MJ (2000) Regional maritime regime building: Prospects in Northeast and Southeast Asia. Ocean Development and International Law 31(3):223–247

Valencia MJ, Van Dyke JM, Ludwig NA (1997) Sharing the resources of the South China Sea. University of Hawaii Press, Honolulu

Vasquez JA (1993) The war puzzle. Cambridge University Press, Cambridge

Vasquez JA (2001) Mapping the probability of war and analyzing the possibility of peace: The role of territorial disputes. Conflict Management and Peace Science 18(2):145–174

Vasquez JA, Henehan MT (2001) Territorial disputes and the probability of war, 1816–1992. Journal of Peace Research 38:123–138

Wan M (2003) Economic interdependence and economic cooperation: Mitigating conflict and transforming security order in Asia. In: Alagappa M (ed) Asian security order: Instrumental and normative features. Stanford University Press, Stanford

Wendt A (1999) Social theory of international politics. Cambridge University Press, Cambridge

Chapter 2
Conceptual and Theoretical Framework

2.1 An Overview of a Territorial Bargaining Game

Territorial disputes rarely break out in a political vacuum. They are often fought
in an arena where international, regional, and domestic politics meet. For revisionist countries that challenge an existing territorial *status quo*, the most prominent way to achieve their goal is to acquire the territory in question. The process
of acquisition itself can vary from peaceful (e.g., sale or concession of territory)
to violent (e.g., military conquest). Most contemporary territorial disputes in East
Asia fall between these two extremes: they persist, while neither reaching peaceful resolutions nor escalating into full-scale militarized conflicts.

Building upon Aggarwal (1998) and Huth and Allee (2002), I conceptualize
a territorial bargaining game process along with the principal pathways leading
to different outcomes. From a territorial bargaining game perspective, the process of a shift from a prevailing territorial *status quo* to a new one generally
comes about with an *initial impetus*, which occurs through significant changes
either at the international, regional, or domestic level. The initial impetus may
create some type of externalities that affect the availability of *goods* that territory can provide. When combined with a perception of enduring rivalry harbored by territorial disputants, the initial impetus and subsequent changes in the
value of territory may result in contending *territorial nationalisms*, often manifested in the form of either resource nationalism (focused on tangible values)
or irredentism (focused on intangible values), or both. Countries respond to the
pressure of territorial nationalism in various ways based on their *individual
bargaining situations*, defined by their economic interdependence, geopolitical
postures, domestic power dynamics, and institutional contexts at the regional
and global level. Figure 2.1 illustrates the process of a territorial bargaining
game in its initiation stage.

Set in motion by varying stimuli, these elements of a territorial bargaining
game generate differing payoffs for national and subnational actors. If faced with
undesirable payoffs, some actors may attempt to modify the existing territorial
status quo. A *challenge-the-status-quo stage* is initiated if the challenger country

M.G. Koo, *Island Disputes and Maritime Regime Building in East Asia,*
The Political Economy of the Asia Pacific,
DOI 10.1007/978-0-387-89670-0_2, © Springer Science+Business Media, LLC 2009

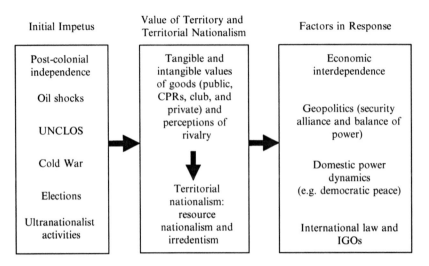

Fig. 2.1 Territorial bargaining game process: initiation stage

registers its revisionist claim through diplomatic or military means such as uni-lateral declaration of boundaries, construction of territorial posts, and threat or show of force. If the challenged target country resists with a strong countermeasure, the initiation phase is likely to escalate into a diplomatic crisis.

If claimant countries choose not to risk a large-scale conflict, they may enter into talks to defuse the tension. If they are committed to resolve their differences in a peaceful manner, talks will continue in a *negotiations stage*. During this stage, claimant countries must decide whether and to what extent to offer any conces-sions over the contested territory. If a settlement is reached through mutually agreeable concessions, the dispute will end (at least for the time being); otherwise, the dispute will persist in a *stalemate stage* and the challenger country will con-sider its policy options, either diplomatic or military, in another round of challenge-the-status-quo stage.

If the challenger country presses the target country even harder and the target country responds with military force, then a *military escalation stage* ensues. At this stage, both countries must decide whether or not to resort to the large-scale use of force. If war breaks out, a decisive victory by one side may end the dispute, whereas a stalemate on the battlefield will lead to the persistence of the dispute in the postwar period, preparing for another round of challenge-the-status-quo. Figure 2.2 illustrates the process of a territorial bargaining game as briefly sketched out above. In the following section, I explain the key components of a territorial bargaining game and show conceptually how these components determine the structure of a territorial bargaining game.

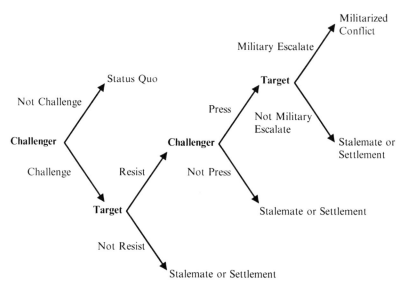

Fig. 2.2 Territorial bargaining game process: challenge-the-status-quo stage and beyond

2.2 Key Components of a Territorial Bargaining Game

2.2.1 Initial Impetus

An initial impetus may alter the context of preexisting territorial *status quo* or equilibrium. Examples include post-colonial independence, the advent and end of the Cold War, international oil shocks, and the introduction of the United Nations Convention on the Law of the Sea (UNCLOS). An impetus can also come from endogenous changes – which are less dramatic but still capable of modifying actors' individual bargaining situations – such as a military coup, the electoral victory of a nationalist government, and the activities of ultranationalist groups. These changes, which can be either directly related to the territorial issues at hand or affect the broader regional context within which a territorial issue is being contested, will create differing incentives for actors.

2.2.2 Value of Goods, Perceptions of Rivalry, and Territorial Nationalism

An initial impetus may create either positive or negative externalities on countries that are not immediate participants in the precipitating event, thereby stimulating or impeding the supply of certain types of goods that pertain to the contested territory.

Four types of goods are in order: public goods, common pool resources (CPRs), inclusive club goods, and private goods.[1]

Public goods are characterized by nonrivalry and nonexcludability in consumption. In this case, actors face a collective action dilemma or the *n*-person prisoners' dilemma, in which actors' dominant strategy is to defect, thereby resulting in undersupply of the goods. For example, positive security externalities of stable boundaries – namely greater certainty and lower transactions costs to neighboring countries – can be considered regional public goods.[2]

CPRs are characterized by rivalry and nonexcludability. They are probably a source of the so-called tragedy of the commons, which refers to a dilemma where self-interested actors can eventually destroy a shared resource even where it is clear that it is not in anyone's long-term interest for this to happen (Hardin 1982). Examples include global commons such as maritime resources in the High Sea and Antarctica. The sustainable use of CPRs can be achieved by resolving the collective action problem through contractual arrangements that can regulate the preservation, maintenance, and consumption of the goods.

Inclusive club goods refer to the type of goods that exhibit nonrivalry and excludability in consumption, at least until reaching a point where congestion occurs. Examples include trade liberalization through the World Trade Organization (WTO) and preferential trading agreements (PTAs) and economic stability through the International Monetary Fund (IMF) and the World Bank. Inclusive club goods can solve the collective action problem by eliminating the possibility of free-riding and by offering its members benefits that can actually be captured by the individual.

Finally, *private goods* have the property of rivalry and excludability, and they are the principal type of goods that territory can provide. Most territorial disputes inherently represent a zero-sum game in which actors seek to acquire or restore their territorial sovereignty at the expense of others. Territorial sovereignty can be created anew from the transformation of different types of goods into private goods. For example, the introduction of UNCLOS has considerably expanded national maritime boundaries through the adoption of a wider definition of territorial waters, continental shelves, and EEZs, thereby transforming erstwhile

---

[1]The distinction between different types of goods is made along two dimensions: *rivalry*, which refers to the extent to which one actor's consumption of goods affects that of the other; and *excludability*, which refers to the possibility of excluding non-contributors to the provision of goods from consuming them. For a discussion of these types of goods and actors' motivations to provide them, see Aggarwal (1996, 1998). On CPRs in particular, see Ostrom (1990) and Keohane and Ostrom (1995). For earlier insights, see Snidal (1979). The best summary of the literature on goods can be found in Cornes and Sandler (1996).

[2]Simmons (2003) argues that territorial borders provide essential benefits since institutionalized border arrangements can increase certainty and reduce transactions costs, thus facilitating international cooperation.

CPRs into (quasi-)private goods.[3] Not surprisingly, the transformation process is not an easy task, and a number of maritime boundaries remain contested across the world.

National territory as a private good is the primary concern of scholars in the realist tradition. For them, territory not only places physical limits on the exercise of state sovereignty, but also makes the material space available for the provision of national security under anarchy. In a realist world, states have historically given top priority to the conquest of territory in order to advance their economic, security, and other interests (Gilpin 1981: 23). As Kenneth Waltz (1979: 106) argues, the anarchic structure of international politics makes states worry about their vulnerability, compelling them to "control what they depend on or to lessen the extent of their dependency." For Waltz, this "simple thought" explains their imperial thrusts to widen the scope of their control.[4]

The value of territory can be divided into *tangible* and *intangible* dimensions (Newman 1999) or *intrinsic* and *relational* aspects (Goertz and Diehl 1992). This category is most, if not exclusively, relevant for private goods. Knowledge of the types and nature of goods gives us a first cut into understanding the type of problems that actors face and their incentives.

Control of *tangibly-valued territory* can make a country more powerful or richer. It is widely accepted that if a certain territory is known to have natural resources of economic value for exclusively private use, it is more likely to be a target of dispute initiation and higher levels of escalation. It is not a coincidence that a number of territorial disputes in East Asia have unfolded as an issue of *resource nationalism* concerning hydrocarbon potential near barren offshore islands and rocks at a time of rising prices of oil and other raw materials (Park 1973; O'Brien 1977; Hayashi 1991;

---

[3] A long-awaited UNCLOS was adopted in 1982 and finally entered into force in 1994. It sets down rules for measuring maritime zones and contains guidelines for mediation and settlement of disputes. In brief, the UNCLOS establishes parameters for defining a territorial sea, a contiguous zone, an EEZ and a continental shelf, and it specifies terms for deciding what is and what is not an island, as well as the criteria to be met in order for an island to generate a maritime zone beyond a 12-nautical-mile (nm) territorial sea. Article 121(1) of UNCLOS defines an island as "a naturally formed area of land, surrounded by water, which is above water at high tide." Article 121(3) specifies that "[r]ocks which cannot sustain human habitation or economic life of their own shall have no exclusive economic zone or continental shelf." In the meantime, Article 121(2) states that "[e]xcept as provided in paragraph 3, the territorial sea, the contiguous zone, the exclusive economic zone, and the continental shelf of an island are determined in accordance with the provisions of this Convention applicable to other land territory. Despite the major innovation in regulation of international norms afforded by the UNCLOS, it has exacerbated problems of delimitation, most acutely with respect to EEZs in enclosed seas like the South China Sea (Burgess 2003: 8–9).

[4] In a similar vein, John Mearsheimer (1992: 223) contends that countries requiring vital goods fear being cut off, and thus seek to extend political control to the source of supply, giving rise to conflict with the source or with its other customers.

Charney 1995; Lu 1995; Valencia 1995, 2000; Calder 1997; Catley and Keliat 1997; Paik 1997; Valencia et al. 1997).[5]

Intangibly-valued territory, which is characterized by its relational and social significance, largely falls within the category of indivisible private goods. A group of people values a certain piece of territory not because it physically enhances their power, but because the territory has symbolic value such as being where the group's ancestors once lived, where important religious sites are located, or where ethnic kin currently lives (Tir 2001: 5).[6] As territory becomes the focus of symbolism, contestants imbue specific sites with historic and religious importance, often through the use of historical and archeological narratives, as a means of proving priority, duration, and exclusivity to the territory in question (Burghardt 1973). As a result, competing territorial claims frequently take on the prominent form of *irredentism*, which refers to claiming a right to territories belonging to another state on the grounds of common ethnicity and/or prior historical possession, actual or alleged (Suganuma 2000: 3–10).[7]

The rise of territorial nationalism in the form of resource nationalism and irredentism is often fueled by the perceptions of rivalry held by countries about the other countries involved in territorial disputes. In fact, enduring rivalry is a near-permanent feature of East Asian territorial politics. In a highly competitive atmosphere, territorial disputes frequently revolve around the perceptions of rivalry coupled with historical animosities. From this viewpoint, the most serious barrier to achieving mutually agreeable resolutions of many territorial disputes in East Asia is unassuaged historical grievances and rivalry between territorial contestants

---

[5] Another tangible manifestation of territory is its role as a strategic resource. Undoubtedly, retaining control of territory with important strategic and military values is critical to national security. In East Asia, as the traditional balance of power began to erode in the post-Cold War period, a sense of insecurity concerning the critical sea-lanes in the South and East China Seas is increasingly becoming pervasive. As demands for energy and other raw materials have expanded, the region's rising import dependency and reliance on long-haul shipping has also increased its vulnerability to a disruption of supply. The strategic significance of this region lies on not only the commercial and oil transportation, but also its potential to be bases for air and naval operations (Valencia 1995; Snyder 1996).

[6] Symbolic attachment of territory to national identity and pride can make territorial conflicts all the more intractable and difficult to resolve, even when pragmatic solutions – for example, setting aside sovereignty claims in favor of shared ownership – may appear applicable in theory (Newman 1999; Hassner 2003).

[7] A number of territorial disputes among East Asian countries have often been fought on irredentist grounds. In particular, China has attracted the most scholarly attention. Since the Sino-Indian border war of 1962, China's policies towards territorial disputes have allegedly been dictated by insatiable irredentist ambitions. According to this view, China believes that territory once won for civilization must not be given back to barbarism; therefore, territory which was once Chinese must forever remain so, and, if lost, must be recovered at the first opportunity to regain the full territory and standing of the Chinese Empire at its peak (Fitzgerald 1964). Unmistakably, China's growing irredentist tendency increases the likelihood of territorial conflicts by fueling nationalist sentiments in its neighbors (Roy 1994: 149; Segal 1996: 160; Mearsheimer 2001: 375).

rather than differing interpretations of past treaties, competition over resources, or strategic interests (Solomon 1970; Samuels 1982; Deans 1996, 2000; Till 1996; Mack 1997; Sin 1997; Anwar 1998; Blanchard 2000).

Indeed economic/strategic resources and enduring rivalry are a dangerous combination in East Asia. Most importantly, combined with Japan's more assertive territorial nationalism, the irredentism of China, which is a party to many of the maritime and territorial disputes, is adding fuel to potential fires. Some claimant countries have made progress toward hammering out terms for jointly exploring and developing maritime resources. But it remains highly likely that miscalculation could lead to a worsening of relations, inhibiting development and investment.

The emergence of territorial nationalism in East Asia provides the baseline for a territorial bargaining game process. Territorial nationalism is likely to motivate countries to initiate and escalate a dispute to higher levels of hostility rather than to accept the territorial *status quo*, while preventing them from making concessions in negotiations over disputed territory. Yet the rise of contending territorial nationalism alone falls short of capturing the full complexity of conflict behaviors. The actual outcomes of a territorial bargaining game, either peaceful or violent, are in fact determined by *individual bargaining situations* as discussed in the following section.

2.2.3   Individual Bargaining Situations

While there are many factors that might affect national preferences for territorial policy, the most significant elements that influence responses to an initial impetus and subsequent change in the provision of certain types of goods (and the rise of territorial nationalism) are contestant countries': (1) complex economic interdependence; (2) geopolitical postures; (3) domestic power dynamics; and (4) the institutional context at the regional and global levels. The objective of this section is to provide the theoretical groundwork for each of these explanatory components with a special focus on the role of complex economic interdependence in containing, if not resolving, individual territorial disputes. The hypotheses developed in this section are further elaborated and tailored in the following chapters.

2.2.3.1   Complex Economic Interdependence

There exist at least three different channels of economic interdependence. First of all, the early liberal thinkers emphasized international trade as a natural pacifier, arguing that peace gradually emerges from commerce (Keohane 1990). Secondly, the mobility of capital is often linked to peace and conflict. Montesquieu (1989 [1748]) argues that "movable wealth" encourages peace between states, because capital can easily penalize those countries that behave otherwise. Finally, international monetary relations may also be a source of economic interdependence. States may choose to subordinate monetary sovereignty to a foreign power through a fixed exchange-rate regime, pool sovereignty in a monetary union, or assert their own sovereignty under a floating exchange-rate regime (Cohen 1998). Although they reduce state autonomy in monetary policymaking, higher levels of monetary dependence raise the external economic stability by reducing the costs of doing business – such as foreign exchange risk (including the cost of hedging such risk) and transactions costs – with the partner country (Frankel et al. 1997). Furthermore, monetary interdependence can promote peace by creating a mechanism that allows credible signals of political resolve to maintain peaceful economic relations (Gartzke et al. 2001).

In the postwar period, particularly since China adopted its reform policy in 1978, the economic integration of East Asian countries has been truly impressive, as manifested by soaring intra-regional flows of trade, capital, long-term investments, and technology (Frankel et al. 1997; Katzenstein 1997). Intra-East Asian trade has expanded dramatically in recent years with China replacing the U.S. as a number one trading partner to many in the region. For example, China became the largest trading partner for both South Korea and Japan in 2004. According to China's Customs Statistics, Chinese exports to Japan increased by 23.7%, reaching $73.5 billion, while its exports to South Korea increased by 38.4%, reaching $27.8 billion in 2004. In the same year, Chinese imports from Japan increased by 27.3%, reaching $94.4 billion, while its imports from South Korea increased by 44.3%, reaching $62.2 billion. As of 2009, Japan is China's third largest trading partner only after the EU and the U.S., and South Korea is China's fifth largest trading partner, if Hong Kong is not included.

Undoubtedly, cross-border economic relationships in East Asia are far broader than just trade. Regional capital markets dwarf the exchange of goods and services. While developing East Asian countries remain important recipients of FDI flows, many East Asian countries have become increasingly important FDI donors over the last few years. According to UNCTAD data, annual average of FDI inflows to East Asia grew from US$48.8 billion between 1990 and 2000 to US$127.7 billion between 2004 and 2007. At the same time, annual average of FDI outflows from East Asia grew from US$29.5 billion to US$74.5 billion for the respective periods. The East Asian portion of world gross inward and outward FDI is 8.5 and 5.2%, respectively. On average, about 57% of FDI inflows to East Asia have been to China during the period of 2004–2007. China is also becoming an important source of FDI outflows with about 22% of gross FDI outflows from East Asia in 2007 (US$102.9 billion) originating from mainland China. Around 40% of FDI flows to East Asia between 1997 and 2004 have come from within the region including Japan (Rajan 2008; UNCTAD 2008).

A series of recent events also indicate growing monetary interdependence among East Asian countries. Most notably, the role of the Japanese yen has undoubtedly been on the rise. Although a yen bloc remains a remote possibility, the weights given to the yen in exchange rate policies of East Asian countries have increased since the 1980s. Regional monetary interdependence was on full display when the financial crisis that started in Thailand in July 1997 spread like wildfire to the rest of East Asia. When financial crisis hit the region, Japan proposed an Asian Monetary Fund (AMF) as an East Asian solution to regional financial and monetary problems, only to fail in the face of strong opposition from the U.S. (and China). Alternatively, ten ASEAN member countries and three Northeast Asian countries (China, Japan, and South Korea) set up a currency swap scheme in Chiang Mai, Thailand, in 2000 to better manage their deepening monetary interdependence (Pempel 1999; Amyx 2003). The global financial crisis that started from the U.S. in 2008 opened the door to accelerated talks and created new momentum for East Asia's financial and monetary integration. Looking beyond the 2000 Chiang Mai Initiative (CMI), which only allowed for country-to-country currency swaps, the ASEAN Plus Three (APT) countries agreed in Bali in May 2009 on the governing mechanisms and implementation plan for the multilateralization of the CMI, comprising at least $120 billion of reserves.   Further talks are currently underway to combine some of region's over US$3 trillion in foreign reserves to help central banks shield their currencies from speculative attacks. The Plus Three countries would provide 80% of the fund, while the 10 ASEAN countries would provide the rest. Interestingly, there were no objections to the proposal this time around, which indicates the region's growing clout, its substantial monetary reserves, and the desire to embed as many safety measures into the regional system as possible (*Japan Times*, October 29, 2008; Volz 2009).

The rapid economic integration of East Asia sets the backdrop of the liberal peace debate about whether or not economic interdependence fosters peaceful relations by giving states an economic incentive to avoid costly disputes (Shirk and Twomey 1996; Harris and Mack 1997; Mochizuki 1998; Wan 2003). Liberals would argue that territorial disputes in East Asia remain a potential source of conflict, but their salience has been in steady decline due to increasing economic interdependence. In sharp contrast, realists remain skeptical about the mitigating influence of economic interdependence.[8]

As one of the three legs in the Kantian tripod for "perpetual peace," [9] the question of liberal peace has long puzzled international relations scholars because economic interdependence has a dual aspect. As Albert Hirschman's (1980 [1945]) classic work points out, the concept of interdependence has both beneficial and potentially costly components. Richard Cooper (1968: 4) concurs by noting that a country can "abandon unilaterally the tacit international code of good behavior only if it is prepared to accept the adverse reaction of other states." In a similar vein, Robert Keohane and Joseph Nye (1977) define the components of interdependence as

---

[8] Despite growing scholarly interests in the pacific effect of economic interdependence, however, few studies have been dedicated to territorial disputes as a distinct category of regional conflicts.

[9] Immanuel Kant's vision of perpetual peace (Kant 1957 [1795]) was built on a tripod of complementary influences: (1) republican constitutions and democracy that constrain autocratic caprice in waging war; (2) international law and intergovernmental organizations that, building on an understanding of the legitimate rights of all citizens and of all republics, provide the moral and legal edifice for the peaceful resolution of conflicts; and (3) a "commercial spirit" of trade and economic interdependence that reinforces structural constraints and liberal norms by creating transnational ties that encourage accommodation rather than conflict (Doyle 1983a, b; Russett et al. 1998).

sensitivity and vulnerability. Sensitivity is the extent to which one country is affected by the actions of another, whereas vulnerability is the extent to which a country can insulate itself from the costly effects of events that occur elsewhere. For Keohane and Nye, interdependence therefore means "mutual dependence," a condition in which states are both highly sensitive and vulnerable to each other. An examination of the empirical literature indicates that one can easily find support for either positive or negative aspects of economic interdependence (Copeland 1999/2000; Mastanduno 1999/2000).[10]

Early arguments that connected economic interdependence with less conflict were based on the hope that international trade would somehow quell the passion for territorial conquest that seemed so prevalent in the seventieth and eightieth centuries. As found in the writings of David Hume, the Baron de Montesquieu, Adam Smith, Richard Cobden, and John Stuart Mill, classical liberals hoped that the rejection of mercantilism and the strict limitation on sovereign states' intervention in private, entrepreneurial activities would diminish the temptation to impose their own conflicts upon other states (Doyle 1997: 233–4).

Norman Angell (1910) restated this view in the early twentieth century, arguing that war, by destroying trade ties, is "commercially suicidal." Theories about complex economic interdependence, which emerged in the 1970s, carried such integration arguments one step further (Cooper 1968; Keohane and Nye 1977). As an intellectual heir to Angell, Richard Rosecrance (1986, 1996) argues that modern conditions push states to be "trading states" rather than "territorial states" obsessed with territorial expansion. One of the most recent empirical studies with liberal overtones finds that democratic leaders should be more averse than autocratic leaders to initiating military conflicts with trading partners, as such conflicts might damage commercial ties and hamper politically important economic growth on which many democratic leaders rely on for political survival (Gelpi and Grieco 2008). Though not all contemporary adherents of liberal peace go as far as Kenichi Ohmae (1993), who asserts that the world is now "borderless," it is rather commonly accepted that territorial borders are declining in economic significance (Stopford and Strange 1991; O'Brien 1992; Strange 1996) as well as socio-cultural significance (Agnew and Duncan 1989; Appadurai 1996).

---

[10] Of the twenty studies reviewed, McMillan (1997) found that ten support the liberal hypothesis (i.e., Polachek 1980, 1992; Arad and Hirsch 1981; Gasiorowski and Polachek 1982; Domke 1988; Polachek and McDonald 1992; Stein 1993; Mansfield 1994; Copeland 1996; Oneal et al. 1996); six produce mixed or conditional results (i.e., Gasiorowski 1986; Sayrs 1989; de Vries 1990; Barbieri 1995, 1996a, b); and four support the realist hypotheses (i.e., Russett 1967; Uchitel 1993; Kim 1995; Blanchard and Ripsman 1996). In addition to the liberal-realist debate over the positive and negative aspects of economic interdependence, recent empirical works suggest that trade and conflict affect each other simultaneously. A useful survey of the empirical literature on the simultaneous equations to disentangle the reciprocal relations between trade and conflict is found in Reuveny (1999/2000).

Realists turn liberal peace theory on its head.[11] They argue that economic interdependence not only fails to promote peace, but in fact also heightens the likelihood of conflict because interdependence tends to foster asymmetry as a result of dependence and inequality between economic partners in an anarchic setting (Hirschman 1980 [1945]; Hoffman 1963; Waltz 1970). Particularly for structural realists, it is the distribution of power rather than interdependence that keeps peace under anarchy; therefore, it does not matter whether states are interdependent trading states or not, because the frequency of war is a function of their international standing rather than the attributes of states (Kindleberger 1973; Gilpin 1975, 1981; Krasner 1976; Waltz 1979; Mearsheimer 2001). As Waltz (1970) notes, increased interdependence at the system level may lead to increased conflict because increased contact creates potential opportunities for discord.[12] Furthermore, state actors under anarchy must worry that others will gain more from cooperation than they will, as those relative gains might later be turned into military advantage (Grieco 1990; Gowa 1994).[13] As some realists note, the inference that trade promotes peace may be spurious, because the conditions that facilitate trade – such as nuclear deterrence (Buzan 1984) and military alliance (Gowa 1994) – simultaneously promote peace (Blainey 1988). Realist concerns about dependence and relative gains are not limited to international trade. International financial and monetary relations may also increase uncertainty about policy acts, thereby promoting disputes (Kirshner 1995; Gartzke et al. 2001).

This modern realist understanding of economic interdependence follows the early mercantilist logic that states, locked in a competition for relative power and wealth, are often tempted to reduce their dependence on others through territorial conquest (Viner 1948; Liberman 1996). The mercantilist view of the world is hinged upon the assumption that most economic relations tend to be unequal and tension-ridden rather than equal and harmonious. It is most likely that asymmetric dependence confers

---

[11] For philosophical foundations, realists often draw on the works of J.J. Rousseau, who argued that interdependence breeds suspicion and incompatibility rather than accommodation and harmony. Rousseau viewed inequality between states as a source of insecurity and thus a key source of world conflict. Although he recognized that commerce brought wealth, he concluded that the inequality it also brought was more dangerous for world politics (Hoffman 1963).

[12] Forbes (1997) reviews a body of theoretical and empirical literature on the *contact hypothesis* that contact has a positive impact on relations between individuals, and that close contact reduces prejudices between people and countries and to foster peaceful relations. The majority of the empirical evidence reviewed suggests that contact between individuals breaks down prejudices and improves relationships, but increased contact between aggregate groups such as nation-states tends to result in conflict.

[13] Gowa (1994) assesses the security externalities associated with trade and argues that states choose to trade with allies in order to avoid granting the gain from trade to adversaries, which creates security externalities. She argues that it is not the increased income that is of greatest concern in trade with an adversary, but the ability of the adversary to enjoy the gains arising from specialization. Permitting an adversary the opportunity to increase its productive efficiency and redirect resources away from alternative productive ventures could allow it to increase production of military resources, which would pose a potential challenge.

unequal power to the less dependent country. The advantaged bargaining position of the less dependent country may be used to gain concessions on economic or political issues. Conversely, asymmetric interdependence can foster aggressive action from the more dependent country, particularly when its political leaders attempt to divert public frustration and aggression toward an outside target. Gasiorowski (1986) provides evidence that states that are more dependent on trade as a source of national income are more hostile toward states on which they are dependent.[14]

An even more pessimistic view than realism about the relationship between economic interdependence and peace can be found in the Marxist understanding of international capitalism. The most prominent formulation of this pessimism is Lenin's theory of imperialism, which predicts that the unstoppable imperial expansion can cause international wars in two ways: imperial rivalry among advanced capitalist states and nationalist rebellions in the colonies against the yoke of imperial oppression (Tucker 1975; Doyle 1997). Perhaps with a more pessimistic overtone, dependency theorists argue that the interdependence of capitalist economies prevents less developed countries from developing their economies (Frank 1967; Brewer 1980). Immanuel Wallerstein and followers of his modern world system theory see the capitalist interdependence as divided hierarchically into three tiers: the core, the semi-periphery, and the periphery. In this rendering, economic interdependence occurs on the basis of an unequal differentiation and systemic exploitation from the top to the bottom tier (Wallerstein 1979: 1–36, 66–94). For Wallerstein, the logic of world capitalism would inevitably lead to an erosion of the hegemonic power's economic edge and its alliance network, thereby destabilizing the international system and making the world ripe for another great power conflict (Wallerstein 1984: 37–46, Wallerstein 1995: 25–45).

Finally, a game-theoretic perspective argues that higher trade flows do not necessarily have a determinate effect on the likelihood of dispute escalation, since the threat of the loss of trade could either deter the prospective challenger from initiating a dispute, or intimidate its target into making concessions, thereby motivating the prospective challenger to initiate and escalate a dispute. According to the latter logic, the challenger may misinterpret the target country's conciliatory actions as a signal that the target lacks resolve or willingness to risk conflict, and thus believe that the challenger itself can exploit the target country's fear of conflict by standing firm and thereby improving its own strategic or economic position (Morrow 1999). Yet there is an important qualification to this argument. As James Morrow (1999: 487) notes, higher trade flows could create a way to avoid escalation to war by providing states with an opportunity to send a credible, costly signal to one another about their unobservable resolve.

In sum, the causal links between economic interdependence and conflict are neither simple nor self-evident. Liberals clearly emphasize the beneficial aspects, whereas realists emphasize the conflictual aspects of international transactions. From this different starting point, liberals claim that economic interdependence has a pacifying effect, whereas realists come to the conclusion that interdependence

---

[14] See also Heldt (2003).

either increases the likelihood of conflict or is not related to conflict initiation at all. In this study, I test these competing theories by examining how and to what extent economic ties affect the manner in which East Asian countries deal with their conflicts of territorial and maritime interest.

2.2.3.2   Shifting Alliances and Balance of Power

After World War II, U.S.–Soviet antagonism was heating up to a boiling point, and, as a result of complicated situations within the U.S. and overseas, the issue of concluding a peace treaty with Japan had been delayed. Yet the outbreak of the Korean War in June 1950 prompted the U.S. to conclude it swiftly. The new political-economic order – which was created as a result of the San Francisco Peace Treaty of 1951, popularly known as the "San Francisco System" – reconfigured Japan's role to become a linchpin of America's anti-communist front in East Asia.[15]

The regional order as codified in San Francisco has had both positive and negative effects on interstate relations in East Asia. On the positive side, the U.S. has not only served as the principal architect of regional order, but has also kept two regional rivals – Japan and China – at bay. Through its alliance and commitment to defend Japan, the U.S. has made it possible for Japan to avoid confronting China directly (Cumings 1997; Katzenstein 1997; Mastanduno 2003: 153–4). U.S. hegemony has also played a critical role in mitigating the security concerns of smaller countries and keeping the disputes between subregional rivals from spiraling in a dangerous direction (Lo 1989; Cha 1996; Kim 2000).

Yet U.S. preponderance did not always promote a Pax Americana in East Asia during the Cold War period. On the one hand, the balance-of-power politics under the quasi-bipolar system in the region exacerbated local conflicts occasionally, if not frequently. The ideological competition between the U.S. and the Soviet Union provided an incentive for superpower intervention in local conflicts to maintain the credibility of their regional commitments (Goldstein 2003: 172–4). On the other hand, the political vacuum left by the Soviet–U.S. *détente* in the 1970s was exploited by regional powers to advance their own interests. For instance, the emergence of territorial disputes between China and Vietnam coincided with the shift in the strategic landscape in Indochina. Hanoi's role had been transformed from Beijing's

---

[15] In Europe, the U.S.–U.K.–USSR Yalta Agreement of 1945 had survived as the basis of the Cold War structure until it collapsed in the late 1980s. In December 1989, when Presidents Gorbachev and Bush announced the "end of the Cold War" declaration in Malta, the expression "from Yalta to Malta" symbolized the advent of the post-Cold War era in the Western world. In East Asia, however, the backbone of the Cold War system was the San Francisco System rather than the Yalta system. Therefore, the sense of a new era remained unclear at best (Hara 2001: 361–2; Calder and Ye 2003: 1–2). Calder (2004: 138–40) outlines the defining features of the San Francisco System as follows: (1) a dense network of bilateral alliances; (2) an absence of multilateral security structures; (3) strong asymmetry in alliance relations, both in security and economics; (4) special precedence to Japan; and (5) liberal trade access to U.S. markets, coupled with relatively limited development assistance.

ally to its archenemy in the late 1960s and early 1970s when Soviet expansion became China's principal security concern in the region. At the dawn of the 1974 Sino–Vietnamese battle for the Paracel Islands, critical damage to their bilateral relations was inflicted by Beijing when it invited U.S. President Richard Nixon to visit China in 1972 (Lo 1989: 68–9). Subsequently, with the U.S. decision to withdraw from Indochina, China became less restrained in forcefully denouncing Hanoi's claim to sovereignty over the Paracel and Spratly Islands. By contrast, China's attitude toward the other two claimants, the Philippines and Malaysia, remained much more restrained, as they assumed a new, positive role in China's anti-Soviet united front (Lo 1989: 38–9).

In the post-Cold War era, two major trends have opened a new horizon of regional peace and security. The first trend has been associated with the overall reconfiguration of the East Asian regional system from the Cold War's (quasi-) bipolar confrontation to unipolar American dominance. Many experts agree that the U.S. Cold War military structure still dominates in matters of regional security (Cumings 1997; Mearsheimer 2001). The second and more important feature of the post-Cold War East Asian security order is the rise of China. In East Asia, China's economic and military growth is more likely to give rise to bipolarity within the region in the near future. Although not all draw worst-case scenarios about the rise of China, uncertainty about the ways in which a more capable China would exercise its power has alerted many in the region to scramble to balance against the possible dangers (Shambaugh 1995; Mochizuki 1998; Goldstein 2003, 2005; Friedberg 2005). It is worth noting that during the Cold War period, the U.S. and the Soviet Union both had geopolitical interests of their own, but not territorial ambitions. In sharp contrast, China as an emerging regional hegemon presents a different landscape of the future of East Asian territorial disputes because it has both geopolitical *and* territorial ambitions.[16]

2.2.3.3 Domestic Power Politics

Changes in the provision of goods provided by contested territory may touch off resource nationalism and irredentism, both of which point to nationalism as a principal source of territorial disputes. Nationalist sentiments are not immutable.

---

[16] As pointed out in Chapter 1 of this book, Johnston (1998) argues that China is more likely to resort to force when disputes involve territory and occur during periods in which the perceived gap between ascribed and desired international status is large or growing. Fravel (2003) disagrees by contending that China has been more cooperative and peaceful in its territorial disputes than is commonly believed. He finds that China has participated in 23 unique disputes with its neighbors on land and at sea since 1949, of which it has settled 18 peacefully. Moreover, China has usually received less than 50% of disputed land in these settlements. While China has used force in five disputes, military action has usually not been undertaken to seize large amounts of contested land on the battlefield. Instead, China has only occupied some Nationalist-held coastal islands and contested reefs in the South China Sea. Fravel concludes that China has been more likely to compromise over disputed territory and less likely to seize it through force than many think. For another benign view of China's territorial policy, see Huang (2004).

However, they inevitably take time both to form and to change because they are the result of accumulated, collective experience, reinforced by education or government propaganda. On the one hand, governments can be influenced by an intensively nationalistic atmosphere. Directed nationalism – for example, overt expressions of opinion from nationalist groups, rightist intellectuals, and the conservative mass media – can have more impact on government policymaking, whereas popular nationalism has only an indeterminate effect. On the other hand, governments can take a determined action to manipulate nationalist sentiments into a certain direction in favor of their political legitimacy (Mansfield and Snyder 1995; Snyder 2000; Heldt 2003).

To examine exactly how and to what extent contending territorial nationalisms are translated into actual disputes, a theory of state–society relations needs to be elaborated. The domestic power politics approach examines how state elites' desire to remain in office allows domestic coalitions and electoral politics to influence their decisions on conflict behavior. This approach often focuses on whether or not the tug-of-war within and between ruling and opposition groups encourages territorial disputes. As many East Asian countries move from authoritarianism toward greater political pluralism, a window of opportunity to resolve complex territorial disputes may be closing due to domestic political processes that are more prone to the tyranny of nationalism. As Scott Snyder (1996) points out, the twin challenges of responding to nationalist sentiments and maintaining political legitimacy are major dilemmas for political leaders in East Asia as democratization has taken a greater hold in the region.

The influence of democracy on the likelihood of conflict is one of the most intensively studied issues in international relations scholarship. Liberals have long believed that the democratic and republican constitutions bind or obligate states that are not peace-seeking by their very internal structures under anarchy. As one of the three legs in the Kantian tripod for perpetual peace, the "democratic peace" theory states that the supreme liberal internationalist mechanism is the democratic, self-determining state because international politics can be domesticated by the principle of popular sovereignty, wherein the people have no real interest in war (Doyle 1983a, b; Maoz and Russett 1993).

Even if debates remain as to whether and the extent to which democracies are more peaceful than nondemocracies, a consensus has emerged that (1) *stable* democracies are much less likely to engage in militarized conflicts *with one another*; (2) once in wars, high level of intensity and longer duration are expected because democracies face higher "audience costs," which refer to the political pressures on the leaders when they back down in the face of challenge from other states; and (3) democratizing states (or transitional democracies) have a higher probability of conflict than either stable democracies or autocracies (Bueno de Mesquita and Lalman 1992; Lake 1992; Fearon 1994; Spiro 1994; Farber and Gowa 1995; Mansfield and Snyder 1995; Schultz 1999; Snyder 2000; Gelpi and Griesdorf 2001).

In the East Asian context, the works of Mansfield and Snyder (1995) and Snyder (2000) on transitional democracy are of particular relevance and importance. They outline two principal mechanisms through which democratization leads to militarized disputes. First, in democratizing states, both new and established elites tend to play the nationalist card. Elites have incentives to mobilize the mass populace because of the need to counter political threats at the mass level. Second, democratization engages a variety of groups with a wide range of interests. During transitions, political elites who seek domestic allies are likely to form coalitions that are often unstable and incoherent. At least some of those coalitions may have an interest in assertive foreign policies and nationalist political agenda.[17]

Territorial disputes in East Asia can be seen as an arena of foreign policy competition in which state elites – be they democratic or authoritarian – attempt to enhance their political legitimacy. At a time of legitimacy deficit, state elites tend to resort to aggressive territorial policies in order to capitalize on nationalist and irredentist sentiments. Otherwise, they take a more pragmatic stance to pursue tangible foreign policy goals such as national security and economic development (Downs and Saunders 1998/1999; Deans 2000; Bong 2002).[18]

2.2.3.4 International Law and Intergovernmental Organizations (IGOs)

Aside from democratic peace theory, there is a long history of plans for world peace in Western political thought. Thinkers such as Emeric Cruce, Abbe de Saint-Pierre, and William Penn, among others, are well-known early advocates of international organization. Although not liberal in an ideological sense, such thinkers left an important legacy of designing institutions of law and dispute settlement mechanism to pacify interstate relations. Early liberal thinkers such as John Locke adopted the view that such institutions could serve to secure more peaceful international politics by reducing the uncertainty that prevailed among sovereign states. Locke applied this view of domestic politics to interstate relations. For him, an international society of sovereign states is not necessarily in a state of war of all against all if cooperative norms and institutions can be established to minimize misunderstanding and poor judgment on the part of state leaders (Franceschet 2002: 72–4).

One of the earliest examples of international law and IGOs is the Congress system for European security in the nineteenth century. The League of Nations was the first multipurpose, quasi-universal IGO in the twentieth century. In the post-World War II era, the representative international organizations included the United

---

[17]Some scholars argue that the timing, method, and intensity of the territorial claims in East Asia have been dictated not only by the state elites, but also by domestic opposition groups not fully within the control of the governments. The issue of control and ownership of disputed territories provides a mechanism through which opponents of the government can mobilize popular support for their own nationalist agenda, thus damaging foreign policy initiatives of the incumbent government (Deans 2000; Chung 2004).

[18]The legitimization strategy model is also referred to as the "diversionary" theory. In either variant, it is commonly assumed that state elites' desire to remain in office allows considerations of domestic dissatisfaction, and thus domestic politics, to influence decisions on interstate conflict behavior. For a useful review of the diversionary version, see Heldt (2003).

Nations (UN) proper, various specialized agencies, and other regional organizations that deal with either security or economic issues (Russett et al. 1998; Simmons and Martin 2002). This research program was enriched by neoliberal institutionalists of the 1980s who asserted that international regimes alter state strategies in favor of cooperation by lengthening the shadow of the future, increasing the reputational costs for cheating, monitoring compliance, facilitating issue linkages, and offering salient solutions (Keohane 1984). Recent empirical findings, though much contested, indicate that dense networks of IGO membership make an independent contribution to the avoidance of serious militarized disputes (Russett et al. 1998; Mansfield and Pevehouse 2003).

Yet seen in comparative regional perspective, East Asia – particularly Northeast Asia – has the most pronounced formal "organization gap" of any area (Calder 2004: 191). Katzenstein (1997) presents a widely cited framework to explain the organization gap in East Asia. He argues that two institutional features of East Asian countries contribute to the lack of formal regional institutions: (1) hierarchic state–society relationships; and (2) distinctive state structures. For him, the concept of community, especially horizontal and associational community, is underdeveloped in East Asia.

Indeed, the San Francisco System provided East Asian countries with a bilateral–multilateral institutional mix. It offered them access to U.S. markets in return for a bilateral security alliance with the U.S. It also encouraged America's East Asian allies to participate in broad-based, multilateral forums in both areas of security – e.g., the UN – and trade – e.g., the General Agreement on Tariffs and Trade (GATT) and the WTO. This system, which proved relatively beneficial for most East Asian countries, created little incentives for them to develop rigorous regional institutions (Cumings 1997; Grieco 1997).[19]

Particularly on the security front, East Asia lacks the equivalent of the North Atlantic Treaty Organization (NATO) for Europe and the U.S., and alliance relationships in East Asia tend to be bilateral, leaving security coordination at the minilateral level under-institutionalized. During the Cold War period, together with large U.S. military forces stationed in Japan, South Korea, the Philippines, South Vietnam, and Guam, these bilateral security treaties became the backbone of the U.S. strategy of a "hub and spokes" network to contain Communist forces.

---

[19] For examples, since its creation in 1967, ASEAN has shown a certain degree of institutional capacity in both security and trade matters. Yet ASEAN remains a remarkably modest organization with only scattered signs of institutional deepening and widening. APEC, a transregional agreement and Asia Pacific's most ambitious institutional experiment, remains an essentially consultative forum – even after 15 years since its birth, with most members continuing to prefer "loose family-type linkages" to "a formal institution" (Aggarwal and Morrison 1998; Ravenhill 2001). Several proposals for a more exclusive East Asian club failed throughout the 1990s. The most oft-cited example is the fate of the East Asian Economic Group (EAEG), proposed by Former Malaysian Prime Minister Mahathir. Strong U.S. opposition, Japan's hesitation, and lukewarm support from most East Asian neighbors led to a downgrading of his idea to the creation of an East Asian Economic Caucus (EAEC) in 1993 (Higgott and Stubbs 1995; Terada 2003).

The ASEAN Regional Forum (ARF), which was launched in 1994, is virtually the only intergovernmental forum for security dialogue in East Asia. The idea for such a forum originally came from Japan in 1992 as part of its effort to promote region-wide dialogues and cooperation through the ASEAN Post-Ministerial Conference as well as APEC. Although support for such a multinational forum to discuss political and security issues was lukewarm at first, the Japanese initiative bore fruit when the members of ASEAN decided to take the lead. ARF has formed several working groups for intensive discussions on confidence-building measures, preventive diplomacy, and the management and resolution of regional conflicts. Nevertheless, East Asian countries have yet to put their full weight behind ARF (Smith 1997; Garofano 1999).

More recently, the traditional institutional equilibrium in East Asia – a combination of bilateral and multilateral approaches to both security and trade issues – is in flux. The erosion of Asian countries' traditional confidence in bilateral alliances and multilateral globalism is increasingly visible, manifesting itself in the burgeoning interest in intra- and extra-regional free trade agreements (FTAs), regional financial institutions, and cooperative security dialogues. Only a decade ago, it was widely believed that East Asian countries were inherently incapable of managing their own economic and security affairs in an institutionalized manner. East Asia seemed to be very poor soil for implanting a sense of community and regional institutions in the post-World War II era, even when other parts of the world were busy surfing the wave of regionalism. In recent years, however, we have seen dramatic changes in perceptions about and responses to East Asia's long-standing trade, financial, and security order. While the traditional postwar trade, financial, and security order focused on bilateral alliance structures, global economic and security institutions, and informal corporate and ethnic solutions, the new institutional environment in East Asia now revolves around the proliferation of FTAs, regional financial cooperation, and bilateral and minilateral security dialogues (Aggarwal and Koo 2008).

References

Aggarwal VK (1996) Debt games: Strategic interaction in interaction in interaction in international debt rescheduling. Cambridge University Press, Cambridge

Aggarwal VK (1998) Reconciling multiple institutions: Bargaining, linkages, and nesting. In: Aggarwal VK (ed) Institutional designs for a complex world: Bargaining, linkages, and nesting. Cornell University Press, Ithaca

Aggarwal VK, Koo MG (eds) (2008) Asia's new institutional architecture: Evolving structures for managing trade, financial, and security relations. Springer, New York

Aggarwal VK, Morrison CE (eds) (1998) Asia-Pacific crossroads: Regime creation and the future of APEC. St. Martin's Press, New York

Agnew JA, Duncan JS (1989) The power of place: Bringing together geographical and sociological imaginations. Unwin Hyman, Winchester

Amyx J (2003) Japan and the evolution of regional financial arrangements in East Asia. In: Krauss E, Pempel TJ (eds) Beyond bilateralism: U.S.–Japan relations in the new Asia-Pacific. Stanford University Press, Stanford

Angell N (1910) The great illusion: A study of the relation of military power in nations to their economic and social advantage. Putnam, New York

Anwar DF (1998) Indonesia: Domestic priorities define national security. In: Alagappa M (ed) Asian security practice: Material and ideational influences. Stanford University Press, Stanford

Appadurai A (1996) Modernity at large: Cultural dimensions of globalization. University of Minnesota Press, Minneapolis

Arad R, Hirsch S (1981) Peacemaking and vested interests: International economic transactions. International Studies Quarterly 25:439–468

Barbieri K (1995) Economic interdependence and militarized interstate conflict, 1870–1985. Paper presented at the annual meeting of the International Studies Association, Chicago, IL

Barbieri K (1996a) Economic interdependence: A path to peace or source of interstate conflict? Journal of Peace Research 33(1):29–49

Barbieri K (1996b) Explaining discrepant findings in the trade-conflict literature. Paper presented at the annual meeting of the International Studies Association, San Diego, CA

Blainey G (1988) The causes of war. Free Press, New York

Blanchard JM, Ripsman N (1996) Measuring vulnerability interdependence: The strategic goods test. Geopolitics 1(3):225–246

Blanchard JM (2000) The U.S. role in the Sino–Japanese dispute over the Diaoyu (Senkaku) Island, 1945–1971. China Quarterly 161:95–123

Bong YD (2002) Flashpoints at sea? Legitimization strategy and East Asian Island disputes. PhD Dissertation in Political Science, University of Pennsylvania, Philadelphia

Brewer A (1980) Marxist theories of imperialism: A critical survey. Routledge and Kegan Paul, London

Bueno de Mesquita B, Lalman D (1992) War and reason. Yale University Press, New Haven

Burgess PJ (2003) The politics of the South China Sea: Territoriality and international law. Security Dialogue 34(1):7–10

Burghardt A (1973) The bases of territorial claims. Geographical Review 63:225–245

Buzan B (1984) Economic structure and international security. International Organization 38(4):597–624

Calder KE (1997) Asia's deadly triangle: How arms, energy and growth threaten to destabilize Asia-Pacific. Nicholas Brealy, London

Calder KE (2004) Securing security through prosperity: The San Francisco system in comparative perspective. The Pacific Review 17(1):135–157

Calder KE, Ye M (2003) Northeast Asia: Ripe for regionalism? BASC News 6(1)

Catley R, Keliat M (1997) Spratlys: The dispute in the South China Sea. Ashgate, Brookfield

Cha VD (1996) Bridging the gap: The strategic context of the 1965 Korea–Japan normalization treaty. Korean Studies 20:123–160

Charney JI (1995) Central East Asian maritime boundaries and the law of the sea. The American Journal of International Law 89:724–749

Chung C (2004) Domestic politics, international bargaining and China's territorial disputes. Routledge, New York

Cohen B (1998) The geography of money. Cornell University Press, Ithaca

Cooper R (1968) The economic interdependence: Economic policy in the Atlantic community. McGraw-Hill, New York

Copeland D (1996) Economic interdependence and war: A theory of trade expectations. International Security 20(4):5–41

Copeland D (1999/2000) Trade expectations and the outbreak of peace: Détente 1970–74 and the end of the cold war 1985–91. Security Studies 9(1/2):15–58

Cornes R, Sandler T (1996) The theory of externalities, public goods, and club goods. Cambridge University Press, Cambridge

Cumings B (1997) Japan and Northeast Asia into the twenty-first century. In: Katzenstein PJ, Shiraishi T (eds) Network power: Japan and Asia. Cornell University Press, Ithaca

de Vries MS (1990) Interdependence, cooperation and conflict: An empirical analysis. Journal of Peace Research 27(4):429–444

Deans P (1996) The Diaoyutai/Senkaku dispute: The unwanted controversy. Kent Papers in Politics and International Relations 6

Deans P (2000) Contending nationalisms and the Diaoyutai/Senkaku dispute. Security Dialogue 31(1):119–131

Domke WK (1988) War and the changing global system. Yale University Press, New Haven

Downs ES, Saunders PC (1998/1999) Legitimacy and the limits of nationalism: China and the Diaoyu Islands. International Security 23(3):114–146

Doyle MW (1983a) Kant, liberal legacies and foreign affairs. Philosophy and Public Affairs 12:205–235

Doyle MW (1983b) Kant, liberal legacies and foreign affairs, Part 2. Philosophy and Public Affairs 12:323–353

Doyle MW (1997) Ways of war and peace: Realism, liberalism, and socialism. W.W. Norton, New York

Farber H, Gowa J (1995) Polities and peace. International Security 20(2):123–147

Fearon J (1994) Domestic political audiences and the escalation of international disputes. American Political Science Review 90(3):715–735

Fitzgerald CP (1964) The Chinese view of their place in the world. Oxford University Press, London

Forbes HD (1997) Ethnic conflict: Commerce, culture, and the contact hypothesis. Yale University Press, New Haven

Franceschet A (2002) Kant and liberal internationalism. Palgrave Macmillan, New York

Frank AG (1967) Capitalism and underdevelopment in Latin America. Monthly Review Press, New York

Frankel JA, Stein E, Wei S (1997) Regional trading blocs in the world economic system. Institute for International Economics, Washington, DC

Fravel MT (2003) The long march to peace: Explaining China's settlement of territorial disputes. PhD Dissertation in Political Science, Stanford University, Stanford

Friedberg A (2005) The future of U.S.–China relations: Is conflict inevitable? International Security 30(2):7–45

Garofano J (1999) Flexibility or irrelevance? Ways forward for the ARF. Contemporary Southeast Asia 21(1):74–94

Gartzke E, Li Q, Boehmer C (2001) Investing in the peace: Economic interdependence and international conflict. International Organization 55(2):391–438

Gasiorowski MJ (1986) Economic interdependence and international conflict: Some cross-national evidence. International Studies Quarterly 30(1):23–38

Gasiorowski MJ, Polachek S (1982) Conflict and interdependence: East–West trade linkages in the era of détente. Journal of Conflict Resolution 26(4):709–729

Gelpi CF, Grieco JM (2008) Democracy, interdependence, and the source of the liberal peace. Journal of Peace Research 45(1):17–36

Gelpi CF, Griesdorf M (2001) Winners or losers? Democracies in international crises, 1918–1994. American Political Science Review 95(3):633–647

Gilpin R (1975) U.S. power and multinational corporation: The political economy of foreign direct investment, Basic Books, New York

Gilpin R (1981) War and change in world politics. Cambridge University Press, Cambridge

Goertz G, Diehl PF (1992) Territorial changes and international conflict. Routledge, London

Goldstein A (2003) Balance-of-power politics: Consequences for Asian security order. In: Alagappa M (ed) Asian security order: Instrumental and normative features. Stanford University Press, Stanford

Goldstein A (2005) Rising to the challenge: China's grand strategy and international security. Stanford University Press, Stanford

Gowa J (1994) Allies, adversaries, and international trade. Princeton University Press, Princeton

Grieco JM (1990) Cooperation among nations: Europe, America, and nontariff barriers to trade. Cornell University Press, Ithaca

Grieco JM (1997) System sources of variation in regional institutionalization in Western Europe, East Asia, and the America. In: Mansfield E, Milner H (eds) The political economy of regionalism. Columbia University Press, New York

Hara K (2001) 50 Years from San Francisco: Re-examining the peace treaty and Japan's territorial problems. Pacific Affairs 74(3):361–382

Hardin R (1982) Collective action. John Hopkins University Press for Resources for the Future, Baltimore

Harris S, Mack A (eds) (1997) Asia-Pacific security: The economics-politics nexus. Allen & Unwin Australia, St. Leonards

Hassner RE (2003) The path to indivisibility: The role of ideas in the resolution of intractable territorial disputes. PhD Dissertation in Political Science, Stanford University, Stanford

Hayashi M (1991) Fisheries in the North Pacific: Japan at a turning point. Ocean Development and International Law 22:343–364

Heldt B (2003) Domestic politics, absolute deprivation, and the use of armed force in interstate territorial disputes, 1950–1990. The Journal of Conflict Resolution 43(4):451–478

Higgott R, Stubbs R (1995) Competing conceptions of economic regionalism: APEC versus EAEC in the Asia Pacific. Review of International Political Economy 2(3):516–535

Hirschman AO (1980 [1945]) National power and the structure of foreign trade. University of California Press, Berkeley

Hoffman S (1963) Rousseau on war and peace. American Political Science Review 57(2): 317–333

Huang T (2004) State preferences and international institutions: Boolean analysis of China's use of force and South China Sea territorial disputes. Journal of East Asia Studies 4(2):227–262

Huth PK, Allee TL (2002) The democratic peace and territorial conflict in the 20th century. Cambridge University Press, Cambridge

Johnston AI (1998) China's militarized interstate dispute behavior, 1949–1992: A first cut at the data. China Quarterly 153:1–30

Kant I (1957 [1795]) Perpetual peace. Edited with an introduction by Beck LW (ed) Liberal Arts Press, New York

Katzenstein PJ (1997) Introduction: Asian regionalism in contemporary perspective. In: Katzenstein PJ, Shiraishi T (eds) Network power: Japan and Asia. Cornell University Press, Ithaca

Keohane RO (1984) After hegemony: Cooperation and discord in the world economy. Princeton University Press, Princeton

Keohane RO (1990) International liberalism reconsidered. In: Dunn J (ed) The economic limits to modern politics. Cambridge University Press, Cambridge

Keohane RO, Nye JS (1977) Power and interdependence: World politics in transition. Little, Brown, Boston

Keohane RO, Ostrom E (eds) (1995) Local commons and global interdependence. Sage Publications, London

Kim D (2000) Naval strategy in Northeast Asia: Geo-strategic goals, policies, and prospects. Frank Cass, London

Kim SY (1995) Bilateral conflict and trade, 1948–86: The role of economic interdependence in conflict processes. Paper presented at the annual meeting of the American Political Science Association, Chicago, IL

Kindleberger C (1973) The world in depression 1929–1939. University of California Press, Berkeley

Kirshner J (1995) Currency and coercion: The political economy of international monetary power. Princeton University Press, Princeton

Krasner S (1976) State power and the structure of international trade. World Politics 28:317–347

Lake D (1992) Powerful pacifists: Democratic states and war. American Political Science Review 86(1):24–38

Liberman P (1996) Does conquest pay? The exploitation of occupied industrial societies. Princeton University Press, Princeton

Lo C (1989) China's policy towards territorial disputes: The case of the South China Sea islands. Routledge, New York

Lu N (1995) Flashpoint: Spratlys. Dolphin Books, Singapore

Mack A (1997) Island disputes in Northeast Asia. Working Paper No. 1997/2, Australian National University, Canberra, http://rspas.anu.edu.au/ir/pubs/work_papers/97–2.pdf, Accessed 10 February 2009

Mansfield ED (1994) Power, trade, and war. Princeton University Press, Princeton

Mansfield ED, Pevehouse J (2003) Institutions, interdependence, and international conflict. In: Schneider G, Barbieri K, Gleditsch NP (eds) Globalization and armed conflict. Rowman and Littlefield, Lanham

Mansfield ED, Snyder J (1995) Democratization and the danger of war. International Security 20(1):5–38

Maoz Z, Russett B (1993) Normative and structural causes of democratic peace, 1946–1986. American Political Science Review 87(3):624–638

Mastanduno M (1999/2000) Economic statecraft, interdependence, and national security: agendas for research. Security Studies 9(1–2):288–316

Mastanduno M (2003) Incomplete hegemony: The United States and security order in Asia. In: Alagappa M (ed) Asian security order: Instrumental and normative features. Stanford University Press, Stanford

McMillan S (1997) Interdependence and conflict. Mershon International Studies Review 41(1):33–58

Mearsheimer J (1992) Disorder restored. In: Allison G, Treverton G (eds) Rethinking America's security. W.W. Norton, New York

Mearsheimer J (2001) The tragedy of great power politics. W.W. Norton, New York

Mochizuki MM (1998) Security and economic interdependence in Northeast Asia. Asia/Pacific Research Center Working Paper, Stanford University, Stanford

Montesquieu CS (1989 [1748]) In: Cohler AM, Miller BC, Stone HS (eds) The spirit of the laws. Cambridge University Press, Cambridge

Morrow J (1999) How could trade affect conflict? Journal of Peace Research 36(4):481–489

Newman D (1999) Real spaces, symbolic spaces: Interrelated notions of territory in the Arab-Israeli conflict. In: Diehl PF (ed) A road map to war: territorial dimensions of international conflict. Vanderbilt University Press, Nashville and London

O'Brien R (1977) South China Sea oil: Two problems of ownership and development. Occasional Paper, 47, Institute of Southeast Asian Studies, Singapore

O'Brien R (1992) Global financial integration: The end of geography. Council on Foreign Relations Press, New York

Ohmae K (1993) The borderless world: Power and strategies in the interlinked economy. Harper Business, New York

Oneal JR, Oneal FH, Maoz Z, Russett BM (1996) The liberal peace: Interdependence, democracy, and international conflict, 1950–1985. Journal of Peace Research 33(1):11–28

Ostrom E (1990) Governing the commons: The evolution of institutions for collective action. Cambridge University Press, Cambridge

Paik J (1997) Exclusive economic zones in Northeast Asia: Source of conflict or avenues toward cooperation? Korea and World Affairs 21(4):586–599

Park C (1973) Oil under troubled waters: The Northeast Asia sea-bed controversy. Harvard International Law Journal 14(2):212–260

Pempel TJ (1999) Regional ups, regional downs. In: Pempel TJ (ed) The politics of the Asian economic crisis. Cornell University Press, Ithaca

Polachek S (1980) Conflict and trade. Journal of Conflict Resolution 24(1):55–78

Polachek S (1992) Conflict and trade: An economics approach to political international interactions. In: Isard W, Anderton C (eds) Economics of arms reduction and the peace process: Contributions from peace economics and peace science. North-Holland, Amsterdam

Polachek S, McDonald J (1992) Strategic trade and the incentive for cooperation. In: Chatterji M, Forcey LR (eds) Disarmament, economic conversion, and management of peace. Praeger, New York

Rajan R (2008) Foreign direct investment flows within developing Asia. Asia EconoMonitor, May 21, http://www.rgemonitor.com/asiamonitor/252649/foreign_direct_investment_flows_within_developing_asia, Accessed 10 February 2009

Ravenhill J (2001) APEC and the construction of Asia-Pacific regionalism. Cambridge University Press, Cambridge

Reuveny R (1999/2000) The trade and conflict debate: A survey of theory, evidence and future research. Peace Economics, Peace Science and Public Policy 6(1):23–49

Rosecrance RN (1986) The rise of the trading state: Commerce and conquest in the modern world. Basic Books, New York

Rosecrance RN (1996) The rise of the virtual state: Territory becomes passé. Foreign Affairs 75(4):45–61

Roy D (1994) Hegemon on the horizon? China's threat to East Asian security. International Security 19(1):149–168

Russett B (1967) International regions and the international system. Rand McNally, Chicago

Russett B, Oneal J, Davis D (1998) The third leg of the Kantian tripod for peace: International organizations and militarized disputes, 1950–85. International Organization 52(3):441–467

Samuels MS (1982) Contest for the South China Sea. Methuen, New York

Sayrs L (1989) Trade and conflict revisited: Do politics matter? International Interactions 15:155–175

Schultz K (1999) Do democratic institutions constrain or inform? Contrasting two institutional perspectives on democracy and war. International Organization 53(2):233–266

Segal G (1996) East Asia and the containment of China. International Security 20(4):107–135

Shambaugh D (1995) Greater China: The next superpower. Oxford University Press, Oxford

Shirk SL, Twomey CP (eds) (1996) Power and prosperity: Economics and security linkages in Asia-Pacific. Transaction Publishers, New Brunswick

Simmons BA (2003) Trade and territorial conflict: International borders as institutions. Paper presented at the annual meeting of the American Political Science Association, Philadelphia, PA

Simmons BA, Martin L (2002) International organizations and institutions. In: Carlsnaes W, Risse T, Simmons BA (eds) Handbook of international relations. Sage Publications, London

Sin Y (1997) Korea's territorial rights to Dokdo: An historical study. Dokdo Research Association (in Korean), Seoul

Smith GJ (1997) Multilateralism and regional security in Asia: The ASEAN regional forum (ARF) and APEC's geopolitical value. Weatherhead Center for International Affairs, Harvard University, Cambridge

Snidal D (1979) Public goods, property rights, and political organization. International Studies Quarterly 23(4):532–566

Snyder J (2000) From voting to violence: Democratization and nationalist conflict. W.W. Norton, New York

Snyder S (1996) The South China Sea dispute prospects for preventive diplomacy. Special Report, 18, United Sates Institute of Peace, Washington, DC

Solomon R (1970) Boundary concepts and practices in Southeast Asia. World Politics 23(1):3–16

Spiro D (1994) The insignificance of the democratic peace. International Security 19(2):50–86

Stein A (1993) Governments, economic interdependence, and international cooperation. In: Tetlock P, Husbands J, Jervis R, Stern PC, Tilly C (eds) Behavior, society and international conflict. Oxford University Press, New York

Stopford J, Strange S (1991) Rival states, rival firms: Competition for world market shares. Cambridge University Press, Cambridge

Strange S (1996) The retreat of the state: The diffusion of power in the world economy. Cambridge University Press, Cambridge

Suganuma U (2000) Sovereign rights and territorial space in Sino-Japanese relations: Irredentism and the Diaoyu/Senkaku islands. University of Hawaii Press, Honolulu

Terada T (2003) Constructing an 'East Asian' concept and growing regional identity: From EAEC to ASEAN+3. The Pacific Review 16(2):251–277

Till G (1996) Maritime disputes in the Western Pacific. Geopolitics and International Boundaries 1(3):327–345

Tir J (2001) Never-ending conflicts? Transfers, partitions, and unifications as potential solutions for territorial disputes. PhD Dissertation in Political Science, University of Illinois, Urbana-Champaign

Tucker RC (ed) (1975) The Lenin anthology. W.W. Norton, New York

Uchitel A (1993) Interdependence and instability. In: Snyder J, Jervis R (eds) Coping with complexity in the international system. Westview Press, Boulder

UNCTAD (2008), World investment report 2008, United Nations Conference on Trade and Development, Geneva, http://www.unctad.org/wir, Accessed 10 February 2009

Valencia MJ (1995) China and the South China Sea disputes: Conflicting claims and potential solutions in the South China Sea. Adelphi Paper 298, The International Institute for Strategic Studies, London

Valencia MJ (2000) Regional maritime regime building: Prospects in Northeast and Southeast Asia. Ocean Development and International Law 31(3):223–247

Valencia MJ, Van Dyke JM, Ludwig NA (1997) Sharing the resources of the South China Sea. University of Hawaii Press, Honolulu

Viner J (1948) Power versus plenty as objectives of foreign policy in the seventeenth and eighteenth centuries. World Politics 1(1):1–19

Volz U (2009) A new era of financial cooperation. Far Eastern Economic Review, June 2, http://www.feer.com/economics/2009/june53/A-New-Era-of-Financial-Cooperation, Accessed 17 July 2009

Wallerstein I (1979) The capitalist world economy. Cambridge University Press, Cambridge

Wallerstein I (1984) The politics of the world economy. Cambridge University Press, Cambridge

Wallerstein I (1995) After liberalism. The New Press, New York

Waltz K (1970) The myth of interdependence. In: Kindleberger CP (ed) The international corporation. MIT Press, Cambridge

Waltz K (1979) Theory of international politics. Random House, New York

Wan M (2003) Economic interdependence and economic cooperation: Mitigating conflict and transforming security order in Asia. In: Alagappa M (ed) Asian security order: Instrumental and normative features. Stanford University Press, Stanford

Chapter 3
Quantitative Analysis of East Asian Island Disputes

3.1 Introduction

A number of statistical studies of international peace and conflict have produced many useful and important findings in recent decades.[1] Yet few quantitative attempts have been made thus far to focus on East Asian territorial disputes. As one of the first quantitative efforts to yield generalizable knowledge about East Asian territorial disputes, this chapter presents a novel attempt to unravel why and to what extent a given dispute becomes more or less heated over time. More specifically, I examine what factors affect the dual nature of continuity and mutual restraint in the disputes over Dokdo, the Senkakus, the Paracels, and the Spratlys using large N quantitative analysis. In so doing, I assess the empirical accuracy and generalizability of the territorial bargaining game approach and provide groundwork for the qualitative analyses in the following chapters.

The remaining chapter proceeds in three sections. Section 3.2 develops the methodology and describes the time-series cross-section data. The dependent variable is defined as the level of hostility reached in a given dyad-year. In defining the dependent variable, I focus on the annual variation in the dispute intensity between three pairs of countries: South Korea and Japan, Japan and China, and China and Vietnam. Due to data limitation, the period under investigation is from 1952 to 2005 for the Dokdo dispute, and from 1960 to 2005 for the Senkaku and the Paracel–Spratly disputes. The measurements of explanatory variables are also provided in this section. Section 3.3 reports the findings. Empirical results based on the ordinary least squares (OLS) and binary logistic regressions show that economic interdependence is significantly connected to the reduction in the intensity

---

[1] See Polachek (1980), Vasquez (1993), Huth (1996), Oneal and Russett (1997, 1999a, 1999b), Russett et al. (1998), Hensel (2001), Gartzke et al. (2001), Barbieri (2002), Huth and Allee (2002), Chiozza and Choi (2003), Choi and James (2003), Gartzke and Li (2003), Senese and Vasquez (2003), and Simmons (2005).

M.G. Koo, *Island Disputes and Maritime Regime Building in East Asia,*
The Political Economy of the Asia Pacific,
DOI 10.1007/978-0-387-89670-0_3, © Springer Science+Business Media, LLC 2009

and the likelihood of the three island disputes. Section 3.4 summarizes the findings and draws policy implications.

3.2   Data and Methods

3.2.1   Estimation Model

I test time-series cross-section data using OLS and binary logistic regression models with fixed effects.[2] I focus on two closely related dependent variables: the intensity of dispute and the initiation of dispute. The intensity of dispute is a five-point scale, categorical dependent variable that measures the highest level of hostility reached in a given territorial dyad-year. The initiation of dispute is a dichotomous dependent variable that measures whether or not a dispute occurs.

Data analysis unfolds in two different but closely related ways. In the first approach, I estimate the parameters of OLS models by treating the five-point scale dependent variable as though it were continuous. Although this is a widely used practice, particularly when the dependent variable has five or more categories, caution is required because an ordinal scale is inherently incapable of distinguishing the magnitude of difference across the categories. In the second approach, therefore, I recode the five-point scale data dichotomously and run a binary logistic regression model. I set a threshold level of hostility for dispute occurrence at the value of 1 (verbal disputes) or higher (coded 1 if the five-point scale measure is greater than 0; coded 0 otherwise).[3]

I use the often-replicated Oneal and Russett's (1997, 1999a, b) research design with some modifications. I include a lagged dependent variable to control for

---

[2] Fixed-effects models permit each unit – each dispute dyad in this chapter – to have a different time-invariant error term. For a discussion of the utility of the fixed-effects approach, see Beck and Katz (2001), Green et al. (2001), King (2001), and Oneal and Russett (2001).

[3] Binary logistic regression is a form of regression that is used when the dependent is a dichotomy and the independents are of any type. Logistic regression estimates the probability of a certain event occurrence. While OLS seeks to minimize the sum of squared distances of the data points to the regression line, logistic regression applies maximum likelihood estimation after transforming the dependent into a logit variable (the natural log of the odds of the dependent occurring or not). The use of a dichotomous dependent variable in OLS regression violates the assumptions of normality as a normal distribution is impossible with only two values. Also, the error term will violate the assumption of homoscedasticity (equal variances) when a dichotomy is used as a dependent. Unlike OLS regression, logistic regression does not assume linearity of relationship between dependent and independent variables; does not require normally distributed variables; does not assume homoscedasticity; and in general has less stringent requirements. It does, however, require that observations are independent and that the logit of the independent variables is linearly related to the dependent variables.

whether or not a particular dyad experiences a dispute in the previous year. I employ a 1-year lag for all the explanatory variables in order to reduce the problems posed by the reciprocal relationship between the outcome and explanatory variables. The baseline model for a given dispute dyad (countries i and j) is as follows:

$$Y_{ij,t} = \beta_0 + \beta_1 Y_{ij,t-1} + \beta_2 X_{ij,t-1} + \gamma Z_{ij,t-1} + u_{ij} + e_{ij,t},$$

where Y is the dependent variable, Y_{t-1} is a one-period lag of the dependent variable, X is a vector of independent variables, Z is a vector of control variables, u is a unit-specific error term, and e is an error term.

3.2.2 Dependent Variable

Many scholars agree that there tends to be a temporal sequence between mild rhetorical disputes and intensive wars. Building upon the existing literature, I develop a five-point scale measure to code the highest level of hostility reached in a given territorial dyad-year. The scale to be used in this chapter is as follows:

0 = Minimal or no diplomatic conflict over disputed territory. The challenger may be involved in a territorial dispute, but there is very limited evidence of public confrontation over territory.

1 = Moderate to high levels of diplomatic conflict over disputed territory. The actions and counter-actions of challenger and target countries may include exchange of hostile rhetoric, public recriminations, and soliciting of third-party support in order to pressure each other into making concessions.

2 = Either a challenger or a target country, in addition to active and confrontational diplomatic actions, may use sanctions on bilateral diplomatic, economic, or military ties; seize civilians in disputed areas; and threaten to use military force to reinforce its territorial claim.

3 = Mild physical clashes and isolated incidents between police or armed forces may take place.

4 = If the circumstances continue to escalate, a military escalation may follow with an outbreak of a MID or a full-fledged war.

I collected outcome data drawing upon Zeev Maoz's Correlates of War (COW)-revised Dyadic Militarized Interstate Dispute (MID) dataset (DYMID 1.1) as well as other national sources.[4] Figs. 3.1–3.3 illustrate the value assigned to each dyad-year of the three island disputes.

---

[4] There will undoubtedly be some debate and questions concerning the coding of specific cases. More systematic effort by Paul R. Hensel is under way to collect a dataset on territorial disputes in East Asia. Further information on the Issue Correlates of War (ICOW) project by Hensel can be found at http://www.paulhensel.org/icow.html (accessed February 10, 2009). At the moment, the data collection used in this chapter is one of the most extensive and detailed datasets available for East Asian island disputes.

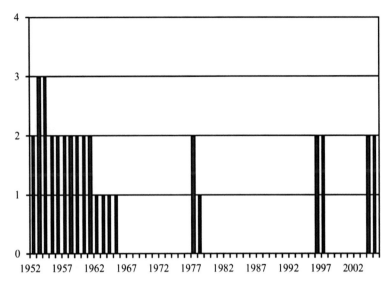

Fig. 3.1 Intensity of the Dokdo dispute (1952–2005)

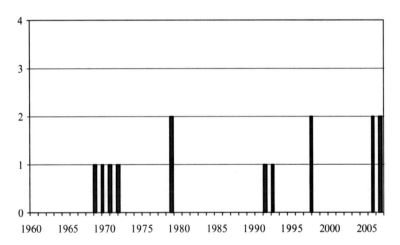

Fig. 3.2 Intensity of the Senkaku dispute (1960–2005)

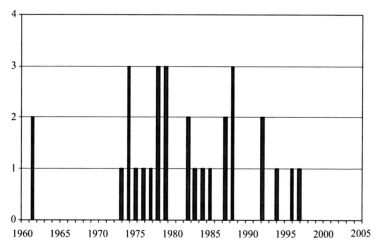

Fig. 3.3 Intensity of the Paracel and Spratly dispute (1960–2005)

3.2.3 Independent Variables

Following the liberal peace argument, I hypothesize the relationship between territorial disputes and economic interdependence as follows:

Hypothesis 1.1: If pairs of countries have low (high) levels of economic ties, they will engage in higher (lower) levels of hostility with regard to their disputed territory.

Hypothesis 1.2: If pairs of countries have low (high) levels of economic ties, they are more (less) likely to initiate (and escalate) a territorial dispute (to higher levels of hostility).

There is no consensus on how best to measure economic interdependence, because there are at least three different channels of economic relations. First, early liberal thinkers emphasized international trade as a natural pacifier (Keohane 1990). Second, the mobility of capital is often linked to peace and conflict (Gartzke et al. 2001). And third, international monetary relations based on exchange rate commitments may also be a source of economic interdependence (Cohen 1998).

With regard to the three dispute dyads examined in this chapter, capital flows have co-varied with trade flows, or remained very limited until recently (Ito and Krueger 2000). Also, because most East Asian currencies were pegged to the U.S. dollar during most of the postwar period, their monetary interdependence at the bilateral level remained analytically insignificant (Katada 2004). As a result, I choose to use bilateral trade as a proxy for bilateral economic interdependence.

Different studies use a wide variety of indicators of trade interdependence – such as trade volumes and values, systemic trade levels, trade as a proportion of gross domestic product (GDP), elasticity of supply and demand, and the trade of strategic goods. One of the simplest ways to capture the dyadic levels of trade interdependence is to construct a trade dependence index, defined as the share of dyadic trade flow (the sum of imports and exports) in GDP.[5]

Although based on the same baseline measure of trade dependence, Oneal and Russett (1997, 1999a, b) and Barbieri (2002) offer two of the most different constructions of trade interdependence. Oneal and Russett use a less dependent country's trade dependence score as an indicator of dyadic interdependence. The rationale for this measure is that the least dependent country is the "weakest link," in Dixon's (1993) terms; it is less constrained to refrain from force, because it needs the relationship less. By contrast, Barbieri argues that it is problematic to employ the characteristics of only one country when describing the characteristics of a dyad. Hence she defines trade interdependence as a product of the salience and symmetry of trade dependence.[6]

For my baseline specification, I use target and challenger countries' respective trade dependence scores, and their interaction term, as separate indicators of dyadic trade interdependence. There is good reason to expect that target and challenger countries may respond to their island disputes in a different manner depending on the level of their trade dependence on each other. Unlike Oneal and Russett, I do not adopt the weakest link hypothesis in my baseline model because I believe that both countries in a dyad constitute the composition of bilateral economic interdependence. I do not use Barbieri's measures for my baseline model, either, because trade dependence scores by definition already reflect the dyadic nature of trade.

---

[5] Formally,

$$\text{Trade Dependence}_i = \frac{(\text{Imports}_{ij} + \text{Exports}_{ij})}{\text{GDP}_i} = \frac{\text{Trade}_{ij}}{\text{GDP}_i},$$

where Trade_{ij} denotes bilateral trade between states i and j. I collect trade and GDP data from a variety of sources including the International Monetary Fund's *Direction of Trade Statistics* (CD-ROM), the World Bank's *World Development Indicators* (CD-ROM), the World Trade Organization's *International Trade Statistics*, the United Nation's *Monthly Bulletin of Statistics*, the Asian Development Bank's *Key Indicators of Developing Asian and Pacific Countries*, and other national statistics. With regard to the Paracel and Spratly dispute, I use South Vietnam's data for the period of 1960–75 because North Vietnam remained silent on the territorial issues in the South China Sea before the re-unification of Vietnam in 1975.

[6] For Barbieri (2002), 53–62, the salience measure for a pair of countries, defined as the geometric mean of two trade dependence scores, captures the extent to which the trading partners are important to each other ($\text{Salience}_{ij} = \sqrt{\text{Trade Dependence}_i \times \text{Trade Dependence}_j}$). For example, higher dyadic-salience score indicates that the trade relationship is important for both countries, thereby providing the necessary bonds to deter conflict. Barbieri defines the *symmetry* of dependence as the difference of trade dependence scores of a pair of countries ($\text{Symmetry}_{ij} = 1 - |\text{Trade Dependence}_i - \text{Trade Dependence}_j|$). This measure is designed to capture the realist concern that unequal trade dependence may exert a negative influence on peace by conferring coercive power to a less dependent country and/or touching off nationalist sentiments in a more dependent country.

Yet for the purpose of comparison, I include Oneal and Russett's and Barbieri's interdependence measures for alternative specifications.[7] Trade dependence scores of each dispute dyad are presented in Figs. 3.4–3.9.[8]

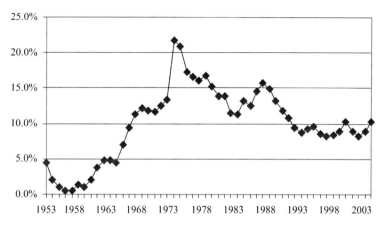

Fig. 3.4 South Korea's trade dependence on Japan (1953–2004)

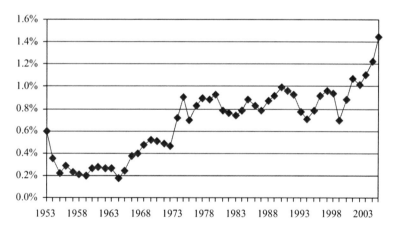

Fig. 3.5 Japan's trade dependence on South Korea (1953–2004)

---

[7]Given the fact that the distribution of the salience measure for her sample has much greater variance than the symmetry measure, Barbieri (2002, 60–1) standardizes salience and symmetry by creating z-scores for each variable as well as and create an interdependence index that is the product of the z-scores of salience and symmetry in order to allow each component of interdependence to contribute equal proportions to an interdependence index. Yet I use the direct product of salience and symmetry for an alternative specification because I do not face the same problem with my cases (variance of salience = 0.000203; variance of symmetry = 0.002483). Nevertheless, this formulation still produces an index of interdependence that is highly correlated with the salience variable (corr = 0.997), creating a serious multicollinearity problem.

[8]Sources: The International Monetary Fund, *Direction of Trade Statistics*; The World Bank, *World Development Indicators*.

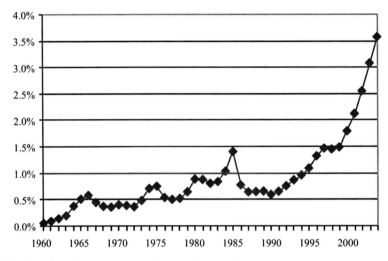

Fig. 3.6 Japan's trade dependence on China (1960–2004)

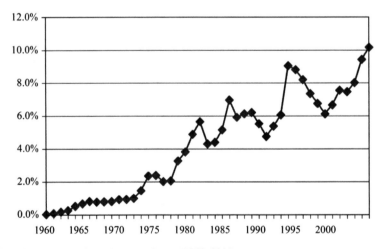

Fig. 3.7 China's trade dependence on Japan (1960–2004)

First, South Korea's trade dependence on Japan has fluctuated widely over time. By contrast, Japan's trade dependence on South Korea has been on a steady rise, but its level is much lower than that of South Korea's in absolute terms. These trade dependence scores indicate that trade with Japan has been more important to South Korea than trade with South Korea has been to Japan. Second, Japan's trade dependence on China fluctuated at levels less than 1.5% during the period of 1960–1990, but began to take off exponentially after 1991, reaching 3.59% in 2004.

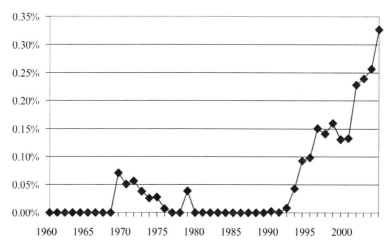

Fig. 3.8 China's trade dependence on Vietnam (1960–2003)

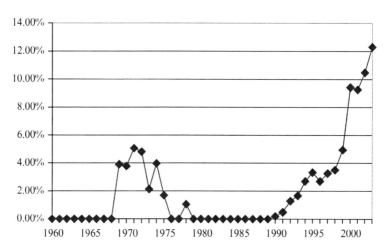

Fig. 3.9 Vietnam's trade dependence on China (1960–2003)

China's trade dependence on Japan also indicates an overall rise, but has fluctuated more widely and with much higher levels of dependence in absolute terms than did those of Japan's on China. These trade dependence scores indicate that bilateral trade is increasingly becoming important for both China and Japan, although trade with Japan has traditionally been more important to China than trade with China has been to Japan until recently.

Finally, the commercial links between China and Vietnam had been virtually severed during the Cold War period except for the early 1970s. By contrast, mutual trade dependence has been on a dramatic rise since 1991, particularly for Vietnam in both absolute and relative terms.

3.2.4   Control Variables

Following Oneal and Russett (1997, 1999a, b), I include a set of control variables that could influence bilateral conflict: challenger country's relative material capability, joint democracy, and joint membership in IGOs.[9] I also take into account whether or not the Cold War, accession to the UNCLOS, and oil prices have affected the dependent variable.

3.2.4.1   Relative Power

I hypothesize that if a challenger country experiences faster growth in material capability than its target country, it is more likely to initiate and escalate a dispute to higher levels of hostility.[10] To test this hypothesis, I employ the widely used Composite Index of National Capability (CINC) from the COW II-based National Material Capabilities dataset (Version 3.02, June 2005).[11] The relative power measures the challenger country's share in a dyadic power equation (challenger's CINC/[challenger's CINC + target's CINC]).

3.2.4.2   Joint Democracy

I include a combined polity score to test if pairs of more democratic countries are less likely to initiate and escalate a dispute to higher levels of hostility. I code the degree to which the political system of challenger and target countries are democratic as opposed to authoritarian. I utilize the POLITY IV data set to create a net-democracy score, which ranges in value from −10 to +10 (Marshall and Jaggers 2002). This 21-point net-democracy score is created by subtracting each country's autocracy score (which ranges from 0 to 10) from its democracy score (which also ranges from 0 to 10).[12]

---

[9] The other two variables in the neo-Kantian model from Oneal and Russett – geography and alliance – are not included in this chapter because disputant countries are geographically close to each other without formal alliance ties.

[10] See Organski and Kugler (1980), Doran (1991), and Geller (1993). In a more nuanced study, Sweeney (2003) finds that dyads with similar interests have less severe disputes, and that under the condition of interest dissimilarity, balances rather than preponderances of military capabilities are associated with less severe disputes.

[11] This index is based on annual values for total population, urban population, iron and steel production, energy consumption, military personnel, and military expenditure of all state members, currently from 1816 to 2001.

[12] See Rousseau et al. (1996).

3.2.4.3 Shared IGO Membership

I hypothesize that if pairs of countries have joint membership in regional and/or global IGOs, they are less likely to initiate and escalate a dispute to higher levels of hostility.[13] Given the pronounced formal "organization gap" in East Asia, my measure for joint IGO membership focuses on two multilateral IGOs: the GATT/WTO and APEC.[14] If both countries in a dyad-year share joint membership of either IGO, the case is coded as 1; otherwise, it is coded as 0.[15]

3.2.4.4 Cold War

This variable, designed to control for the effect of the Cold War, assigns a value of 1 for the years during the Cold War and 0 for the years after 1990. It can be argued that in the wake of superpower confrontation between the U.S. and the Soviet Union during the Cold War period, regional territorial quarrels were muted significantly, if not completely.

3.2.4.5 Accession to the UNCLOS

It is often argued that the global trend to adopt the UNCLOS has further heightened the possibility of bilateral conflict at sea by increasing the tangible value of those otherwise barren islands. I include the UNCLOS variable to control the impact that a country's accession to the UN Law of the Sea might have on the intensity and the likelihood of island disputes. If both countries in a given dyad-year are signatories of UNCLOS, the case is coded as 1; otherwise, it is coded as 0.[16]

---

[13] Realists often dismiss IGOs as unimportant because they typically lack means of enforcement that are independent of the international distribution of power (Mearsheimer 2001). Yet a close look at various IGOs indicates that they may serve any of six functions: coercing norm breakers; mediating among conflicting parties; reducing uncertainty by conveying information; problem-solving, including expanding states' conception of their self-interest to be more inclusive and long-term; socialization and shaping norms; and generating narratives of mutual identification (Russett et al. 1998, 444–45).

[14] For more details about the organization gap in East Asia, see Calder and Ye (2004).

[15] Japan joined the GATT in 1955, while South Korea joined the organization in 1967. Both countries were founding members of APEC in 1989. China joined APEC in 1991 and the GATT/WTO in 2001. Vietnam joined APEC in 1998 and is currently working on its application for WTO admission.

[16] Vietnam signed the Convention in 1994, and South Korea, Japan and China all signed it in 1996.

3.2.4.6 Oil Prices

Finally, I include the oil prices in a given dyad-year to control the impact that the annual average crude oil prices might have on the intensity and the likelihood of island disputes.[17]

3.3 Estimation Results

The results of my data analysis are mixed, but favor the pacific benefits of economic interdependence. The coefficients relating the trade dependence score of a target country to the intensity and the likelihood of dispute is statistically significant at $p < 0.004$ and at $p < 0.08$, respectively. This implies that economic interdependence measured in terms of trade dependence scores has a major explanatory effect on the process of the three island disputes examined in this chapter. Yet, neither Oneal and Russett's nor Barbieri's measure of economic interdependence is effective in capturing the pacific benefits of economic interdependence. Aside from the lagged dependent variable, the other control variables vary considerably in their magnitudes and statistical significance, but there is evidence that joint democracy and joint accession to the UNCLOS both have a statistically significant influence on the likelihood of dispute occurrence.

3.3.1 OLS Regression

Table 3.1 reports the estimation results of OLS regressions. The first column is based on the baseline specification. Following Oneal and Russett, the second column reports the result based on a less dependent country's trade dependence score in a given dyad-year. Finally, the third column presents the estimation result based on Barbieri's measures. As shown in the first column, a target country's trade dependence on a challenger country has a statistically significant negative impact on the dispute intensity across time and space ($p < 0.004$). As predicted by the liberal peace proposition, this indicates that the more (less) dependent on the challenger country the target country becomes for trade than other dispute dyads and/or in other periods, the two countries in a given dyad-year will engage in lower (higher) levels of hostility vis-à-vis island disputes. By contrast, the challenger country's trade dependence on the target country has little statistical significance, although it has a correct sign as hypothesized.

---

[17] Because the prices are annual averages, they do not show the absolute peak price and differ slightly from daily and monthly averages. Source: http://inflationdata.com/inflation/Inflation_Rate/Historical_Oil_Prices_Table.asp accessed February 10, 2009.

Table 3.1 Effect of economic interdependence on dispute intensity: fixed-effects OLS panel regression result

Variables	I	II	III
Target's trade dependence (TD)	−13.418 (−2.94)[a]		
Challenger's TD	−3.485 (−0.79)		
Target's TD×Challenger's TD	737.866 (1.89)[b]		
Less dependent country's TD		25.866 (0.78)	
Salience			24.949 (0.19)
Symmetry			11.240 (2.01)[c]
Salience×Symmetry			5.892 (0.04)
Challenger's relative power	−0.126 (−0.06)	−1.066 (−0.49)	0.368 (0.16)
Cold War	−0.123 (−0.53)	−0.312 (−1.40)	−0.219 (−0.96)
Joint democracy	−0.031 (−1.45)	−0.027 (−1.22)	−0.035 (−1.49)
Joint IGO membership	−0.163 (−0.52)	−0.599 (−2.31)[c]	−0.217 (−0.69)
Joint accession to the UNCLOS	−0.422 (−1.65)	−0.299 (−1.13)	−0.388 (−1.47)
Oil prices	−0.006 (−0.83)	−0.007 (−0.095)	−0.008 (−0.098)
Lagged dispute intensity	0.264 (3.00)[a]	0.354 (4.20)[a]	0.296 (3.41)[a]
R²	0.113	0.145	0.180
Number of groups	3	3	3
Number of observations	133	133	133

Note: The *t*-statistics appear in parentheses.
[a]Significant at the 0.01 level;
[b]Significant at the 0.10 level;
[c]Significant at the 0.05 level

How can we explain such an unbalanced result vis-à-vis the pacific effect of economic interdependence? At first glance, this may appear puzzling. Yet if we look beneath the surface, this reflects the volatility in the target-challenger relationship in all of the three island disputes under investigation. Although target countries exercise physical control of disputed islands in one way or the other, their claims remain highly contested and unstable. Under these circumstances, and other things being equal, target countries may be more (less) constrained to respond to sovereignty issues with high levels of hostility, if they become more (less) dependent on their challenger countries.

Interestingly, the interaction term (target's trade dependence×challenger's trade dependence) has a statistically significant but positive impact on the dispute intensity ($p < 0.061$). This indicates that the impact of the target's trade dependence on conflict depends on the level of the challenger's trade dependence and vice versa. One of the easiest ways to interpret the conditional effect of an interaction term is to consider the first derivative of the estimation equation with respect to the target's trade dependence score: $-13.418 + 737.866 \times$ challenger's trade dependence score. If we solve this first derivative for the challenger's trade dependence score, any score below 0.01819 will be associated with a negative, pacifying impact of marginal increase in the target's trade dependence score on the dispute intensity.

Otherwise, a marginal increase in the target's trade dependence score will have a positive, aggravating influence.[18] As such, the positive coefficient of an interaction term does not necessarily invalidate the pacific effect of the target country's trade dependence score. As predicted, the lagged dispute intensity has a statistically significant positive impact on the dispute intensity in present time ($p < 0.003$). Yet the other control variables do not have a statistically significant impact, although some of them show correct signs.

The second column reports the estimation result based on Oneal and Russett's construction of economic interdependence. Surprisingly, a less dependent country's trade dependence score has no statistically significant influence on the dispute intensity. In the cases of the Senkaku and the Paracel and Spratly disputes, a less dependent country's trade dependence scores are virtually identical to a target country's trade dependence scores. Japan as a target country in the Senkaku dispute has been less dependent on China for trade than China has been on Japan, except for the year 1960 during the period under study.

In the meantime, China as a target in the Paracel and Spratly dispute has been less dependent on Vietnam for trade than Vietnam has been on China. By contrast, in the Dokdo case, Japan as a challenger has been less dependent on South Korea for trade than South Korea has been on Japan. This indicates that the inclusion of the trade dependence scores of South Korea as a target in my baseline model made a significant difference in the estimation results as compared to the result from the alternative specification based on Oneal and Russett's interdependence measure. Finally, both the joint IGO membership and the past dispute intensity have a statistically significant impact as hypothesized.

According to Barbieri, both symmetry and salience measures are hypothesized to have a negative impact on conflict. Yet as shown in the third column, her symmetry index produced statistically significant positive influence, whereas salience index has little statistical significance. In fact, this is not surprising because there are a large number of dyad-years in which bilateral trade relations are "equally" unimportant to each other. For instance, the trade ties between China and Vietnam had largely been severed during the Cold War period, making the two disputants "symmetrically" independent of each other for trade (symmetry score coded 1). As discussed in the previous section, the two countries repeatedly collided over the island issue in a violent manner until they normalized diplomatic and economic relations in 1991. Apparently, Barbieri's construction of symmetry index cannot capture such an anomaly.[19] Finally, consistent with the first two columns, the lagged dependent variable has a statistically significant positive influence on the dispute intensity.

---

[18] Out of 142 total observations of the challenger country's trade dependence score, 94 cases (about 66%) have values below .01819 (mean = 0.024; median = 0.009; standard deviation = 0.03; minimum = 0; maximum = 0.1485).

[19] It should be noted that Barbieri's interdependence index (salience × symmetry) shows no sign of statistical significance, either. Both conceptually and empirically, I found her interdependence measure problematic because it is a product of an interaction term (salience) and an additive term (symmetry). Aside from the statistical problem of high multicollinearity, such a double-product conditional term is too complicated to make a valid measure of economic interdependence.

3.3.2 Binary Logistic Regression

Table 3.2 summarizes the estimation results of binary logistic regressions. The first column is based on the baseline specification. The second column reports the result based on a less dependent country's trade dependence score. Finally, the third column presents the estimation result based on Barbieri's measures.

As shown in the first column, a target country's trade dependence on a challenger country has a statistically significant negative impact on the log likelihood of dispute occurrence ($p < 0.08$). Consistent with the result in the first column of Table 3.1, this evidence strongly supports the liberal peace proposition, indicating that if the target country becomes more dependent on the challenger for trade, both parties are less likely to initiate and escalate their island dispute to higher levels of hostility. Yet the challenger country's trade dependence on the target country has little statistical significance. The interaction term (target's trade dependence × challenger's trade dependence) has no statistical significance, either.

As for the control variables, the lagged dependent variable has a statistically significant positive impact on the log likelihood of dispute occurrence ($p < 0.001$). In contrast to the OLS estimation result, joint democracy has a statistically significant negative influence on the dispute likelihood ($p < 0.073$). That is, pairs of more democratic countries are less likely to initiate and escalate a dispute to higher levels of hostility. In addition, joint accession to the UNCLOS has a statistically significant impact on the dispute likelihood ($p < 0.082$), indicating that the UN Law of the Sea plays a pacific role by reducing the likelihood of island disputes.

As shown in the second and third columns, the alternative specifications based on Oneal and Russett's and Barbieri's interdependence measure produced no statistical significance, except for the lagged dependent variables and, in the second column, joint IGO membership ($p < 0.026$).

Finally, I set higher threshold levels of dispute occurrence to assess the sensitivity of logistic regression results to different coding approaches to the dependent variable. With a threshold level of dispute occurrence set at the value of 2 in a five-point scale (1 = seizures, threat or show of force, or higher levels of hostility; 0 = minimal or verbal diplomatic conflict), the estimation result of my baseline binary logistic regression model is largely consistent with the one reported in the first column of Table 3.2.[20] With a threshold level of dispute occurrence set at the value of 3 in a five-point scale (1 = mild physical clashes, isolated incidents between police and armed forces, or an outbreak of a MID/full-fledged war; 0 = threat or

---

[20] The coefficient of the target country's trade dependence ($\beta = -86.186$) is statistically significant at $p < 0.003$. The parameter estimation of the interaction term ($\beta = 5265.010$) is also statistically significant at $p < 0.031$. Finally, joint access to the UNCLOS is the only control variable ($\beta = -2.639$) that is statistically significant ($p < 0.079$). In alternative specifications based on Oneal and Russett's and Barbieri's interdependence measure, none of the parameters show any statistical significance, except for symmetry score, which has a positive impact on the dispute likelihood ($p < 0.011$).

Table 3.2 Effect of economic interdependence on the log likelihood of dispute occurrence: fixed-effects binary logistic panel regression result

Variables	I	II	III
Target's TD	−57.700 (1.75)[a]		
Challenger's TD	0.206 (0.01)		
Target's TD×Challenger's TD	2708.670 (1.26)		
Less dependent country's TD		27.824 (0.16)	
Salience			−165.876 (−0.25)
Symmetry			18.686 (0.68)
Salience×Symmetry			245.992 (0.35)
Challenger's relative power	−13.008 (−1.13)	−11.188 (−1.13)	−6.651 (−0.63)
Cold War	−0.853 (−1.06)	−1.161 (−1.49)	−1.044 (−1.30)
Joint democracy	−0.301 (−1.79)[a]	−0.148 (−1.56)	−0.181 (−1.59)
Joint IGO membership	−1.837 (−1.35)	−2.613 (−2.22)[b]	−1.846 (−1.33)
Joint accession to the UNCLOS	−1.931 (−1.74)[a]	−1.686 (−1.40)	−1.770 (−1.51)
Oil prices	−0.027 (−0.91)	−0.013 (−0.43)	−0.033 (−0.67)
Lagged dispute occurrence	1.676 (3.19)[c]	1.847 (3.49)[c]	1.787 (3.42)[c]
LR Chi-square	52.97	48.03	48.99
Log likelihood	−47.531	−50.003	−49.525
Number of observations	133	133	133

Note: The z-statistics appear in parentheses.
[a]Significant at the 0.10 level;
[b]Significant at the 0.05 level;
[c]Significant at the 0.01 level

show of force, or lower levels of hostility), none of the models produced statistically significant estimation results. This may not be surprising considering the fact that, out of 142 total observations of the outcome variable, there are only 6 cases (4.2%) that fall within this category.

3.4 Conclusion

The three dispute cases examined in this chapter provide an ideal laboratory to test the liberal peace argument, not only because disputant countries have engaged in various patterns of diplomatic and military behaviors in addressing their respective territorial claims, but also because economic interdependence of individual dyads has varied significantly over time.

I tested time-series cross-section data using OLS and binary logistic regression models with fixed effects. The estimation results are mixed, but favor the pacific benefits of economic interdependence. The coefficients relating the trade dependence score of a target country to the intensity and the likelihood of dispute is statistically significant at the $p<0.004$ and at the $p<0.08$, respectively. This implies that economic interdependence measured in terms of trade dependence scores has a major explanatory effect on the process of the three island disputes. Yet neither Oneal and Russett's nor Barbieri's measure is effective in capturing the impact of economic interdependence.

These findings provide theoretically and empirically interesting implications for liberal peace theory. The empirical results suggest that an indicator of trade dependence focusing on target–challenger relationship in a dispute dyad directly captures the effects of economic interdependence on the process of island disputes with respect to their intensity and likelihood of dispute occurrence.

Aside from the lagged dependent variable, the other variables to control for spurious relationships between the dependent and independent variables vary considerably in their magnitude and statistical significance, but there is evidence that both joint democracy and joint accession to the UNCLOS have a statistically significant influence on the likelihood of dispute occurrence. Largely consistent with existing explanations, joint democracy has a pacifying effect on the likelihood of dispute occurrence. In contrast to conventional wisdom, however, the UNCLOS has a pacifying effect on the dispute likelihood.

To conclude, my quantitative efforts to unravel what factors affect the dual nature of continuity and mutual restraint in the disputes over the Dokdo Islands, the Senkakus, and the Paracels and the Spratlys constitute one of the first attempts to focus on East Asian island disputes from a large N perspective. I believe that the findings of this chapter fill a significant gap in the empirical studies of East Asian territorial disputes. Yet, as with any kind of regression analysis with a relatively small N, these statistical findings require a cautionary interpretation. Also, given the historical complexity surrounding these island disputes, there remain stories to be explained in a qualitative manner. Building upon these quantitative findings, I turn to in-depth analyses in the following three chapters.

References

Barbieri K (2002) The liberal illusion: Does trade promote peace?. University of Michigan Press, Ann Arbor

Beck N, Katz JN (2001) Throwing out the baby with the bath water: A comment on Green, Kim, and Yoon. International Organization 55(2):487–495

Calder KE, Ye M (2004) Regionalism and critical junctures: Explaining the "Organization Gap" in Northeast Asia. The Journal of East Asian Studies 4(2):191–226

Chiozza G, Choi A (2003) Guess who did what: Political leaders and the management of territorial disputes, 1950–1990. Journal of Conflict Resolution 47(3):251–278

Choi S, James P (2003) No professional soldiers, no militarized interstate disputes? A new question for neo-Kantianism. Journal of Conflict Resolution 47(6):796–816

Cohen B (1998) The geography of money. Cornell University Press, Ithaca

Dixon WJ (1993) Democracy and the management of international conflict. Journal of Conflict Resolution 37(1):42–68

Doran CF (1991) Systems in crisis: New imperatives of high politics at century's end. Cambridge University Press, Cambridge

Gartzke E, Li Q (2003) War, peace, and the invisible hand: positive political externalities of economic globalization. International Studies Quarterly 47(4):561–586

Gartzke E, Li Q, Boehmer C (2001) Investing in the peace: Economic interdependence and international conflict. International Organization 55(2):391–438

Geller DS (1993) Power differentials and war in rival dyads. International Studies Quarterly 37(2):173–194

Ghosn F, Palmer G, Bremer S (2004) The MID3 data set, 1993–2001: Procedures, coding rules, and description. Conflict Management and Peace Science 21:133–154

Green DP, Kim SY, Yoon DH (2001) Dirty pool. International Organization 55(2):441–468

Hensel PR (2001) Contentious issues and world politics: Territorial claims in the Americas, 1816–1992. International Studies Quarterly 45(1):81–109

Huth PK (1996) Standing your ground: Territorial disputes and international conflict. University of Michigan Press, Ann Arbor

Huth PK, Allee TL (2002) The democratic peace and territorial conflict in the 20th century. Cambridge University Press, Cambridge

Ito T, Krueger AO (eds) (2000) The role of foreign direct investment in East Asian economic development. University of Chicago Press, Chicago

Katada SN (2004) Japan's counterweight strategy: U.S.–Japan cooperation and competition in international finance. In: Krauss ES, Pempel TJ (eds) Beyond bilateralism: U.S.–Japan relations in the new Asia-Pacific. Stanford University Press, Stanford

Keohane RO (1990) International liberalism reconsidered. In: Dunn J (ed) The economic limits to modern politics. Cambridge University Press, Cambridge

King G (2001) Proper nouns and methodological propriety: Pooling dyads in international relations data. International Organization 55(2):497–507

Marshall MG, Jaggers K (2002) Political regime characteristics and transitions, 1800–2002: Dataset users' manual. Center for International Development and Conflict Management (CIDCM), University of Maryland, College Park

Mearsheimer J (2001) The tragedy of great power politics. W.W. Norton, New York

Oneal JR, Russett BM (1997) The classical liberals were right: Democracy, interdependence, and conflict, 1950–85. International Studies Quarterly 41(2):267–293

Oneal JR, Russett BM (1999a) Assessing the liberal peace with alternative specifications: Trade still reduces conflict. Journal of Peace Research 36(4):423–442

Oneal JR, Russett BM (1999b) The Kantian peace: The pacific benefits of democracy, interdependence, and international organizations, 1885–1992. World Politics 52(1):1–37

Oneal JR, Russett BM (2001) Clear and clean: The fixed effects of the liberal peace. International Organization 55(2):469–485

Organski AFK, Kugler J (1980) The war ledger. University of Chicago Press, Chicago

Polachek S (1980) Conflict and trade. Journal of Conflict Resolution 24(1):55–78

Rousseau D, Gelpi C, Reiter D, Huth P (1996) Assessing the dyadic nature of the democratic peace. American Political Science Review 90(3):512–544

Russett B, Oneal J, Davis D (1998) The third leg of the Kantian tripod for peace: International organizations and militarized disputes, 1950–85. International Organization 52(3):441–467

Senese PD, Vasquez JA (2003) A unified explanation of territorial conflict: Testing the impact of sampling bias, 1919–1992. International Studies Quarterly 47(2):275–298

Simmons BA (2005) Rules over real estate: Trade, territorial conflict, and international borders as institutions. Journal of Conflict Resolution 49(6):823–848

Sweeney KJ (2003) The severity of interstate disputes: Are dyadic capability preponderances really more pacific? Journal of Conflict Resolution 47(6):728–750

Vasquez JA (1993) The war puzzle. Cambridge University Press, Cambridge

Chapter 4
The Island and Maritime Disputes in the East Sea/Sea of Japan

4.1 Introduction

South Korea has recalled ambassadors only four times in its modern history – three times from Japan. The latest recall in July 2008 followed Japan's renewed claim to the Dokdo Islands in a new guideline for junior high school teachers and textbook publishers. The islands are *de facto* controlled by South Korea, but Japan does not recognize South Korea's *de jure* sovereignty over the islands.[1] The Lee Myung-bak administration, which has made improving ties with Japan a major policy goal, said it was an "intolerable act" that Japan restated its territorial claim (*The New York Times*, July 15, 2008).

The conflict between Seoul and Tokyo over the Dokdo Islands is a textbook case of East Asian maritime disputes, in which a chain of responses and counter-responses have led to the present stalemate. Tokyo has pressed for a judicial settlement, claiming that the islands have been Japanese since Japan formally annexed them in February 1905, following the Russo–Japanese War, which was 5 years before Korea was forced to sign the treaty of annexation.[2] Seoul does not recognize the existence of a territorial dispute, but prefers low-key diplomacy in the hope

---

[1] The Dokdo Islands consist of two tiny, barely habitable rocky islets surrounded by 33 smaller rocks and reefs. As illustrated in Map. 4.1, they are located about 50 nautical miles east of South Korea's Ullung Island and about 90 nm northwest of Japan's Oki Islands. Their approximate total surface area is 0.186 square kilometers (56 acres) (Lovmo 2002).

[2] While there is historical evidence that the islands were occasionally visited by Japanese fishermen harvesting abalone and sea lions, Japan's fundamental legal claim stems from February 22, 1905 when the government of Shimane Prefecture issued Notification Decree #40 which placed the islands under the administrative control of its local authorities in the Oki Islands. The prefecture's decree was based on the Decision of Parliament (January 28, 1905) concerning the Territorial Incorporation of Takeshima which was claimed to be *terra nullius* – uninhabited land exhibiting no evidence of being in the possession of any other country (Park 1969: 79–80).

M.G. Koo, *Island Disputes and Maritime Regime Building in East Asia*,   63
The Political Economy of the Asia Pacific,
DOI 10.1007/978-0-387-89670-0_4, © Springer Science+Business Media, LLC 2009

China

North Korea

East Sea/Sea of Japan

Dokdo/Takeshima

Japan

South Korea

Yellow Sea

East China Sea

Map. 4.1   The Dokdo/Takeshima Islands and the East Sea/Sea of Japan

to prevent the dispute from escalating to the point where pressures would build up to have it arbitrated by a third party.[3]

For outsiders, the dispute over a collection of barren rocks that seem to have little economic value might seem mysterious. But for those Koreans who still remember Japan's brutal occupation of their country, the dispute is both real and emotional. One the one hand, fishing resources near the islands have been one of its most salient material concerns. On the other hand, South Korea's claim to the

---

[3] The Koreans lay their claim to Dokdo based on earlier and numerous precedents than Japan. They point to the document that named it as a territory that was first incorporated into the Shilla Dynasty in 512 AD. They also point to ancient land surveys and maps that show the islands within Korean territory. The Koreans also complain that the Japanese took advantage of Korea's political weakness vis-à-vis Japan in 1905, when the islands were registered as a part of Shimane Prefecture of Japan. As of 1905, Japan had already taken control of the foreign affairs of Korea via the Protectorate Treaty of 1905, the ratification of which had been forced on Korea by the Japanese colonialists without the endorsement by King Kojong (1852–1919) (Lovmo 2002).

islands has emotional content far beyond any material significance because giving way on the island issue to Japan would be considered as once again compromising the sovereignty over the whole Korean peninsula. For Japan, the Dokdo issue may lack the same degree of strategic and economic values and emotional appeal as the other two territorial disputes that Japan has had with Russia and the two Chinas – namely the Northern Territories/Southern Kurile Islands and the Senkaku Islands, respectively. Nevertheless, fishing resources and the maritime boundary issues became highly salient with the introduction of UNCLOS. Also, the legal, political, and economic issues surrounding Dokdo are all intertwined with Japan's other territorial disputes to the extent that concessions of sovereignty on any of these island disputes could jeopardize claims or negotiations concerning the rest.

South Korea and Japan have forged a deeper diplomatic and economic partnership over the past decade. A new spirit of partnership after the landmark joint declaration of 1998 culminated in the successful co-hosting of the World Cup 2002. At the end of 2003 the two neighbors began to negotiate an FTA to further strengthen their already close economic ties. South Korea's decades-long embargo on Japanese cultural products has now been lifted, while a number of South Korean pop stars are currently sweeping across Japan, creating the so-called "Korean Wave" fever. A pragmatic calculation of national interests would thus suggest cooperative behavior. Yet beneath the surface, few years have passed since the end of Japanese colonial rule in 1945 without dangerous undercurrents capable of causing a diplomatic crisis across the East Sea/Sea of Japan. Any insensitive, seemingly sovereign actions – such as the authorization of history textbooks, a prime ministerial visit to a war shrine, and the issuance of postage stamps – can fuel the persistent hostility between these two quasi-allies.

The sovereignty question of Dokdo has indeed been one of the most fundamental barriers to better bilateral relations throughout the postwar period. Competing sovereignty claims emerged as a byproduct of the San Francisco Peace Treaty negotiations between the Allied Powers and Japan, and escalated into a near crisis in the early 1950s when South Korea took physical control of the islands. In 1965, South Korea and Japan reached an agreement to normalize their bilateral relationship, but the island question was left unresolved. The sovereignty issue surfaced again in 1977 when Japan proclaimed new exclusive fishing zones. The island question flared up in 1996 when both countries demonstrated an unusually hardline territorial and maritime policy. In 2004, the two countries collided again over the island issue using postage stamps to wage a surrogate conflict. In 2005, the diplomatic spat over the Japanese designation of "Takeshima Day" and official approval of history textbooks that reinforce Japan's claim to the disputed islands unleashed a flood of nationalist venom in South Korea. In the first half of 2006, a serious diplomatic row flared up between Seoul and Tokyo over the issue of naming seabed features and maritime survey near the islands. Most recently, the summer of 2008 had its share of confrontation owing to the Japanese Ministry of Education's decision to issue a new manual for teachers and textbook publishers urging them to instruct junior high school students that ownership of the Dokdo Islands is in dispute.

This brief chronological overview raises two closely related questions. Why does the Dokdo dispute persist? And why has the island dispute been contained within certain confines despite regular outbreak of tension? In what follows, I show that a territorial bargaining game approach can systematically explain the transition between, and conclusion of, multiple rounds of dispute that have unfolded in the postwar period. Coupled with growing resource competition, the clash of rival nationalisms between South Korea and Japan has had an enduring influence on the initiation and escalation of the recurring rounds of dispute. Yet the pacific influence of increasingly salient economic interdependence – along with the geo-strategic situation in Northeast Asia – has prevented the maritime issues from spinning out of control. Both the South Korean and Japanese governments have found it a convenient strategy to continue to shelve the final resolution of the island and maritime dispute in favor of more pragmatic concerns. Yet again, popular nationalist passions on both sides may move the issue beyond the absolute calculation of political elites, particularly if South Korea's trade dependence on Japan continues to decline in the face of increasingly fluid geopolitics in the Korean peninsula in a post-9-11 world.

4.2 The First Round of Dispute (1952–65)

The first two postwar decades witnessed a growing tension between South Korea and Japan. During the first round of Dokdo dispute, South Korea restored *de facto*, if not *de jure*, control over the islands, and Japan began to seek to overturn the new territorial *status quo* in the East Sea/Sea of Japan, occasionally backed by threat or use of force. During this period, South Korean–Japanese economic ties were insignificant, as indicated by the low trade dependence scores of both South Korea and Japan, which remained at the level of less than 5% (See Table 4.1). All else constant, the absence of the mitigating forces of mutual gains from trade would mean the lack of economic deterrent to dispute. The first round was catalyzed by America's Cold War policy in favor of Japan and was magnified by resource competition and domestic politics loaded with hostile nationalist sentiments. Yet by the mid-1960s, the island issue eventually took a back seat as the need for trade and investment cooperation between South Korea and Japan became increasingly urgent. The containment or de-escalation of the first round of Dokdo flare-up indicates the pacifying effect of economic interdependence.

4.2.1 Initiation and Escalation Phase

The Dokdo problem arose both directly and indirectly as a consequence of U.S. Cold War policy in Northeast Asia. The initial impetus for the first round of the challenge-the-status-quo came with Japan's defeat in the Pacific War in August 1945. South Korea gained independence but was soon divided at the thirty-eighth

Table 4.1 GDP and trade statistics of Korea and Japan (1953–2004) (US$ million)

	South Korea					Japan				
	GDP	Export to Japan	Import from Japan	Bilateral trade balance	TD on Japan (%)	GDP	Export to Korea	Import from Korea	Bilateral trade balance	TD on Korea (%)
1953	2,633	9	107	−98	4.41	19,446	107	9	98	0.60
1954	3,644	8	69	−61	2.11	21,610	69	8	61	0.36
1955	2,262	7	17	−10	1.06	23,197	40	10	30	0.22
1956	3,002	8	9	−1	0.57	26,115	64	11	53	0.29
1957	3,914	11	12	−1	0.59	30,190	57	12	45	0.23
1958	4,066	10	48	−38	1.41	32,078	57	11	46	0.21
1959	4,320	13	32	−19	1.03	36,721	62	12	50	0.20
1960	3,892	20	58	−38	2.00	44,622	100	19	82	0.27
1961	2,357	19	69	−50	3.77	53,888	126	23	103	0.28
1962	2,746	24	109	−86	4.83	61,154	138	29	110	0.27
1963	3,864	25	162	−137	4.82	69,991	160	27	133	0.27
1964	3,358	38	110	−72	4.42	82,329	109	42	67	0.18
1965	3,018	44	167	−123	6.98	91,596	180	41	139	0.24
1966	3,806	66	294	−228	9.44	106,378	335	72	263	0.38
1967	4,703	85	443	−358	11.22	124,661	407	92	315	0.40
1968	5,955	100	624	−524	12.15	147,642	603	102	501	0.48
1969	7,476	133	755	−621	11.88	173,427	767	134	633	0.52
1970	8,900	234	809	−575	11.72	204,409	818	229	589	0.51
1971	9,851	262	962	−700	12.42	230,889	857	274	584	0.49
1972	10,735	408	1,031	−623	13.41	305,765	996	433	563	0.47
1973	13,691	1,242	1,727	−485	21.68	415,418	1,793	1,206	587	0.72
1974	19,229	1,380	2,621	−1,240	20.81	461,127	2,655	1,567	1,088	0.92
1975	21,459	1,293	2,434	−1,141	17.37	501,426	2,246	1,307	939	0.71
1976	29,555	1,802	3,099	−1,298	16.58	563,554	2,828	1,919	909	0.84
1977	37,926	2,148	3,927	−1,778	16.02	693,587	4,113	2,160	1,953	0.90
1978	51,125	2,627	5,982	−3,355	16.84	974,518	6,056	2,630	3,426	0.89
1979	65,562	3,353	6,657	−3,304	15.27	1,014,321	6,201	3,358	2,843	0.94

(continued)

Table 4.1 (continued)

	South Korea					Japan				
	GDP	Export to Japan	Import from Japan	Bilateral trade balance	TD on Japan (%)	GDP	Export to Korea	Import from Korea	Bilateral trade balance	TD on Korea (%)
1980	63,810	3,039	5,858	-2,819	13.94	1,062,752	5,392	3,040	2,352	0.79
1981	71,469	3,503	6,374	-2,871	13.82	1,174,567	5,640	3,395	2,245	0.77
1982	76,209	3,405	5,305	-1,900	11.43	1,091,583	4,869	3,270	1,599	0.75
1983	84,511	3,383	6,239	-2,856	11.39	1,190,692	6,006	3,407	2,599	0.79
1984	93,212	4,610	7,640	-3,030	13.14	1,266,999	7,211	4,205	3,006	0.90
1985	96,620	4,546	7,557	-3,011	12.53	1,356,363	7,159	4,144	3,015	0.83
1986	111,305	5,426	10,869	-5,443	14.64	2,009,699	10,557	5,334	5,223	0.79
1987	140,007	8,437	13,657	-5,220	15.78	2,437,335	13,344	8,173	5,171	0.88
1988	187,448	12,004	15,847	-3,843	14.86	2,959,386	15,442	11,827	3,615	0.92
1989	230,474	13,167	17,167	-4,000	13.16	2,961,160	16,491	12,931	3,560	0.99
1990	263,775	12,638	18,574	-5,936	11.83	3,039,693	17,499	11,743	5,756	0.96
1991	308,194	12,356	21,120	-8,764	10.86	3,475,955	20,088	12,381	7,707	0.93
1992	329,877	11,599	19,458	-7,859	9.41	3,793,819	17,786	11,596	6,190	0.77
1993	362,195	11,564	20,016	-8,452	8.72	4,354,707	19,192	11,742	7,450	0.71
1994	423,265	13,523	25,390	-11,867	9.19	4,794,206	24,361	13,524	10,837	0.79
1995	517,129	17,088	32,597	-15,509	9.61	5,283,057	31,292	17,330	13,962	0.92
1996	557,638	16,002	31,396	-15,394	8.50	4,688,254	29,369	15,980	13,389	0.97
1997	517,044	14,780	27,840	-13,060	8.24	4,305,591	26,097	14,606	11,491	0.95
1998	345,003	12,262	16,843	-4,582	8.44	3,931,051	15,400	12,142	3,258	0.70
1999	445,168	15,863	24,142	-8,279	8.99	4,452,977	23,089	16,138	6,951	0.88
2000	511,928	20,466	31,828	-11,362	10.22	4,746,068	30,703	20,454	10,249	1.08
2001	481,969	16,506	26,633	-10,128	8.95	4,162,363	25,292	17,221	8,071	1.02
2002	546,713	15,143	29,856	-14,713	8.23	3,972,485	28,612	15,498	13,114	1.11
2003	605,331	17,276	36,313	-19,037	8.85	4,300,858	34,823	17,931	16,892	1.23
2004	663,200	21,701	46,144	-24,443	10.23	4,685,400	46,144	21,701	24,443	1.45

Sources: The International Monetary Fund, *The Direction of Trade Statistics* (CD-Rom); The World Bank, *World Development Indicators* (CD-Rom)

parallel into the Soviet zone to the north and the U.S. zone to the south. The U.S. provided a hegemonic balance between the two quasi-enemies – South Korea and Japan – and defined their postwar strategies. Under these circumstances, South Korea and Japan communicated with each other primarily through the U.S. as the hub country in a hierarchical regime solidified through bilateral defense treaties. In addition, the political economy of the region was primarily bilateral with the U.S. whose bulk aid grant sustained many developing countries including South Korea (Cumings 1997: 135, 159).

In the early postwar years, the boundary issue in the East Sea/Sea of Japan remained both contentious and unpredictable. In September 1945, the U.S. occupation forces placed the Dokdo Islands within the Japan-based U.S. Sixth Army's area of responsibility. In less than a year, the so-called MacArthur Line replaced the occupation boundaries, thus including Dokdo under the command of the U.S. XXIV Corps, which was in charge of all of South Korea and its various outlying islands (Lovmo 2002).[4]

It was the San Francisco Peace Treaty of 1951 between the Allies and Japan that eventually left the location of sovereignty over the islands undefined, thereby sowing the seeds of disagreement between South Korea and Japan. During the treaty negotiations, both South Korea and Japan lobbied the U.S. for ultimate sovereignty over Dokdo. From late 1946, the U.S. State Department prepared nine drafts of a peace treaty with Japan. The first five drafts explicitly mentioned Dokdo as among the "offshore Korean islands" that Japan was to renounce. Yet the sixth draft deliberately indicated that "Takeshima" was Japanese territory, as a result of the intensive Japanese lobbying effort. However, other "associated powers" such as the U.K., Australia, and New Zealand disagreed with the U.S. version. Therefore, the final drafts (seventh–ninth) did not mention the name of Dokdo. Many experts believe that the U.S. decision to remain neutral on the Dokdo issue was designed to leave some potential wedges for defense of Japan in the wake of communist expansion in Northeast Asia (Hara 2001: 368–74).

The 1951 Peace Treaty states that "Japan, recognizing the independence of Korea, renounces all right, title, and claim to Korea, including the islands of Quelpart (Jeju Island), Port Hamilton (Komun Island), and Dagelet (Ullung Island)," while formally abolishing the MacArthur Line. However, it did not make explicit determination of Dokdo's sovereignty, leaving interpretations of the documentary evidence put forward by the South Korean and Japanese governments open to conflict.

The South Korean position is that the islands named in the San Francisco Peace Treaty were cited as an illustration rather than as enumeration and, therefore, that the Dokdo Islands should be included in Japan's overall renunciation of its pre-World War II imperial territories "taken by greed and violence." Also, South Korea argues that Dokdo is clearly South Korean territory in that: (1) they were not explicitly stipulated as Japanese territory in the Treaty, either; (2) they were covered as territory

---

[4] General MacArthur's Directives to the Japanese Government, Supreme Commander for the Allied Powers Instruction (SCAPIN) 1033, June 22, 1946. SCAPIN 677 of January 29, 1946 also detached Dokdo from Japan.

to be stripped of Japan by Cairo, Potsdam, and the surrender documents; (3) they had been separated administratively from Japan by SCAPIN 677 and 1033; and (4) they were under the effective control of the South Korean government since the Republic of Korea regained formal independence in 1948 (Park 1969: 19–20).

Japan, on the other hand, contends that none of these texts, nor any other internationally valid postwar instrument, amounted to a definitive territorial settlement requiring the surrender of its claim to sovereignty over the Dokdo Islands. Japan maintains that SCAPIN 677 simply defined administrative functions rather than sovereignty *per se*. Japan also emphasizes that the MacArthur Line established under SCAPIN 1033 was abolished on April 25, 1952 as a result of the San Francisco Peace Treaty, which allegedly reverted the islands to Japan as part of Shimane Prefecture (Day 1987: 337–8; Sin 1997: 145–8; Kajimura 1997: 459–60).

These initial impetuses greatly changed the value of territory perceived by the two rival countries. From the beginning, the issue of fishing in the East Sea/Sea of Japan became a surrogate battlefield for the Dokdo dispute. For centuries, Japanese fishing in the coastal and offshore waters of the Korean peninsula has been a major source of controversy between the two neighbors (Park 1983a: 143–4). In the postwar years, the fishery dispute emerged again with South Korea's unilateral proclamation of the Peace Line.[5] In the following years, the relations of the two countries went from bad to worse as South Korea continued to seize Japanese fishing vessels found within the Peace Line.[6]

Japan took a variety of retaliatory measures against South Korea, sometimes effectively and sometimes in vain. The Shimane prefectural authorities of Japan began to issue licenses for fishing and sea lion hunting near Dokdo in March 1953 when a joint U.S.–Japanese decision lifted the designation of the area as a bombing range.[7] In the following months, Japan sent naval ships to expel South Korean fishermen who were found to conduct fishing activities on the islands and in their nearby waters. As a warning against unauthorized fishing activities by South Koreans, the Japanese government planted several signposts on the islands, but they were quickly removed by South Korean fishermen and volunteer guards (*The New York Times*, October 8, 1953).

---

[5] On January 18, 1952, upon the impending abolition of the MacArthur Line, the Syngman Rhee government (1948–1960) declared the Peace Line (or Rhee Line) to include Dokdo within South Korean territory, as well as to delineate the zone of maritime defense and fishing in South Korea's favor. This delimitation ran 60 nm on average from the South Korean coast and 170 nm at its farthest point. The Peace Line effectively excluded Japanese fishermen from some of the richest fishing grounds in the East Sea/Sea of Japan, and was taken by Japan as the equivalent of declaring war against Japan (Park 1983b: 62; Day 1987: 338; Cha 1996: 130).

[6] This practice, which started in September 1953, reached a climax in August 1955. For example, during the single week of August 3–9, 1955, eleven Japanese vessels with 266 men on board were seized and four more fired on by the South Korean maritime forces (*Keesing's Record of World Events*, April 1960).

[7] SCAPIN 1778 established the Dokdo Islands as an aerial bombing range on September 16, 1947. The physical dangers arising from this status was demonstrated by an incident near the islands in June 1948 when sixteen Korean fishermen were killed and four of their boats were destroyed by U.S. Air Force planes engaged in bombing practice (Lovmo 2002).

Unintended victims of Japanese retaliatory pressure were the 600,000 Koreans residing in Japan, who had to face every conceivable form of discrimination against them. Japan also refused to import South Korean sea products and to export fishing gear and nets to South Korea, thus further deteriorating bilateral relations. Serious physical clashes between South Korean and Japanese maritime forces were only a matter of time. In July 1953, a Japanese patrol boat ordering South Korean fishermen to leave the islands was fired upon allegedly by armed South Korean maritime paramilitary vigilantes. In April 1954, three Japanese patrol boats arrived to stage their typical show of force. Upon arriving at the Dokdo Islands, these ships came under mortar fire from South Korean forces. The Japanese lost one boat and suffered sixteen casualties, including several deaths (Park 1983b: 61–4; Day 1987: 338–9; Lovmo 2002).[8]

Having emerged as an outcome of Cold War politics and resource competition, the Dokdo question quickly became an icon of the contending nationalisms of South Korea and Japan in the 1950s. Often fueled by the competitive political atmosphere in the immediate postwar years, the cognitive biases held by the leadership both in Seoul and Tokyo essentially made compromise or concession in negotiations amount to treason (Cha 1996: 127).

On the Japanese side, throughout the U.S. occupation period (1945–52), the Supreme Commander for the Allied Powers (SCAP) as well as the Japanese government struggled with the problem of Korean residents in Japan, the majority of whom had been forced to move to Japan to support Japan's war mobilization against the U.S. Some of these Koreans, who chose to remain in Japan, allegedly engaged in smuggling and black market activities. More problematically for Japan, many of them cooperated with the Japanese Communist Party and instigated civil unrest against the U.S. and Japanese authorities. The Japanese government branded most of the Koreans in Japan as communists and was anxious to repatriate as many of them as possible (Cheong 1992: 91).[9]

Rhee Syngman, the first president of South Korea, held profound contempt for Japan although his government had to rely on Korean collaborators with Japanese colonialism for practical reasons. Not surprisingly, Rhee's entire political career before attaining the presidency was built upon his anti-Japanese activities during the occupation period. In the eyes of many South Koreans, hostility towards Japan

---

[8] In a provocative show of will to reinforce its territorial claim, South Korea took physical control of the islands in July 1954 by stationing a small number of garrison guards. In the following months and years, South Korea and Japan continued to clash over the islands, exchanging gun and mortar fire on a number of occasions (Day 1987: 338).

[9] In particular, Japanese Prime Minister Shigeru Yoshida (1948–54) held not only negative images of Korea but also an intense personal dislike of Rhee. He once referred to Koreans living in Japan as "insects in the stomach of a lion with the potential to kill the lion itself if not checked" (Lee 1985: 176). Such negative attitudes were further exacerbated by a Japanese superiority complex towards the Koreans. The prewar Japanese militarists and intellectuals disguised their expansionist ambitions as pan-Asianism, while implicitly regarding the neighboring countries as inferior. Despite cultural affinity with their colonial peoples, the Japanese disparaged them for failing to modernize as effectively as the Japanese did (Bridges 1993: 25).

was deeply intertwined with national identity, and postwar Korean nationalism was thus imbued with anti-Japanese sentiments. For South Korean political leaders, both ruling and opposition, "Japan-bashing" provided a powerful rhetorical tool with which to manipulate public opinion and undercut political opponents in a fierce struggle for power. Virtually all political entities tried to capitalize on the anti-Japanese sentiments, although many of them had dubious careers during the colonial times (Cumings 1984; Eckert et al. 1990; Cheong 1992: 89–90).

The historical animosity was further fueled by the negative view held by the South Koreans about their economic relations with Japan. After the outbreak of the Korean War, sales to U.S. forces in Japan led to a special procurement boom. The result was a rapid reconstruction of the Japanese economy, paving the way for a subsequent era of high growth. This made many in South Korea to believe that the Japanese economic miracle came at the expense of Korean lives. After a brief trade boom during the Korean War, the two countries returned to quasi-enemy status by the mid-1950s. In 1954, for instance, Japan's export to South Korea was worth $69 million while its import $8 million; in 1959, its export to South Korea was $62 million and its import was $12 million. The bilateral trade as a share of GDP mattered equally little to both countries as it was extremely limited between 1954 and 1960 (See Table 4.1).

Even for the U.S., it was not always easy to bring the two *quasi-enemies* together. It was only with the restoration of Japanese sovereignty in 1952 that the first formal but reluctant contact between South Korea and Japan began. The negotiations for normalization faced a rocky start from the very first meeting held in February 1952 and were to continue, acrimoniously and intermittently, for 14 years and through seven official rounds of talks. In all, it took five Japanese Prime Ministers, from Shigeru Yoshida to Eisaku Sato, and three South Korean Presidents from Syngman Rhee to Park Chung Hee, before the normalization process could come to fruition in 1965. The two sides tried to settle their differences over a wide range of issues, such as the property claims, Korean residents in Japan, fishery/Peace Line disputes, the sovereignty over Dokdo, and Japan's relations with North Korea, just to name the major ones (Bridges 1993: 9–10).

Although initial progress was made on some minor questions during the first three official talks, virtually all negotiations were suspended by 1956. In 1957, negotiations resumed over the terms of the release of the Japanese detainees as well as other pending issues, while tension grew as the seizure of Japanese vessels and crews continued in the East Sea/Sea of Japan.[10] The progress of the negotiations,

---

[10] Eventually an agreement was signed in Tokyo on December 31, 1957, whereby 850 Japanese fishermen who had completed their sentences would be sent back to Japan; 100 more would be sent back on completing their sentences; in exchange, 460 South Koreans detained in Japan who had lived there before 1945 would be released or allowed to remain in Japan; and 1,100 illegal immigrants would be deported to South Korea. It was also agreed that formal negotiations on the establishment of normal diplomatic relations, trade, fisheries, and problems concerning Koreans in Japan should begin in Tokyo on March 1, 1958 (*Keesing's Record of World Events*, April 1960).

however, was again hampered by South Korea's refusal to make concessions on the Peace Line, and the continued seizure of Japanese fishing boats and their crews. The fourth official talks, which started in April 1958, came to an abrupt end since Japanese Prime Minister Nobusuke Kishi's (1957–60) decision to allow repatriation of Korean residents to North Korea provoked President Rhee. As a protest against the Japanese assertion on the repatriation question as well as the Peace Line, the South Korean government cut off all trade exchanges with Japan on June 15, 1959. It took more than a year before full trade relations and official normalization talks resumed. But the fifth official talks that were resumed in October 1960 were again called off in May 1961 when a military coup led by General Park Chung Hee over-threw the fledgling democratic regime that had replaced Rhee's in the previous year (Bridges 1993: 9–10; Lee 1995a: 76–9).

Japan showed a lukewarm attitude towards the sixth official talks that started in October 1961 owing to complex power dynamics. Prime Minister Hayato Ikeda (1960–64) worried that the financial and political responsibilities that would result from a normalization treaty might possibly backfire on him as the Upper House and the ruling Liberal Democratic Party (LDP) elections drew near in July 1962. For the Ikeda administration, the Dokdo issue was a convenient excuse to delay normal-ization talks (Lee 1995b: 60–2).

During this stage, the Dokdo question was discussed occasionally, but it was never placed on the official agenda because of its thorny nature. In a 1962 statement before the Diet, Foreign Minister Masayoshi Ohira stated that relations with South Korea would not be normalized until the sovereignty question had been fully resolved (House of Representatives, fortieth Session, Standing Committee on Foreign Affairs, No. 27, April 27, 1962). During a series of formal and informal meetings with South Korea, Japan continued to insist that the territorial problem be written down in the treaty and that South Korea agree to take the case to the ICJ. From South Korea's view, there could be no dispute about the title to the islands, since they were indisputably within the territorial jurisdiction of South Korea. Therefore, taking the case to the ICJ would lure South Korea into a diplomatic and legal trap only in favor of Japan (Kajimura 1997: 465).

4.2.2   De-escalation Phase

The hostile situation abruptly changed after Park Chung Hee (1961–79) seized power in South Korea. The island question continued to serve as one of the most vexing and intractable bilateral problems, jeopardizing the final stage of normaliza-tion negotiations. Yet the sovereignty question eventually took a back seat in favor of more pressing diplomatic and economic affairs. Once South Korea and Japan both felt a strong urge to improve their bilateral relations, they made the conscious choice to shelve territorial issues, while giving fishery negotiations a higher priority than before, thereby opening the way to conclude the prolonged normalization negotiations. Among others, President Park realized that he could not delay the treaty negotiations any longer and, in October 1962, sent his right hand man, Korean Central Intelligence Agency (KCIA) Director Kim Jong-pil, to Tokyo as a chief negotiator to conclude prolonged negotiations.

To be sure, the path to the final agreement was not an easy one. In their second meeting in November, Kim and Ohira reached a secret agreement on the amount of a financial reparation package.[11] Yet again, Ohira brought up the territorial issue, asking Kim to agree to take the case to the ICJ. Available evidence suggests that President Park gave Kim a specific instruction that the Dokdo Islands should not be a treaty agenda. Obsessed with concluding financial deals, however, Kim failed to strongly protest Ohira's claim. It remains unclear whether Kim ignored Park's personal guidelines intentionally or not (Lee 1995b: 125–31).

The 1962 Kim–Ohira secret agreement was a breakthrough in the stalemated talks, but left many problems. The diplomatic atmosphere between South Korea and Japan became dangerously charged with mutual suspicion when the Kim–Ohira memorandum was released in January 1963. In South Korea, the secretive, if not collusive, manner in which Kim had handled the issue sparked public fear of a national sellout. It was rumored that Kim had agreed in the memorandum that South Korea would give up sovereignty claim to the Dokdo Islands in return for Japan's generous "economic aid" or "gift for Korean independence," instead of "reparations" for Japan's past atrocities. He was also mistakenly known to have suggested that the islands be detonated if no peaceful resolution of the sovereignty question were possible (*The Korea Times*, February 11, 1996).[12] The revelation touched off South Korean nationalism, leading to nationwide demonstrations against normalization talks. Intense public outcry forced Kim Jong-pil into an 8-month political exile (February–October 1963), leaving negotiations at a standstill (Oda 1967: 54–5).

Having just barely won the presidential election held in August 1963, General-turned-President Park had to contend with the public's growing sense of

---

[11] The Kim–Ohira memorandum states: (1) Japan would pay $300 million as a grant over the following 10 years; (2) Japan would loan a further $200 million, from the Overseas Economic Cooperation Fund, over the following 10 years with a repayment schedule of 20 years at 3.5% interest deferred for 7 years; and (3) Japan would arrange for private loans over $100 million through its Ex-Im Bank (Lee 1995a: 124–5).

[12] To do Kim justice, the idea of bombing away the islands was not new. At a preliminary meeting held on September 3, 1962, Director of the Northeast Asian Division of Japanese Ministry of Foreign Affairs, Yujiro Iseki, told his South Korean counterparts that the Dokdo Islands were useless, so that they could be exploded in order to clear the way for normalization talks. But the underlying intention was to take the issue to the ICJ (Lee 1995a: 80). During the final stage of negotiations, the U.S. Secretary of State Dean Rusk suggested visiting President Park in May of 1965 that South Korea and Japan erect a jointly operated lighthouse on the islands, allowing both sides a share of the islands and gradually diffusing the issue. Park responded by saying that "Even if the Dokdo issue is a small one in the diplomatic relations negotiations, it is one that makes one angry…I wish I could bomb the islands out of existence just to solve the problem" (*Yonhap News*, June 20, 2004).

indignation. Overconfident in his grip over domestic politics, Park rehabilitated Kim in March 1964 and sent him again to Tokyo as presidential envoy to resume the stalemated talks. The announcement in Tokyo that month that a treaty draft was imminent drew allegations in South Korea that Kim had secretly cut another deal with Tokyo by conceding South Korea's negotiating position in exchange for vast amount of Japanese funds for his own profit and ruling party coffers. Although Park removed Kim in the middle of the Tokyo negotiations, domestic protests continued to attack Kim's association with widespread corruption in the ruling Democratic Republican Party (DRP), in which Kim held the party chairmanship. In addition, factions developed within the ruling party between pro and anti-Kim forces, threatening the stability of the entire government. The entire turmoil resulted in Kim's resignation from the DRP chairmanship in June 1964 and his departure for the U.S. on an extended leave of absence (Lee 1990: 169–70; Lee 1995b: 200–1; Cha 1996: 135).

The momentum created by the Kim–Ohira secret memorandum stalled even further at the end of March 1964 over South Korean seizures of Japanese fishing vessels. South Korea claimed Japanese fishing vessels violated its territorial integrity as established by the Peace Line. Japan refused to recognize the line and protested the seizures as unlawful acts of aggression. Acrimonious outbursts by both sides led to a suspension of the fishery subcommittee talks in April 1964. The potential for armed clashes was high as the Japanese maritime police introduced naval patrols to protect fishing vessels from further harassment (*Japan Times*, September 21, 1964; Cha 1996: 134).

In Japan, the anti-normalization movement – primarily led by Socialist, Communist, and other leftist elements – gained momentum, especially with the support of pro-Pyongyang Federation of Korean Residents in Japan that organized demonstrations effectively through its elaborate, nationwide network (Lee 1995b: 60–2). Seen comparatively, however, the situation in Japan was not as bad as in South Korea where martial law had to be declared in June 1964 to control the deteriorating situation. Although the voice of anti-normalization was loud in Japan, it was never beyond the government's control. To some extent, the Japanese government took advantage of domestic dissent as a diplomatic leverage to extract concessions from a more desperate South Korea (Lee 1995b: 146–7). In the final phase of negotiations, the question was not whether Japanese Prime Minister Eisaku Sato (1964–72) could handle domestic pressure; it was whether Park could survive the large-scale anti-normalization movement in South Korea (Lee 1990: 170).

Despite the complex domestic power dynamics in both countries, geopolitical conditions began to change dramatically towards South Korean–Japanese rapprochement. It is widely held that the U.S. created the necessary, if not sufficient, momentum for the conclusion of normalization treaty in 1965. Until 1963, the U.S. maintained a somewhat indifferent position towards the normalization talks. While reconciliation between Seoul and Tokyo would be beneficial to U.S. security interests in the region, the issue did not hold a high priority in Washington except among regional experts. By 1964, however, increasingly intense Cold War competition in

East Asia prompted a significant change in the U.S. approach.[13] In the face of growing regional uncertainties, a stable relationship between America's two major allies, South Korea and Japan, became the highest priority. Against this backdrop, the U.S. began to strongly push for a conclusion of prolonged normalization negotiations (Cha 1996: 131–4).

America's hegemonic position certainly ensured that potential bilateral tensions between South Korea and Japan took place within certain confines. During Park's visit to Washington, DC in May 1965, the U.S. government pressed him to jointly control the disputed islands with Japan and to yield to Tokyo in a separate but related dispute on the Peace Line. The controversial U.S. suggestion came at a time when the island dispute was seen as the last obstacle to Washington's efforts to speed up the normalization talks (*Yonhap News*, June 20, 2004). U.S. President Lyndon Johnson reiterated his unconditional backing of a South Korea–Japan settlement and its importance not only for the two countries, but also for the anti-communist front in East Asia. Johnson also confirmed in conversations with Park that American military and economic assistance to South Korea would remain intact after normalization. At the same time, he urged the Japanese to play a more active role in seeking a political compromise on the issues in the East Sea/Sea of Japan. While such American efforts did not solve the dispute itself, they were successful in moderating behavior on both sides (Lee 1995b: 249–50, 351–2; Cha 1996: 134–5, 141).

Aside from the realities of the Cold War containment network and the overriding demands of alliance politics, the high priority given to a stable economic relationship motivated both South Korea and Japan to stop pushing for a definitive and final political showdown over the disputed islands, as well as over other thorny bilateral issues. Despite the growing popular pressures against normalization, a strong political momentum for its conclusion was gathering speed at the top leadership levels on both sides.

In South Korea, the Park government faced a near-desperate situation as the first five-year development plan (1962–66) failed to overcome persistent economic troubles of poverty and low development. A steady decline in U.S. economic aid further exacerbated the grim situation, as it reached a 16-year low in 1965. President Park decided to "live or die" with the normalization issue. South Korea's *chaebol* (business conglomerates) also lobbied strongly for normalization. Especially appealing to these groups was the prospect of acquiring Japanese technology and manufacturing capabilities in industries vacated by Japan's ascension up the product cycle.

---

[13] In the early 1960s, the Chinese communist threat loomed large. Beijing's geopolitical divorce with Moscow, its signing of a mutual defense treaty with North Korea (1961), and its support for Southeast Asian communist movements strongly indicated to U.S. policymakers that an Asian communist front was being consolidated. China's successful nuclear tests in October 1964 and May 1965, coincided with its aggressive rhetoric on Taiwan, further exacerbated threat perceptions in the rest of the region. The security outlook in Southeast Asia appeared even less promising. In April 1965, U.S. commitments to a deteriorating situation in Indochina became complicated with the decision to send U.S. troops into the conflict (Cha 1996: 131–42).

In government white papers for 1965 and numerous public statements, the Park government stressed the pragmatic need to overcome historical animosities – including the island dispute – and to normalize ties with Japan (Lee 1990: 170–1; Cha 1996: 128–9).

In Japan, political elites were aware of their strengths concerning South Korea's desperate economic needs. Prime Minister Sato and the elder LDP politicians, particularly former Prime Minister Kishi, decided to take full advantage of a strong but relatively pro-Japan Korean dictator to accelerate the negotiation process (Lee 1990: 169–70). Voices within the Ministry of Foreign Affairs (MOFA) also pressed strongly for a settlement. As a 1965 MOFA White Paper noted, the re-establishment of ties with South Korea was a "historical inevitability" and Park's urgent need for foreign capital and political legitimacy offered relatively low cost for a normalization agreement with South Korea. The Sato government faced additional pressure from the powerful Japanese business lobby. South Korea was becoming an increasingly important export market for Japan. Park's second five-year plan (1967–71) would offer Japanese firms a plethora of large-scale projects, all of which could be underwritten by the financial package to be followed by normalization settlement (Bridges 1993: 32–3; Cha 1996: 129–30).

Foreign Ministers Etsusaburo Shiina and Lee Tong-won finally signed the Treaty on Basic Relations and four other agreements in Tokyo on June 22, 1965. Among these, the fishery agreement is of great importance vis-à-vis the sovereignty dispute. From the viewpoint of the international law, the bilateral dispute was closely associated with the nature and scope of a coastal state's exclusive right to manage the marine resources adjacent to its coast. With the adoption of the four Geneva Conventions on the Law of the Sea in 1958, the special interest of the coastal state in the exploration of the resources near its coast was officially recognized. However, such a new development was satisfactory neither to South Korea, because it was not strong enough to justify the Peace Line, nor to Japan, because it was not weak enough to completely reject South Korean claims. Notwithstanding, the Geneva Conventions were meaningful enough to suggest reference lines along which mutual disagreement between Seoul and Tokyo could be settled (Park 1983b: 64–5). Accordingly, the fishery agreement defined the 3 nm territorial waters around the islands, the 12 nm exclusive fishing zone, and jointly controlled waters. Yet neither the Peace Line nor the sovereignty over the Dokdo Islands was clearly mentioned in the treaty documents. Therefore, it became a strange form of establishing duplicate fishing rights over the same area. Despite the complex calculations at the state levels, the local fishermen arrived at a tacit understanding that Japanese fishing vessels could not enter into the 3 nm territorial waters, but that they could freely engage in fishing inside the 12 nm exclusive fishing zones near Dokdo. Thereafter, fishing vessels of both countries operated peacefully, and the dispute subsided (Kajimura 1997: 466–7).

The normalization treaty provided a fledgling South Korean economy with the much-needed foreign capital: an $845 million package of government and commercial loans, grants-in-aid, and property claims. The treaty also cleared the way for an extensive expansion of trade relations that helped Japan to surpass the U.S.

as South Korea's number one trading partner within just a year. Also, South Korea became increasingly important to Japan as its market grew to import a greater quantity of Japanese goods (Cha 1996: 124). During the period of 1961–65, South Korea's exports to Japan increased from $19 to $44 million, while its imports increased from $69 to $167 million. As a result, South Korea's trade dependence on Japan as a share of its GDP jumped from 3.77 to 6.98% (See Table 4.1).

Brought together as a marriage of convenience, with the territorial dispute put to shelf, the conclusion of the normalization treaty stood on somewhat shaky ground. Yet it was certainly a big step towards the restoration of amicable relations. On top of the overriding demands of alliance politics at the height of the Cold War, the high priority given to a stable economic relationship motivated both South Korea and Japan to make the conscious choice to shelve territorial issues amid growing nationalism at the popular level. The de-escalation process of the first Dokdo flare-up shows that economic forces indeed gave both countries strong material incentives to avoid costly conflicts.

4.3   The Second Round of Dispute (1977–78)

The first decade after the normalization treaty (1965–74) was an economic honeymoon, as characterized by the high and increasing level of South Korea's trade dependence on Japan. The virtual absence of the island dispute during this period largely supports the liberal hope that international trade and investment will quell competing territorial nationalisms. Although many in South Korea argued that Park's strong pro-Japan and pro-development attitudes had created unequal economic ties with Japan at the expense of national pride, Park managed to effectively silence those grievances through his iron rule. By contrast, the following decade (1975–83) encountered high but falling economic interdependence and the once-smooth economic honeymoon period seemed about to end. Set against this background, the Japanese proclamation of new exclusive fishing zones near the islands catalyzed the second round of Dokdo dispute in 1977. Yet the intensity of dispute remained moderate at worst, as more pressing strategic and economic considerations eventually overrode the sovereignty question.

4.3.1   Initiation and Escalation Phase

The first half of the 1970s was marked by the turbulent geopolitical and political instability in Northeast Asia. Most notably, Prime Minister Kakuei Tanaka (1972–74) abandoned the "One Korea" policy of his predecessor Sato. Following the Nixon shock of Sino–U.S. rapprochement, Tanaka first normalized relations with China in 1972 and, then, tentatively began to explore contacts with North Korea (Bridges 1993: 12).

Frustrated with the advent of regional *détente*, Park himself began to engage in a dialogue with the North, but its failure was used as a justification for the imposition of a highly authoritarian system under the *Yushin* (Restoration) Constitution, a replication of the spirit, if not the letter, of Japan's Meiji Restoration. Park's increasingly dictatorial style of leadership and desire to perpetuate his power also complicated relations with the Tanaka government. Even worse, Park's political nemesis, Kim Dae Jung, who had come close to defeating Park in the 1971 presidential election, was kidnapped in Tokyo by KCIA agents in August 1973. The outrage in Japan over the violation of Japan's sovereignty and Kim's human rights worsened the Tanaka government's perception of Park. Even worse, in August 1974, Mun Se Gwang, a second generation Korean living in Japan, attempted to assassinate Park but succeeded only in killing the First Lady. The Japanese government not only showed little sympathy for South Korea's national tragedy, but also was reluctant to investigate any North Korean connections within Japan that might have inspired Mun. Anti-Japanese feelings ran high, the Japanese Embassy in Seoul was ransacked, and only U.S. intervention managed to prevent a termination of relations (Lee 1985: 81–5).[14]

It was only after Prime Minister Takeo Miki (1974–76) had replaced scandal-plagued Tanaka that the storm clouds gradually subsided. Perturbed by America's withdrawal from Indochina in 1975, and fearful that this might encourage Kim Il Sung in North Korea to contemplate a second invasion of the South, Miki decided to abandon the equidistance policy. He reaffirmed the Korea clause in 1975 along with his commitment regarding bases in Okinawa for the defense of South Korea (Lee 1990: 172; Cha 1999: 15).

Despite a tentative rapprochement between Seoul and Tokyo, the dispute over Dokdo was not avoidable as the global trend towards a 200 nm EEZ regime became even more evident in the late 1970s. The new global trend made the bilateral fishing agreement of 1965 outdated. Among many coastal states, maritime jurisdiction up to a limit of 200 nm became common practice. This practice clearly outdated any obligation for a coastal state to allow foreign fishing immediately outside its 12 nm exclusive fishing zone. As of 1965, few distant water fishermen of South Korea were technically capable of operating within the coastal and offshore waters of Japan, but this became no longer true at the turn of the 1970s. The proclamation of 200 nm fishing zone by the Soviet Union in 1976 ignited fishery disputes between South Korea and Japan because the South Korean distant water fishing vessels that had lost their fishing ground in the Soviet zone in the Northwest Pacific began to swamp the coastal areas of Japan's Hokkaido (Park 1983a: 146–7).

On February 5, 1977, Japanese Prime Minister Takeo Fukuda (1976–78) added fuel to the island dispute by stating "Takeshima is Japanese territory beyond all

---

[14] Infuriated, President Park seriously considered severing diplomatic relations with Japan, but discarded that idea primarily due to the huge economic damage that would likely result from such a decision. Park's sense of diplomatic marginalization, however, led him to launch a secret, indigenous nuclear weapons program in the late 1970s in order to balance against the U.S.–Japan alliance (*Chosun Ilbo*, January 21, 2005).

doubt." Behind this provocative and preemptive statement were the fishery problems and the emerging global trend towards a 200 nm EEZ regime. In response to Fukuda's statement, the South Korean government held its firm position that Japan's territorial claim could not be accepted because "Dokdo is the essential part of South Korea's territory, both on historical and legal grounds." On February 7, the Japanese Foreign Ministry announced that it would take the island case to the ICJ and in addition would raise the issue as part of the official agenda for the Japanese–South Korean Foreign Ministerial meeting scheduled on February 18. Furthermore, departing from the existing maritime regime that had been agreed with South Korea in 1965 and 1974, Japan unilaterally declared a 12 nm territorial waters law and a 200 nm fishing zone law in July 1977.[15] Although the latter was not applied to the coastal waters of South Korea and China under the principle of reciprocity, Japan established the 12 nm territorial waters around Dokdo based on its unilateral theory of "inherent territory"(Hyun 2004: 78).[16] In response, South Korea held its consistent position that there is absolutely no reason to negotiate with Japan vis-à-vis Dokdo. Yet South Korea's opposition groups criticized the weak attitude the South Korean government was taking towards the sovereignty issue, while protesting against Japan's aggressive territorial and maritime claims.[17]

4.3.2 De-escalation Phase

Amid the diplomatic quarrel catalyzed by Japan's unilateral moves, Japanese fishing vessels, which engaged in fishing within the area close to the conventional 3 nm territorial limit of the Dokdo Islands, heightened the level of tension. Yet by early 1978 the sovereignty issue quickly subsided without aggravating the nationalist sentiments on both sides, as an unofficial, tacit agreement was reached to allow the Japanese fishing on occasion within the 12 nm limit of South Korea, thereby maintaining the territorial and maritime *status quo*

---

[15] In addition to the 1965 fishery agreement, South Korea and Japan negotiated two agreements in 1974 in order to deal with exploration and mining rights to areas of their common continental shelves. The northeastern terminus of this boundary lay about 74 nm from the Dokdo Islands, but neither side allowed the sovereignty issue to prevent a delimitation line from being drawn through undisputed areas (Prescott 1985: 242).

[16] For instance, Sato Yoshiyuki, head of the Northeast Asian Division of the Japanese Foreign Ministry stated "our country is taking the position that Takeshima is clearly our inherent territory historically and under international law. Our country has strongly protested and presented to Korea the documents explaining in detail that the Korean claim has no basis, but the Korean side does not agree" (*Asahi News*, March 12, 1978).

[17] In the meantime, North Korea did not take up the Dokdo issue in particular because its influence did not reach the islands. Nevertheless, North Korea regarded Dokdo as traditionally an inherent Korean territory. On February 11, 1977, a commentary in the state-owned *Rodong Shinmun* made clear that position and criticized Park's conciliatory stance on Japan with regard to the territorial issue (Kajimura 1997: 429).

(Kajimura 1997: 471–3). The abrupt de-escalation of the second round of dispute can be attributed to the overriding demands for security and economic cooperation between South Korea and Japan.

First of all, a shared concern over U.S. President Jimmy Carter's plan for a five-year withdrawal of all U.S. ground forces from South Korea, announced in January 1977, belatedly brought Seoul and Tokyo closer to each other. Seoul was particularly worried that the removal of the U.S. deterrent shield would destabilize the peninsula, while Tokyo was concerned about the credibility of the U.S. defense commitment to Japan (Bridges 1993: 13).

Secondly, the destabilizing effect of resource nationalism was eventually kept at bay by the significant level of economic interdependence. South Korea's economy recorded an average annual GDP growth rate of 9.1% from 1965 to 1978. South Korea did benefit from significant U.S. economic aid as well as from its own indigenous efforts to overcome economic backwardness. At the same time, its economic ties with Japan took firm root with the passage of more than a decade since their diplomatic normalization. South Korea's total bilateral trade with Japan remarkably increased from a mere $210 million in 1965 to $8.6 billion in 1978. Yet its trade deficit against Japan continued to worsen, reaching $1.8 billion in 1977, which was even larger than South Korea's total trade deficit of $766 million against the rest of the world for the same year. South Korea's trade dependence on Japan remained at the significantly high level of more than 16% during the period of 1977–78, although it dropped by more than 4% from its peak in 1973 (See Table 4.1). Despite unwavering indications of popular discontent on the South Korean side due to its heavy dependence on Japan for trade and investment, economic cooperation with Japan was one of the principal determinants of South Korea's dazzling economic performance during the period of economic takeoff in the 1970s.[18]

---

[18] In trying to correct the trade imbalance, the South Korean government restricted or completely excluded certain Japanese products from the South Korean market. Under a 1977 government directive to diversify imports, 50 products from Southeast Asian countries were subjected to import approval. Japan was not specifically designated but was the implicit target. In 1980 the list was expanded and the formal restrictions were applied to the country that had been the largest exporter to South Korea in the previous year (i.e., Japan). When, in 1982, Saudi Arabia became the largest import source, this qualification was changed to include the largest import source over the previous 5 years. The length of the list had fluctuated from 162 Japanese products in 1982 to a peak of 344 items in 1988, before falling to a total of 258 in 1991. The problem for the South Korean government was to balance the needs of its own industries for key components and products from Japan against its fears that the Japanese would dominate certain sectors of the domestic market if allowed complete freedom. The Japanese government protested regularly about these restrictions, which it regarded as a violation of GATT principles prohibiting quantitative restrictions, but did nothing to retaliate, since, in practice, Japanese companies were able to get around these restrictions (Bridges 1993: 95–6). This protectionist practice was gradually phased out at the end of the 1990s as a result of the rescue loan package agreement between the IMF and South Korea, which was on the verge of default. Apparently, the elimination of the import diversification rules was influenced by Japan, which was one of the principal patrons of the IMF rescue package for South Korea.

The capital flows that involved private investments and a package of government and commercial loans from Japan to South Korea further consolidated bilateral economic ties. Most notably, small- and medium-sized Japanese businesses carried out the majority of Japanese private investments. During the 1970s, the South Koreans referred to these businesses as "package dealers" – Japanese investors who crossed the Tsushima and Korea Straits with a small amount of investment capital ranging from $50,000 to $100,000. Small- and medium-sized investments usually meant small- and medium-sized technologies transferred to South Korea. Also, most Japanese investment concentrated on labor-intensive manufacturing, which introduced mostly outdated technology to South Korea. In the meantime, commodity loans initially comprised the major part of Japanese official development assistance (ODA), but from the late 1970s yen credits became prominent. By 1980, Japan had provided ¥107 billion in grants and ¥317 billion in loans to South Korea. By that time, the Japanese loans to South Korea were averaging around ¥20 billion per year (Oh 1986: 63; Bridges 1993: 101).

The remarkable economic development of South Korea and its deepening dependence on Japan has been a source of intense scholarly debate. Among others, Bruce Cumings (1984: 3) argues that such a phenomenon cannot be understood outside the context of "the fundamental unity and integrity of the regional effort" that began with Japanese colonialism. For Cumings, this prewar model of economic development survived and was revived in the 1960s, when the Japanese economy regained its prominence in East Asia. The metaphor of "flying geese" has been widely used to describe the manner in which less industrialized East Asian countries developed by following the lead of Japan.[19]

Other scholars contend that what used to be a simple but powerful tool of analysis has become a blunt tool of Japan's hierarchical involvement in regional economic development. Among others, Bernard and Ravenhill (1995) find that the efforts of the Japanese firms to regionalize their production led to the emergence of hierarchical production networks linked both backward to Japanese innovation and forward to American markets. While these production networks opened new opportunities for the entry of producers of sophisticated manufactures,

---

[19] The concept of "flying geese" was first used by Japanese economist Kaname Akamatsu (1937). Akamatsu found that the process of industrialization in the Japanese Empire in the 1920s and 1930s followed three stages: import of new products, import substitution, and export. This process appeared as an inverse "V" shape, resembling the wild flying geese migrating between Japan and Siberia. Akamatsu's product cycle theory was used to justify the hierarchically organized division of labor in the "Greater East Asia Co-Prosperity Sphere," although Akamatsu confined himself as much as possible to the academic field as a scholar (Korhonen 1994). For the adherents of the flying geese model, South Korea and Taiwan in the 1960s, and the later developers Thailand, Malaysia, and Indonesia in the 1990s, grew rapidly as a result of technology and process transfer through the investment and outsourcing of Japanese companies, as these companies followed low-cost production in the later stages of product cycles (Yamazawa 1990; Petri 1993).

they also made East Asian countries highly dependent on Japanese technologies and capital.[20]

Despite some troublesome components, Japanese products, investment, and loans did certainly lubricate the South Korean economy during the period of its economic takeoff. Economic forces thus mitigated the negative impact of territorial nationalism catalyzed by the global trend towards a 200 nm EEZ regime. Pursuing economic interests at the cost of territorial integrity was hardly acceptable to ultra-nationalists on both sides, but economic reality dictated the direction of the Dokdo dispute towards mutual restraint.

4.4 The Interlude (1979–95)

After the second flare-up, the unsettled sovereignty question over Dokdo remained effectively controlled, if not completely dormant, for quite a while. Throughout the 1980s, the combination of the positive impact of cooperative economic relationship and the strong alliance politics among the U.S., South Korea, and Japan helped reduce the occasional tensions in the East Sea/Sea of Japan. Yet the situation began to change at the turn of the 1990s with the end of the Cold War and the democratization of South Korea, eventually leading to the third round of the island dispute in 1996–98.

In the political vacuum left by the assassination of President Park in October 1979, General Chun Doo Hwan (1980–88) seized power through a military coup, which overthrew the interim government in December 1979, and had himself elected as president in August 1980. In the early period of his tenure, Chun was determined to extract a better deal from Japan, as indicated by his close involvement with the proposal to Japan for a $6 billion loan. However, after the settlement of the loan issue in 1983 and, subsequently, his own visit to Japan in 1984, he took less direct interest in policy towards Japan, giving more mandates to his aides and to the Foreign Ministry. During the tenure of his successor, Roh Tae Woo (1988–93), South Korea continued to take a low-key approach to Japan (Bridges 1993: 34–5).

In June 1981, Chun requested $6 billion of Japanese aid over a 5-year period. Chun's rationale was that the security of Japan was closely tied to peace on the Korean peninsula; hence Japan should contribute to regional security rather than

---

[20] In a similar vein, Hatch and Yamamura (1996) argue that East Asia benefited significantly in the short run from Japanese capital and technology exports, but might suffer in the long run as "embraced development" gave way to "captive development." According to Hatch and Yamamura, both statistical and anecdotal data indicate that the once benevolent "lead goose" became a "stingier bird," which was only concerned about replicating its domestic system of hierarchical and potentially exploitative *keiretsu* networking in the region as a whole. As T. J. Pempel (1997) notes, an increasingly integrated East Asia became highly dependent on Japan at its center by the end of 1980s.

free-riding on South Korea. A concrete and visible factor for the loan request lay in the economic condition of South Korea in the aftermath of President Park's assassination. For the first time since its economic takeoff, South Korea experienced negative GDP growth during the chaotic period of 1979–80, and grave economic problems remained in the form of $32 billion in foreign debts and a continuing lack of capital (Oh 1986: 78).

If agreed, the loan request as rationalized by the South Koreans would unnecessarily invoke the impression of a tighter U.S.–Japan–South Korean alliance against the communist bloc. Given the subtlety of the relationship with China, Japan felt that economic cooperation should not be linked to security issues. Yet Japan did not completely reject the loan idea. From the beginning, the point of debate was the alleged linkage of aid to security needs and the size of the loan requested rather than the idea of the loan itself (Oh 1986: 85–7).

Prime Minister Yasuhiro Nakasone (1982–87) took the initiative to resolve the loan issue and made a surprise visit to Seoul in January 1983, breaking the conventional wisdom that a Japanese Prime Minister's first overseas visit would be to Washington. He expressed deep regret for the colonial past and high regard for South Korea's defense efforts, pledged to grant $4 billion in preferential aid to South Korea, and declared that "my visit may mark the beginning of a new and vital stage in our relationship" (Russell et al. 1983). In Japan, the Socialist Party, the Communist Party, and part of the media were critical both of the excessive ODA commitments and the security overtones. Yet the loan agreement was largely well received, especially by the business community, which looked forward to greater commercial opportunities in South Korea. The loan agreement did much to maintain the credibility of South Korea in the international financial market. The climax of improved bilateral relations was President Chun's return state visit to Japan in September 1984 (Kim 1983: 82–7; Bridges 1993: 14–6).

Although the political salience of Dokdo question rarely came to the fore in the 1980s, it was during this period that the sovereignty issue became closely tied to Japanese history textbooks. In July 1982, the Japanese and South Korean media began to report that the Japanese Education Ministry's stricter guidelines for screening history textbooks meant revisions in the descriptions of Japan's pre-war atrocities in Korea and China. Many South Koreans were infuriated to learn that the independence movement of 1919 would be described as a riot and that the Korean workers and soldiers mobilized for Japan's war effort as volunteers. In the face of severe protests from its neighbors, the Japanese government agreed to modify the textbook authorization system and issue teaching guidelines with sensitivity and care. The South Korean government accepted this response in order to finalize the loan negotiations (Bridges 1993: 15).

In 1986, the Japanese Education Ministry authorized a new history textbook compiled by a right-wing group, but only after suggesting partial revisions of the textbook's militaristic overtone under diplomatic pressure from South Korea and China. Yet the outspoken Education Minister, Masayuki Fujio, was greatly upset and publicly denounced South Korea and China. Embarrassed by the controversy provoked by Fujio, Prime Minister Nakasone had to fire him (Bridges 1993: 62).

At the same time, however, Nakasone himself raised the sovereignty issue of Dokdo during the Japanese–South Korean Foreign Ministerial meeting held in September 1986. Towards the end of the meeting, Japanese Foreign Minister Tadashi Kuranari also mentioned the island issue for the purpose of an official record. Kuranari's statement invoked anti-Japanese sentiments in South Korea, which had already been aggravated by Fujio's provocative remark. But South Korean leaders soon recognized that Prime Minister Nakasone and Foreign Ministry officials had to talk openly about "illegal occupation" or the "return" of the disputed islands to pacify conservative elements within the LDP as well as Japanese ultranationalist groups who were infuriated by Fujio's forced departure and Nakasone's low-key diplomacy (Hyun 2004: 79).

The controversy over the history textbooks and Dokdo fell short of undermining the commitment of South Korea and Japan to give priority to friendly bilateral relations. In the 1980s, South Korean GDP grew rapidly at an average rate of 8.6%. In particular, the three-year period of 1986–88 witnessed an unprecedented economic boom with an average GDP growth rate of 10.8%, thanks to the so-called Three Low's (low oil prices, a low yen, and a low exchange rate). South Korea experienced trade surpluses for the first time with a three-year total of $18 billion. Its trade dependence on Japan remained significant at double digits throughout the 1980s although its trade deficit against Japan fell from the peak of $5.4 billion in 1986 to $3.8 billion in 1988 (See Table 4.1). Deeper bilateral economic relations were reinforced by the rise of government aid and FDI, particularly after the 1985 Plaza Accord that pushed the value of the yen to nearly double its value against the U.S. dollar (Bridges 1993: 102–3).

In sum, except for a brief period of freezing relationship after the assassination of President Park in 1979, the pattern of mutual restraint in dealing with the territorial issue continued in the 1980s under Park's two authoritarian successors, Chun and Roh. Both of them were constantly accused of submissive diplomacy over the loan negotiations, the history textbook controversies, and the Dokdo issue. Nevertheless, their authoritarian regimes effectively silenced the domestic grievances and kept the island question on the shelf in favor of a lucrative economic relationship with Japan. The containment continued until South Korean–Japanese relations began to face significant challenges on both security and economic fronts in the first half of the 1990s.

4.5 The Third Round of Dispute (1996–98)

After over 15 years of relative calm, South Korea and Japan seriously collided again over Dokdo from 1996 to 1998, as both governments took unusually aggressive maritime and territorial policies with the advent of UNCLOS in 1994. The extensive confrontation over the maritime and territorial issues drove the overall South Korea–Japan relationship to one of its lowest points in the post-normalization era. This period also coincided with the first decade of the post-Cold War era

and of South Korean democracy after a prolonged spell of military dictator-
ship. The transitional nature of the 1990s greatly contributed to a more contentious diplomacy between the two quasi-allies, but a full-scale diplomatic crisis was
averted by economic forces. In the aftermath of the 1997–98 financial crisis, South
Korea and Japan consciously chose to sidestep the complicated questions of EEZ
delimitation and Dokdo sovereignty; instead, they set up a provisional joint fishing
zone near the disputed islands. Once again, the de-escalation of the third round of
dispute showed the pacifying effect of complex economic interdependence, albeit
limited in its strength and scope.

4.5.1   Initiation and Escalation Phase

Following the introduction of UNCLOS in 1994, South Korea and Japan both
rushed to set their respective maritime boundaries. In January 1996, Japan notified
South Korea that it would promulgate its own EEZ in accordance with the UNCLOS
clauses by early February. Japan also suggested that both governments immediately
start negotiations to settle overlapping terrain in the East Sea/Sea of Japan, where
the distance between some EEZ baselines was less than 400 nm.[21]

On February 9, Japanese Foreign Minister Yukihiko Ikeda dropped a diplomatic bombshell by stating "Takeshima is a part of Japanese territory from the
viewpoint of international law and history," demanding that the South Korean
government immediately remove its facilities and personnel on the islands (*The
New York Times*, February 12, 1996).[22] Clearly this was a preemptive move to
maximize Japan's bargaining position in the impending fishery and EEZ negotiations with South Korea. Ikeda's claim was not entirely inconsistent with Japan's
past claims, but his ill-timed statement unmistakably catalyzed a series of anti-
Japanese demonstrations across South Korea with Japanese flags and his effigies
being burnt. A number of civil and political groups ranging from veterans
organizations to radical student groups formed a united, albeit loose, front under a

---

[21] The UNCLOS does not provide obligatory mechanisms in case of EEZ delimitation and territorial disputes. Article 11 of UNCLOS stipulates that disputes be resolved by peaceful and coordinated diplomatic efforts. In case EEZs overlap, Article 74(1) stipulates that states reach an
"equitable solution." Article 74(3) proposes, in case of prolonged state-to-state negotiations on
EEZ delimitation, that states adopt a provisional memorandum until they reach a final agreement.
From this point of view, the goal of "equitable solution" is to take account of all the "relevant
circumstances" which characterize a particular area, circumstances which might be geographical
or geomorphological. Some view that the solution can be achieved by drawing an adjusted median
line, with due respect to the circumstances in question, even though this is by no means a rule, as
noted by the ICJ in 1982 (Dupuy and Vignes 1991: 13).

[22] Later that year, Ikeda provided another catalyst for territorial dispute with China over the
Senkaku Islands by stating "Senkakus have always been Japan's territory; Japan already effectively governs the islands, so the territorial issue does not exist." See Chapter 5 of this book for
details.

patriotic and nationalist banner and rallied against Japan (*Japan Economic Newswire*, February 9, 10, and 12, 1996).

South Korea's Foreign Ministry, which preferred a traditional low-key approach, was forced to take a backseat in the dispute escalation stage.[23] The Presidential Office directed the Foreign Ministry to refuse to cooperate with Japan for speedy conclusion of EEZ and fishery talks if Japan failed to officially acknowledge South Korea's sovereign rights over the Dokdo Islands (Bong 2002: 103–5, 120–1). President Kim Young Sam (1993–98) canceled a meeting with Japanese officials scheduled on February 12, threatened to scrap a summit meeting in March, and said his government would sternly deal with Japan over the maritime and territorial issues. Kim also ordered his cabinet to develop the islands as a tourist site capable of supporting extended human habitation so that the islands could qualify as a baseline for the South Korean EEZ (*Japan Economic Newswire*, February 10, 1996; *The Washington Post*, February 13, 1996). In order to reaffirm its claim to the islands, the South Korean government increased the number of its garrison guards on the islands from 26 to 34. In a warning to Tokyo, South Korean military forces practiced repelling imaginary enemy vessels around Dokdo (*The New York Times*, February 16, 1996; *Japan Economic Newswire*, February 21, 1996).

Public opinion in Japan on the maritime and territorial issues became increasingly belligerent as well. On February 27, some 400 members of the fishery cooperatives in Shimane Prefecture rallied to urge the government to declare a 200 nm EEZ that would include the disputed islands. They claimed "we have not had one day of relaxed operations in our battle with the fishing boats from South Korea. Now is the once in a lifetime opportunity to bring this to a halt" (*Japan Economic Newswire*, February 27, 1996). Also, the 57 members of the New Progress Party organized a rally and recriminated that the South Korean police activities and wharf construction on the islands as "downright violations of Japanese sovereignty" (*Joongahng Ilbo*, March 1, 1996).

For both countries, the stakes of maritime boundaries were high. Because the existing maritime regime in the East Sea/Sea of Japan favored it, South Korea had no intention to replace the 1965 fishery agreement. Japan's newly announced EEZ would no longer provide South Korea with the exemptions allowed under the old

---

[23] The Ministry of Foreign Affairs and Trade (Ministry of Foreign Affairs before 1998) is involved in handling the day-to-day administration of relations with Japan, and has essentially acted as the voice of reason in disputes with Japan, which often endangers its position in the "politics of patriotism." As in the case of Japan, the increasing complexity of issues on the international agenda has given the growing range of ministries a say in foreign policymaking. Aside from the Presidential Office, the Ministry of Defense is deeply involved in the security dimension of South Korea–Japan relationship, particularly regarding the Dokdo dispute and issues of territorial waters. On foreign economic policy, the Ministry of Strategy and Finance (Ministry of Finance and Economy before 2008) has acted as a very powerful voice, especially through using its enormous institutional and budgetary power over inputs from other economic ministries such as the Ministry of Knowledge Economy (Ministry of Commerce, Industry and Energy before 2008), and the Ministry for Food, Agriculture, Forestry, and Fisheries.

maritime and fishing regime.[24] In August 1996, the two countries opened negotiations aimed at drawing a delimitation line separating their respective 200 nm EEZs, but the negotiation process was rocky at best. Japanese officials proposed separating EEZ delimitation from the revision of fishery agreement in order to promptly conclude the latter. Also, they suggested setting up a temporary joint fishing area around Dokdo and putting aside the sensitive problem of delimiting their respective EEZs around the islands (Mack 1997: 5–6; Kim 1999: 418–21; Bong 2002: 101–2; Kim 2004:251–3). Preferring to maintain the maritime and territorial *status quo*, the South Korean government stalled the revisions.

The situation became more complicated by the shifting domestic politics in both countries. In a possible electoral overture to nationalist sentiments, Japan's ruling LDP asserted a series of sovereignty claims to the disputed islands: the Dokdo, the Senkaku, and the Southern Kurile Islands. The LDP's electoral victories in 1996 were in part a result of its nationalist campaign platform. After winning the Upper House by-election in March, the LDP under Prime Minister Ryutaro Hashimoto's leadership (1996–98) won enough seats to build a single-party cabinet in the October Lower House election. The comeback of the LDP after losing its dominant position in 1993 adversely affected South Korea–Japan relations.[25] With his relatively strong power positions, Hashimoto had a wide range of options for dealing with the Dokdo issue. He chose to prioritize the factional interests – particularly the so-called "maritime tribe (*susanzoku*)" in the LDP – and territorial nationalism over South Korea–Japan relations (Lee 1998: 3–5; Bong 2002: 116–7, 130–2).[26] By June 1997, positions stiffened and the confrontation escalated when Japan began seizing South Korean boats fishing within its unilaterally declared 200 nm EEZ, which

---

[24] Under the "flag state" principle, the 1965 fishery agreement did not permit the Japanese maritime police to seize South Korean fishing boats even if they had violated Japanese territorial waters. The UNCLOS replaced the flag state principle with the "coastal state" principle, giving the legal authority to monitor and regulate illegal fishing by foreign vessels in its EEZ (Bong 2002: 122–3).

[25] Japan's postwar politics can be characterized by the so-called "1955 System" in which the ruling LDP enjoyed an unbroken clear majority over the opposition parties from 1955 to 1993. In the resultant "embedded mercantilism" in Pempel's (1998) terms, the LDP not only gained diffuse electoral support through rapid economic growth itself, but also it earned hard votes by distributing material compensation to favored constituent groups, notably farmers and small businesses, through protection, subsidies and public works spending (Pempel 1998; Vogel 1999). Some scholars argue that the pressures of political scandal and economic downturn in the 1990s have not really changed in the conservative governance system (Johnson 1996). In sharp contrast, Pempel (1998) argues that by the early 1990s, the conservative regime could no longer respond well to domestic and international problems. Vogel (1999) takes a middle ground by arguing that despite enormous pressures for reform, the mercantilist legacy continues to slow the pace and shape the content of Japan's political and economic reforms today.

[26] Furthermore, the collapse of left-wing parties in the 1990s left contemporary Japanese politics dominated almost exclusively by center-right political alignments. In the post-Cold War era devoid of the constraining influences of anti-nationalist left-wing political parties or social movements, a consensus about a "Japan that can say no" and that seeks to become "a normal country" increasingly became appealing to many Japanese nationalists (Launius 2002). Although only a handful in number, the nationalist right-wing groups have been well organized and well financed, and thereby overrepresented in Japanese politics.

would be outside Japanese waters under the normal baseline principle of 1965 agreement. Japan threatened to unilaterally scrap the 1965 fishery agreement if negotiations were not completed satisfactorily by July 20, 1997 (*International Boundary News Database*, June 11, 1997; *The Korea Times*, July 3, 1997).

The South Korean government took assertive action. It demanded the immediate release of the vessels and crew-members, who had allegedly been mistreated by the Japanese government. Infuriated by a series of seizures, tens of thousands South Koreans held anti-Japanese rallies. As the case in Japan, it was not a coincidence that the February 1996 flare-up took place just weeks before elections in South Korea. Since popular antipathy towards Japan was widespread in South Korea, political parties competed to outbid one another in blaming Tokyo (Mack 1997: 10; Bong 2002: 113–6). Furthermore, South Korea's presidential candidates competing for the December 1997 election capitalized on the public anger.[27] It is also widely held that President Kim took an abrasive stance towards Japan in general and the territorial issue in particular in order to garner popular support for his increasingly unpopular regime. As the first civilian president after about 30 years of military rule, Kim initially enjoyed wide support from the people. However, a series of massive man-made disasters and corruption scandals – involving high-profile politicians such as his own son – soon beleaguered his government. Coupled with the disappointing diplomatic performance in the North Korean issue, these political fiascos undermined public support for Kim. Under these circumstances, Kim knew by instinct that Japan-bashing could provide powerful rhetoric with which to manipulate public opinion and undercut political opponents (*The Economist*, February 17, 1996; Lind 2004: 44–5).

Shifting geopolitics in Northeast Asia further escalated the 1996 flare-up. The global superpower confrontation during the Cold War period had cemented the two quasi-allies. As its unifying power receded at the turn of the 1990s, however, regional political factors began to play a more significant, negative role in shaping the course of the island dispute. The 1996 U.S.–Japan Joint Declaration complicated the island issue by increasing South Korea's sense of diplomatic marginalization in the face of mounting uncertainties in the Korean peninsula due to the North Korean nuclear crisis.[28]

On the economic front, South Korea and Japan also felt an increasing distance from each other. Although South Korea's economy grew at an average of 8.5% between 1994 and 1996, its external sector encountered heavy pressure as its total trade deficit tripled from $6.1 billion in 1994 to $19.7 billion in 1996. South Korea's

---

[27] In defiance of the Foreign Ministry's opposition, for example, Yi In Che, one of many promising candidates, flew to Dokdo and presented three big South Korean national flags and a plaque reading "Dokdo is our land" (*Chosun Ilbo*, November 17, 1997).

[28] The U.S.–Japan Joint Declaration issued after the April 1996 Clinton–Hashimoto summit in Tokyo expanded Japan's role in the case of emergency in the Korean peninsula. This emergency clause stipulated close coordination between the U.S. and Japan without requiring consultation with South Korea. In reaction, the South Korean government issued a statement urging the two countries to increase transparency in delineating the limits and requirements for U.S.–Japanese defense cooperation that would affect South Korean sovereign rights and the stability of the Korean peninsula (Bong 2002: 106–13).

trade deficit against Japan was almost doubled from $8.5 billion in 1993 to $15.4 billion in 1996. Certainly, growing trade inequality exercised an aggravating influence on the escalation of the island dispute by adding fuel to the fire of mutual antagonism, particularly in South Korea. At the same time, it is plausible that Kim was less concerned about maintaining stable economic relations with Japan, as South Korea's trade dependence on Japan as the ratio of GDP had in fact continued to decline in the previous years (See Table 4.1). Set against this fluid backdrop, it became clear towards the end of 1997 that the exchange of belligerent diplomacy transformed the initial discord centered on maritime issues into a clash of territorial nationalism.

4.5.2 De-escalation Phase

The 1996–98 flare-up could have been much worse than it actually was. A more serious clash was averted in the winter of 1997–98 when an unusually high level of diplomatic and economic emergencies opened up political space for the new leadership in Seoul and Tokyo to employ a pragmatic approach to territorial and maritime issues.

South Korea's new Kim Dae Jung government's (1998–2003) engagement policy towards North Korea – the so-called "Sunshine Policy" – required Japan's active support, both diplomatic and financial.[29] Deeply concerned about Pyongyang's long-range missile program – which was demonstrated literally over the heads of the Japanese in August 1998 – and about its nuclear adventurism, Tokyo wished Kim's Sunshine Policy could reduce the security threat from the North. For Tokyo, Kim Dae Jung was much more reliable than his predecessor Kim Young Sam (Rozman 2002: 20–2).[30]

More importantly, the advent of the East Asian financial crisis of 1997–98 fundamentally altered the context through which South Korean and Japanese political leaders contemplated their strategies vis-à-vis the island dispute. The complexity of financial interdependence between South Korea and Japan forced the third round of dispute to be sidestepped somewhat abruptly. The South Korean government desperately sought Japan's financial assistance, as well as the International Monetary Fund's rescue loans, in order to alleviate the impact of the financial crisis.

---

[29] In February 1998, Kim announced that he would pursue the "Sunshine Policy" with North Korea, in hopes of encouraging greater discussion and cooperation with Pyongyang. The policy was inspired by the old Aesop's fable about the sun getting more results than the fierce wind. In December 2000, the Norwegian Nobel Committee, in recognition of Kim's "extraordinary and lifelong works for democracy and human rights in South Korea and East Asia in general, and for peace and reconciliation with North Korea in particular," awarded him the Nobel Peace Prize.

[30] Some Japanese Foreign Ministry officials were quoted as saying "Tokyo believes the fundamental policies of the Kim Dae Jung administration will be markedly different from those of his predecessor....the different attitude would be apparent in the approach to such sensitive issues as the long-standing territorial dispute over the ownership of the currently Seoul-controlled Takeshima Islands...Kim Young Sam always stuck to his principles and has caused unnecessary friction with us, while Kim Dae Jung is quite knowledgeable about Japan and places importance on practical dialogue" (*Daily Yomiuri*, February 26, 1998).

Despite the rising anti-Japanese sentiment at home, President Kim Dae Jung used his abundant political capital generated by the nation's financial emergency to forge a compromise on the maritime and territorial issues.

Indeed President Kim Dae Jung consciously sought to prevent any emotional escalation of the maritime and territorial problems. Upon assuming the presidency in January 1998, Kim made it clear that his main foreign policy goal was to significantly amend bilateral relations with Japan. During his first official visit to Japan in October 1998, Kim and his Japanese counterpart, Prime Minister Keizo Obuchi (1998–2000), signed the *Joint Declaration on A New Republic of Korea–Japan Partnership towards the Twenty First Century*. Measures to realize this goal included lifting the embargo on Japanese pop culture commodities and arranging the first historical visit by the Japanese Emperor to South Korea.[31]

Subsequently, South Korea and Japan concluded and signed a new fishery agreement in winter 1998–99, bringing a quick, if not quiet, end to the third round of dispute. The new fishery agreement shelved the sovereignty question by following a complicated formula long advocated by Japan, but heretofore rejected by South Korea (Bong 2002: 153–5; Kim 2004: 254–7).[32] The signing of the new fishery accord and shelving of the territorial question exacted political costs for Kim, but he had few alternatives in the wake of South Korea's near economic collapse and the dire need for emergency loans from Japan.

4.6   The Fourth Round of Dispute (2004–06) and Further Escalation Potential

To many commentators, the 1998 Joint Declaration demonstrated that South Korea and Japan were now inseparably bound together by shared geopolitical and economic interests. The spirit of new partnership seemingly culminated in the successful co-hosting of

---

[31] In addition, the Joint Declaration's emphasis on "direct" security dialogue and coordination between South Korea and Japan to maintain regional stability marked a significant departure from the 1969 Korea clause and the 1983 Chun–Nakasone joint statement, both of which inherently paved a one-way street of security interest designed by the U.S. and financed by Japan. The Joint Declaration specifically cited North Korean missile development as potentially destabilizing for regional stability, although it stopped short of offering concrete steps for dealing with the missile issue, let alone entering into mutually binding security commitments (Manosevitz 2003: 805–9).

[32] The new fishery agreement substantially altered the maritime order in the East Sea/Sea of Japan. First, both governments agreed to apply the "coastal state" principle to illegal fishing within their respective EEZs. Concerning the width of the EEZ, South Korea accepted the Japanese delineation of 35 nm from the baseline of territorial waters. To resolve the problem of overlapping EEZs, both South Korea and Japan agreed to provisionally delimit their overlapping EEZs based upon the 1974 maritime boundary agreement. In particular, both sides agreed to set up two "common water zones," one in the East Sea/Sea of Japan around the Dokdo Islands and the other near Jeju Island. Yet the solution to the Dokdo problem left ample room for confusion and diverse interpretations because the legal status of the common water zone around Dokdo was not clearly defined (Bong 2002: 149–51).

the World Cup 2002. However, if anyone still doubted that there remained a wide gap between these two quasi-allies, the point was well proven in a series of independent but closely intertwined clashes over Dokdo under populist leadership in both countries: President Roh Moo Hyun (2003–2008) and Prime Minister Junichiro Koizumi (2001–2006). In 2004, South Korea and Japan collided over South Korea's Dokdo post-age stamps. In 2005, South Korean–Japanese relations went from bad to worse. In spite of violent anti-Japanese demonstrations in South Korea, a Japanese local government established an annual "Takeshima Day" and the Japanese Education Ministry autho-rized the revisions of new history textbooks that reinforce Japan's symbolic claim to the islands. In 2006, South Korea and Japan became locked in a diplomatic stalemate over the former's plan to register the names of some seabed features near the islands with the International Hydrographic Organization (IHO) and the latter's counter measure to conduct maritime survey in the same area. Further escalation would not have been averted unless North Korea had test-fired a series of missiles, including one thought to be capable of reaching the U.S., thus clearly reminding Seoul and Tokyo of the common security threat from Pyongyang. The confluence of shifting balance of power and rising nationalisms in Northeast Asia makes the danger of conflict escalation loom par-ticularly large. It remains to be seen whether economic interdependence will continue to exercise a pacific effect on the Dokdo dispute.

4.6.1   Initiation and Escalation Phase

In the aftermath of the third round of Dokdo dispute (1996–98), an old rumor resur-faced in South Korea that the sovereignty of the islands would eventually be trans-ferred to Japan as a result of a secret agreement reached during the fishery negotiations.[33] President Kim Dae Jung's political rivals constantly manipulated the controversy to assail his pragmatic and progressive policy towards Japan. In April 1999, for instance, a small group of National Assembly men introduced a bill to increase government's funding for the development of Dokdo. Although the bill was eventually voted down by Kim's ruling party at the National Assembly in December 1999, the controversy certainly tainted Kim's nationalist credentials (Shin 2001: 50–5).

---

[33] For South Korean fishermen, the new fishery agreement, which went into effect on February 6, 1999, was particularly unacceptable. Double-boat dragnet fishing was completely banned in Japan's EEZ under the new fishery agreement. The South Korean government also failed to guar-antee the rights of cuttlefish fishermen to harvest blowfish in Japan's EEZ. Angry South Korean fishermen staged strong protests against the fishery agreement in spring 1999. They called for it to be repealed and eventually forced the South Korea's Minister for Maritime Affairs and Fisheries to resign from his post (*The Korea Herald*, March 1, 20, 1999). In 2000, the dispute over Southern Kurile mackerel fishing zone put additional strain on overall South Korean–Japanese relations and greatly damaged the credentials of the Kim administration. A national sense of urgency motivated the South Koreans to rally around the flag and to mobilize public pressure on the South Korean government to adopt a more assertive territorial policy (Bong 2002: 157).

To make matters worse, old problems reappeared. New Japanese junior high and high school history textbooks – written by Japanese right-wing groups and authorized by the Japanese Education Ministry – became the focus of a diplomatic spat in 2001–02. Although the Japanese government had barred the use of a right-wing text books in the late 1980s, in 2001 the Ministry had little recourse other than forcing several rounds of revisions on the authors of the New History Textbook. Although few local school districts decided to adopt it, this textbook turned out to be a bestseller in bookstores as a result of excessive media attention (Midford and Mitsuhashi 2004: 4).

In April 2001, the South Korean government expressed deep regrets that some history textbooks approved by the Japanese government were compiled "with a historical viewpoint centered only on Japan and include some contents that justify and beautify Japan's past wrongdoing" (*Japan Economic Newswire*, April 3, 2001). In April 2002, the South Koreans were upset again when they learned that the Japanese government approved high school history textbooks that refer to "Takeshima as Japanese territory" over which South Korea is falsely claiming ownership (*The Korea Herald*, April 9, 2002). For many in South Korea, the ongoing textbook controversy was a strong indication of the rise of ultranationalism within Japan's leadership circles. The tension catalyzed by the history textbooks was further compounded by Prime Minister Koizumi's highly controversial visits to Yasukuni shrine to honor Japan's war dead including 14 war criminals convicted by the Allied Powers after the Pacific War (*BBC NEWS ONLINE*, April 9, 2002).

Against this thorny background, the Dokdo issue came under the spotlight in January 2004. The 2004 flare-up followed an announcement by South Korea Post that it would issue stamps illustrating the flora and fauna of the islands. Japanese Foreign Minister Yoriko Kawaguchi wasted no time in urging Seoul to reverse its decision to issue the stamps, but her South Korean counterpart, Foreign Minister Yoon Young-Kwan, rejected her request, citing historical and legal evidence of South Korea's sovereignty rights over the islands. In response, Japan's Home Affairs Minister Taro Aso, who would take the Prime Ministership in September 2008, said Japan would distribute its own stamps. The idea was opposed by Prime Minister Koizumi, but not before he reiterated Japanese claim to the islands. Japan also registered its complaint to the Universal Postal Union (UPU), claiming that portraying the disputed islands on stamps violates the spirit of UPU (*Chosun Ilbo*, January 28, 2004).

South Korea Post, nevertheless, went ahead with its plans.[34] At dawn on the date of first issuance, many South Koreans started lining up outside post offices to buy

---

[34] This was the third time that Dokdo had been featured on South Korean postage stamps. The first issuance in 1954 came two years after President Syngman Rhee announced the Peace Line and was to commemorate the restoration of physical control of the islands. The Japanese government vigorously protested and threatened to send back packages that had the stamp attached. The second issuance in 2002 provoked no reaction from Japan. Later, Japanese government officials said they had not been aware of the second issuance of a Dokdo stamp. As for the third issuance in 2004, a South Korean Post official said, "No questions were raised within our organization this time because no trouble had occurred during the second issuance." Even the South Korea's Foreign Ministry had not been informed about the third stamp issuance until it was publicly announced; thereby permitting South Korean diplomats little time to diffuse the problem (*Asahi News*, February 2, 2004).

their ration of one sheet of 16 stamps, causing the post offices' supplies of 2.2 million sheets to sell out in three hours. South Korean President Roh attempted to cool down the rising diplomatic temperature and not to damage important bilateral relations by largely ignoring Japan's claims over the islands. Yet he could not help but say: "There is no need to refer to the basis of our sovereign right, just as there is no need for one to keep insisting that his wife is his own wife since she's his wife by all means" (*Chosun Ilbo*, January 15, 2004; *The New York Times*, January 27, 2004).[35] The South Korean public had no problems blasting Japanese politicians and government officials, especially those considered revisionist in their interpretation of historical events. Demonstrations were held against Koizumi, Aso, and other right-wing politicians over the postage stamp issue (*Asahi News*, February 2, 2004).

The age-old dispute took a modern twist as well. Following the postage stamp skirmish, Internet users from both sides launched cyber attacks on each other's hostile sites, which was quickly dubbed the "cyber-*imjinwaeran*" referring to the 7-year war of 1592–98 between the two longtime rivals (*South China Morning Post*, February 4, 2004). No particular physical damage was done as a result of this cyber war, but emotions on both sides ran high.

Despite both governments' wishes, contentious rallies continued through the summer of 2004, thanks to the efforts to create diplomatic friction over the territorial issues by those who were outside the governments' full control. Presumably inspired by the seven Chinese activists who landed on the Japan-controlled Senkaku Islands in March the same year, four members of a Japanese right-wing group set sail for the Dokdo Islands in May to set the Japanese flag on them. The group declared that, although they were aware of the danger of being seized, they would push ahead with their plan to go ashore "in respect of the time-honored Japanese national spirit." Reports of this sailing were met with indignation in South Korea. The South Korean maritime police responded by threatening to arrest the intruders and seize their boat, if they had attempted to approach the islands. The Japanese government managed to persuade its citizens at sea to give up their plan, but only after serious diplomatic damage had been done (*Mainichi Daily News*, May 6, 2004; *South China Morning Post*, May 6, 2004).[36]

In early 2005, the Dokdo dispute took a new, unpredictable twist. South Korean nationalism received a wake-up call when a league of Shimane prefectural assembly

---

[35] In fact, Japan Post has been selling customized postage stamps featuring users' favorite photos since June 2003. In earlier February 2004, a Tokyo citizen asked one of post offices to issue customized postage stamps with "Takeshima" pictures and texts. Japan Post rejected the request but, in a separate decision, decided to issue 300 "Takeshima stamps" ordered by a retailer of stamps and coins. In March 2004, 13 lawmakers of the ruling LDP placed orders with the Tokyo Central Post Office for 1,500 custom-made stamps featuring islands that are disputed between Japan and its neighboring countries. But a post office official told lawmakers that the post office could not decide whether to accept the orders (because it was politically too sensitive) (*Japan Economic Newswire*, February 19, March 4, 2004).

[36] Japanese rightist groups had never tried to directly claim the Dokdo Islands, but the May incident sent an alarming wakeup call to South Korean activists. In late May, five local civil groups announced that they would land on the Japanese Island of Tsushima in protest of the Japanese attempt to land on Dokdo. In the meantime, a South Korean company started daily boat tours around the islands in spite of Japan's strong protest (Yonhap News, May 29, June 16, 2004).

members proposed to designate "Takeshima Day" on February 22, which marked the centennial anniversary of the issuance in 1905 of a prefectural ordinance that had incorporated the islands as Japanese territory (*Yonhap News*, February 24, 2005). To add insult to injury, the Japanese ambassador to Seoul claimed "Takeshima is historically and legally Japanese territory" at a press conference held in Seoul (*BBC Monitoring International Reports*, February 24, 2005). In April, the territorial dispute reached a boiling point when Tokyo officially authorized the revisions of the new history textbook in spite of South Korea's strong protest (*Chosun Ilbo*, April 6, 2005).

Unmistakably, the populist governments on both sides provided combustible addition to the contending territorial nationalisms. Koizumi began to employ an aggressive territorial policy by explicitly or implicitly supporting the popular movement for the return of Japan's dislocated territories. He also pushed hard for the revision of Japan's fundamental laws, particularly Article 9 of the Peace Constitution, to allow Japan to maintain regular armed forces despite the worries of South Korea and China (*The Korea Herald*, May 7, 2004). In response, as one of the most democratic but beleaguered presidents, Roh came under heavy pressure for a more definitive territorial policy. In the middle of rising tension, he issued a statement with unusually strong anti-Japanese overtones that his government would risk "diplomatic warfare" unless Japan stopped employing a confrontational territorial policy (*Chosun Ilbo*, March 23, 2005).

Tensions between Seoul and Tokyo escalated to a new level in March 2006, when a Japanese Education Ministry's report revealed that Tokyo had ordered textbook publishers in 2005 to depict the disputed islands as Japanese territory (*Chosun Ilbo*, March 29, 2006). As the dispute over the islands heated up, Seoul announced that it intended to register a set of Korean names for the seabed features near Dokdo with the IHO conference in June 2006. Tokyo reacted with its plan of maritime survey in April, claiming that it was necessary to build its case for retaining the present names that Tokyo had registered in 1978 with the IHO. Under heavy domestic pressure, Roh reiterated Seoul's hard-line policy towards Japan and promised to keep Dokdo under South Korean control by taking "any necessary measures at any expense or sacrifice" (*Xinhua News*, April 25, 2006). Through mid-spring to early summer, the already tense bilateral relations moved closer to the breaking point when Japan began to implement its plan to conduct a maritime survey around Dokdo. In response to the dispatch of Japanese research vessels, Seoul sent 20 gunboats to Dokdo in order to prevent the survey. As the two sides edged towards confrontation, rhetoric escalated and nationalist public opinion was mobilized, particularly in South Korea (Weinstein 2006).

4.6.2   De-escalation Phase

By fall 2006, the diplomatic temperature noticeably cooled down and the quarrel over Dokdo completely subsided. It was largely a result of both governments' conscious efforts to prevent the issue from spinning out of control. Although contending nationalisms helped to escalate the 2004–2006 flare-up, broader strategic and economic conditions prohibited the sovereignty issue from escalating into a full-scale diplomatic crisis.

Among others, North Korea turned out to be the most important, though unintended, agent for defusing the fourth round of dispute, which had continued acrimoniously and intermittently. On July 5, 2006, North Korea test-fired seven missiles into the East Sea/Sea of Japan, including the long-range *Taepodong 2* that is potentially capable of reaching U.S. territory. For many North Korea observers, it was not a coincidence that North Korea test-fired its missiles as the U.S. celebrated its Independence Day holiday and launched the space shuttle from Florida (*BBC NEWS*, July 5, 2006).[37] As an unintended consequence, Pyongyang reminded both Seoul and Tokyo of a common security threat, thus motivating them to form a collective front against Pyongyang.[38]

On the economic front, mutual demand for closer economic ties between South Korea and Japan was clearly manifested by the launch of negotiations to form a bilateral FTA in December 2003. In the wake of the financial crisis of 1997–98, South Korea's policymakers and business community alike recognized the significance of maintaining stable commercial and financial relations with Japan. As Japan began to negotiate bilateral FTAs with those countries that potentially compete with South Korea for the Japanese market, there has been an additional fear that the opportunity cost of not having an FTA with Japan would seriously undermine South Korea's national interest (Koo 2005).

4.6.3   Further Escalation Potential

According to the South Korean Coast Guard, the number of Japanese patrol boats sailing around Dokdo has increased, particularly since the 2004–2006 flare-up (*The New York Times*, August 31, 2008). To be sure, South Korea and

---

[37] The surprise missile tests were an implicit but strong signal to the U.S. to free up North Korean assets in Macau, thus opening a way for Pyongyang to return to the Six Party Talks without losing face. In previous months, North Korea's involvement in counterfeiting U.S. dollars and its reaction to the U.S. government's sanction on a Macau bank, Banco Delta Asia, which had been linked to money laundering for North Korea, had been halting the fifth round of the Six Party Talks to resolve the second North Korean nuclear crisis (Aggarwal and Koo 2006: 38).

[38] In fact, both South Korea and Japan were increasingly feeling the pressure to cooperate together with the U.S. to achieve a peaceful resolution to the second North Korean nuclear crisis that had been set off in October 2002. For the South Korean government, it became a critical task to persuade both the U.S. and North Korea to abandon their antagonistic, assertive diplomacy against each other (Lee and Moon 2003; Lee 2004). The Koizumi government shared South Korea's priority to defuse the nuclear tension in the Korean peninsula. In addition, as public opinion in Japan became alarmed at North Korea's acknowledgment in 2002 of its kidnapping of several Japanese citizens in the past decades, defense and diplomacy began drawing greater public attention. Koizumi spent huge political resources, including his two one-day visits in 2002 and 2004, to resolve the kidnapping issue, for which closer cooperation with South Korea was essential (Cha 2002; *Asahi News*, December 10, 2002; *Japan Economic Newswire*, May 22, 2004).

Japan have too much at stake to use military means to settle their differences over the islands. Yet the slightest misunderstanding over any unilateral act, no matter how colored or allegedly sovereign, can lead to the rupture of the close ties between the two countries.

The summer of 2008 was just another example of what would be on that list. In July, the Japanese Ministry of Education issued a new manual for teachers and textbook publishers urging them to instruct Japanese students that the sovereignty over "Takeshima" is in dispute between Japan and South Korea, implying that the islands rightfully belong to Japan. The South Korean government responded by recalling its ambassador to Tokyo for three weeks, while some of its outraged citizens decapitating pheasants – Japan's national bird – in front of the Japanese Embassy in Seoul. As South Korea and Japan engaged in a diplomatic war over Dokdo, the United States Board on Geographic Names (BGN) added insult to injury to South Korea by changing Dokdo's status from "South Korean" to "undesignated sovereignty." The "technocratic" decision unmistakably infuriated many in South Korea. Although the Bush administration belatedly intervened and ordered the BGN to restore the old designation, many South Koreans already saw it as another instance of their country's fate being arbitrarily decided by a bigger power (*The New York Times*, August 31, 2008).

Interestingly, heightened economic and financial uncertainties in the present period resemble those that prevailed a decade ago. Although no economic forces could deter the initial discord between Seoul and Tokyo on the island issue from developing into heavy storm clouds over the East Sea/Sea of Japan, a serious clash was averted due to high levels of economic emergencies in the late 1990s. In the wake of the global economic crisis that began in the U.S. in fall 2008, South Korea and Japan agreed in December 2008 on a currency swap deal of around $20 billion. That was certainly a positive signal in a climate of name-calling and finger-pointing. During their meeting in Seoul in January 2009, President Lee Myung-bak and Prime Minister Taro Aso, both of whom came to power in 2008, confirmed the importance of resisting protectionism and nationalism, while promising to bring new life to stalemated discussions on a bilateral free trade deal (*The Washington Post*, January 11, 2009).

Prediction is a notoriously risky business in the study of international politics. But a systematic exploration of key variables and their impact may provide us with more precise, albeit contingent, outcomes. As shown in the previous sections, the pacific influence of economic interdependence has repeatedly prevented the sovereignty issue from escalating into a diplomatic crisis. Close economic ties between South Korea and Japan remain significant and this will not change overnight. Yet it is unclear whether their bilateral economic ties will stagnate, decline, or rise in the years to come, as shown in Table 4.1. At the same time, with the remarkable erosion of the U.S. defense commitment to Seoul since the September 11 attacks, the second North Korean nuclear crisis has exposed fundamental differences among Seoul, Tokyo, and Washington rather than bringing them together (Rozman 2002; Lee 2004). Combined with the populist leadership both in Seoul and Tokyo, and Washington's ambivalent commitments to Northeast Asia, even the slightest pessimism about future economic interdependence between South Korea and Japan could possibly spin the island dispute out of control.

4.7   Conclusion

This chapter explored the puzzling pattern of continuity and mutual restraint in the island dispute between South Korea and Japan. The Dokdo dispute has unfolded in multiple rounds since its inception in the early 1950s. The evidence provided here showed that the transition between, and conclusion of, different rounds of the dispute can be systematically explained by the territorial bargaining game approach as developed in Chapter 2.

Consistent with conventional wisdom, I found that the combination of resource competition, fluid geopolitics, and contending nationalisms has regularly brought about the initiation and escalation of Dokdo dispute. Yet I discovered that the pacific influence of economic interdependence has repeatedly prevented the sovereignty question from escalating into a full-scale diplomatic crisis.

From the beginning, the fishery issues in the East Sea/Sea of Japan have served as a surrogate battlefield for the Dokdo dispute. In one way or another, the Dokdo dispute has revolved around the contested maritime and fishing zones in the surrounding area, particularly since UNCLOS' entry into force in 1994. The maritime boundary in the East Sea/Sea of Japan has yet to be settled, thereby leaving competition over the fishing and other maritime resources capable of catalyzing future disputes in the contested area.

From a more strategic point of view, the Dokdo problem arose both directly and indirectly as a consequence of U.S. Cold War policy in Northeast Asia. On the one hand, as the architect of the Dokdo dispute, the U.S. has officially remained neutral on the sovereignty matter, but its hegemonic position has helped to ensure that the sovereignty question takes place within certain confines. To be sure, the common threat from North Korea (and rising China) has consolidated the security triangle among the U.S., South Korea, and Japan. On the other hand, the fluid regional security environment in recent years indicates that the role of the U.S. as an ultimate pacifier is increasingly eroding, although a complete U.S. withdrawal from the region is highly unlikely in the foreseeable future. Furthermore, in a region where the balance of power is shifting because of the rise of China and its perceived threat to American influence, the dispute over Dokdo has significant regional repercussions. If South Korea–Japan relations become strained, an unintended consequence could be to bring South Korea and China together against Japan. This will in turn further motivate Japan to cement its security ties with the U.S., thereby heightening the strategic uncertainties in the region.

It is evident that the combination of competitive domestic politics and enduring rivalry between South Korea and Japan has repeatedly hijacked South Korea–Japan relations. To be sure, a return to the *status quo* that has left the sovereignty issue undefined is satisfactory neither to South Korean nor to Japanese nationalisms.

Conservative politicians and nationalist groups on both sides have applied considerable pressure for a more assertive territorial policies. The Dokdo dispute might not immediately trigger any major conflicts between the two neighbors. Yet the accumulation of grievances and underlying nationalist sentiments could escalate minor quarrels, such as those involving fishing rights near the islands, into major conflicts. On a brighter side, however, greater common economic interests have moved the Dokdo dispute to the periphery of the overall South Korean–Japanese relationship thus far. In spite of the fact that the island dispute remains unresolved, both the South Korean and Japanese governments – particularly foreign policy experts thereof – have found it a convenient strategy to continually shelve final resolution attempts in favor of more pressing economic affairs. Certainly the relationship between territorial dispute and economic interdependence could be explosive, if the latter takes on highly asymmetric characteristics in the face of increasingly fluid geopolitics in the Korean peninsula and the tenacious and pernicious presence of contending nationalisms. Yet, as long as profitable economic opportunities continue for both sides, it is likely that a system of control and restraint will become a permanent feature of Dokdo questions.

References

Aggarwal VK, Koo MG (2006) Shifting ground: Is it finally time for economic and security regionalism? Global Asia 1(1):28–41

Akamatsu K (1937) Shinkoku Koyokoku no Sangyo Hatten. Ueda Teijiro Hakushi Kinen Ronbunshu, 4

Bong YD (2002) Flashpoints at sea? Legitimization strategy and East Asian island disputes. PhD Dissertation in Political Science, University of Pennsylvania, Philadelphia

Bernard M, Ravenhill FJ (1995) Beyond product cycles and flying geese: Regionalization, hierarchy, and the industrialization of East Asia. World Politics 47(2):171–209

Bridges B (1993) Japan and Korea in the 1990s: From antagonism to adjustment. Edward Elgar, Bookfield

Cha VD (1996) Bridging the gap: The strategic context of the 1965 Korea-Japan normalization treaty. Korean Studies 20:123–160

Cha VD (1999) Alignment despite antagonism: The United States-Korea-Japan security triangle. Stanford University Press, Stanford

Cha VD (2002) Mr. Koizumi goes to Pyongyang. Comparative Connections, 4(3), http://www.csis.org/media/csis/pubs/0203qjapan_korea.pdf, Accessed 10 February 2009

Cheong S (1992) The political use of Anti-Japanese sentiment in Korea from 1948 to 1949. Korea Journal 32(4):89–108

Cumings B (1984) The origins and development of the Northeast Asian political economy: Industrial sectors, product cycles and political consequences. International Organization 38(1):1–40

Cumings B (1997) Japan and Northeast Asia into the twenty-first century. In: Katzenstein PJ, Shiraishi T (eds) Network power: Japan and Asia. Cornell University Press, Ithaca

Day AJ (1987) Border and territorial disputes: A Keesing's reference publication, 2nd edn. Longman Group, Burnt Mill

Dupuy RJ, Vignes D (1991) A Handbook on the new law of the sea. Martinus Nijhoff Publishers, Hague/London/New York

Eckert C, Lee K, Lew Y, Robinson M, Wagner EW (1990) Korea old and new: A history. Ilchokak and Harvard University, Seoul

Hara K (2001) 50 Years from San Francisco: Re-examining the peace treaty and Japan's territorial problems. Pacific Affairs 74(3):361–382

Hatch W, Yamamura K (1996) Asia in Japan's embrace: Building a regional production alliance. Cambridge University Press, Cambridge

Hyun DS (2004) Postwar Korea–Japan relationship and territorial dispute: Discourse of Dokdo problem and image in Korea. PhD Dissertation in Political Science, University of Tokyo (in Japanese), Tokyo

Johnson CA (1996) Japan, Who governs? The rise of the developmental state. W.W. Norton, New York

Kajimura H (1997) The question of Takeshima/Tokdo. Korea Observer 28(3):423–475

Kim HN (1983) Politics of Japan's economic aid to South Korea. Asia-Pacific Community, 20

Kim Y (1999) Korea and international maritime laws. Hyosung Publisher (in Korean), Seoul

Kim SP (2004) Maritime delimitation and interim arrangements in Northeast Asia. Martinus Nijhoff Publishers, The Hague/London/New York

Koo MG (2005) From multilateralism to bilateralism? A shift in South Korea's trade strategy. In: Aggarwal VK, Urata S (eds) Bilateral trade arrangements in the Asia-Pacific: Origins, evolution, and implications. Routledge, New York

Korhonen P (1994) The theory of the flying geese pattern of development and its interpretations. Journal of Peace Research 31(1):93–108

Launius MA (2002) The politics of competing territorial claims to Tokdo. Paper presented at the First World Congress of Korean Studies, Academy of Korean Studies, Seoul, July 18–20

Lee C (1985) Japan and Korea: The political dimension. Stanford University Press, Stanford

Lee CM (2004) Rethinking future paths on the Korean peninsula. The Pacific Review 17(2):249–270

Lee D (1995a) A true record of Park Chung Hee and Korea–Japan treaty negotiations: From 5–16 to its conclusion. Hansong (in Korean), Seoul

Lee J (1990) Korean–Japanese relations: The past, present and future. Korea Observer 21(2):159–178

Lee J, Moon C (2003) The North Korean nuclear crisis revisited: The case for a negotiated settlement. Security Dialogue 34(2):135–151

Lee S (1998) The problems and prospects of the termination of the South Korea–Japan fishery accord. Institute of Foreign Affairs and National Security (in Korean), Seoul

Lee WD (1995a) The process of the Korea–Japan treaty. In the Institute of National Issues (ed) The Korea–Japan treaty revisited, Asia Publications (in Korean), Seoul

Lind JM (2004) Democratization and stability in East Asia. Paper presented at the Annual Meeting of the American Political Science Association, Chicago, IL

Lovmo MS (2002) The territorial dispute over Dokdo, http://www.geocities.com/mlovmo/page4.html, Accessed 10 February 2009

Mack A (1997) Island disputes in Northeast Asia. Working Paper No. 1997/2. Australian National University, Canberra, http://rspas.anu.edu.au/ir/pubs/work_papers/97-2.pdf, Accessed 10 February 2009

Manosevitz JU (2003) Japan and South Korea: Security relations reach adolescence. Asian Survey 43(5):801–825

Midford P, Mitsuhashi S (2004) Japan and Korea: The essential irrelevance of history? Paper presented at the Annual Meeting of the American Political Science Association, Chicago, IL

Oda S (1967) The normalization of relations between Japan and the Republic of Korea. American Journal of International Law 61:35–56

Oh K (1986) Japan–Korea rapprochement: A study in political, cultural, and economic cooperation in the 1980s. PhD Dissertation in Asian Studies, University of California, Berkeley

Park C (1983a) South Korea and the law of the sea. In: Park C (ed) East Asia and the law of the sea. Seoul National University Press, Seoul

Park C (1983b) Fishing under troubled waters: The Northeast Asia fisheries controversy. In: Park C (ed) East Asia and the law of the sea. Seoul National University Press, Seoul

Park K (1969) Legal status of 'Dokdo' island. Korea Observer 1(3/4):78–85

Pempel TJ (1997) Transpacific torii: Japan and the emerging Asian regionalism. In: Katzenstein PJ, Shiraishi T (eds) Network power: Japan and Asia. Cornell University Press, Ithaca

Pempel TJ (1998) Regime shift: Comparative dynamics of the Japanese political economy. Cornell University Press, Ithaca

Petri PA (1993) The East Asian trading bloc: An analytical history. In: Frankel JA, Kahler M (eds) Regionalism and rivalry: Japan and the United States in Pacific Asia. University of Chicago Press, Chicago

Prescott JRV (1985) The maritime boundaries of the world. Methuen, London, New York

Rozman G (2002) Japan and Korea: Should the U.S. be worried about their new spat in 2001? The Pacific Review 15(1):1–28

Russell G, Reingold EM, Chang S (1983) To Washington via Seoul. Time, January 24

Shin Y (2001) Domestic laws on the preservation and development of Dokdo. In: Kim M (ed) Special studies on Dokdo. Dokdo Research Association (in Korean), Seoul

Sin Y (1997) Korea's territorial rights to Dokdo: An historical study. Dokdo Research Association (in Korean), Seoul

Vogel SK (1999) When interests are not preferences: The cautionary tale of Japanese consumers. Comparative Politics 31(2):187–207

Weinstein MA (2006) South Korea's and Japan's Dokdo/Takeshima dispute escalates toward confrontation. The Power and Interest News Report, May 10, http://www.pinr.com/report.php?ac=view_report&report_id=487&language_id=1, Accessed 10 February 2009

Yamazawa I (1990) Economic development and international trade: The Japanese model. University of Hawaii Press, Honolulu

Chapter 5
The Island and Maritime Disputes in the East China Sea

5.1 Introduction

Postwar Sino–Japanese relations have been characterized by partnership, competition, and conflict.[1] The uneasy coexistence of economic cooperation, on the one hand, and political wariness and rivalry with deep mutual suspicions, on the other, is most evident in the sovereignty dispute over a group of five islands and three rocky outcroppings in the East China. These offshore islands – known as *Senkaku Retto* (Rocky Hill Islands) in Japan, as *Diaoyutai* (Fishing Platform Islands) in China, and *Tiaoyutai* in Taiwan – are effectively controlled by Japan, but the Chinese challenge its sovereignty claim (See Map 5.1).[2]

The dispute over these small and uninhabited islands may appear paradoxical. China is the world's most populous country and the third largest in land area. Japan is the world's second largest economy and one of the largest maritime countries. Furthermore, the two East Asian giants have forged closer economic ties since their diplomatic rapprochement in 1972, currently making them one of the most important economic partners for each other.[3] Certainly a pragmatic consideration of national interests would suggest more cooperative behavior.

---

[1] This chapter is a revised version of the author's published article entitled "The Senkaku/Diaoyu Dispute and Sino–Japanese Political Economic Relations: Cold Politics and Hot Economics?" (*The Pacific Review*, Vol. 22, No. 2, May 2009, pp. 205–232).

[2] The Japanese name of the Senkaku Islands is relatively new, dating back to 1900 when a study tour of the islands was conducted under private initiative. Although the name of the main island, Diaoyutai, dates back to the early fiftieth century according to an existing Chinese record, the collective use of the name to denote the entire group began with the advent of the controversy between Japan and Taiwan in 1970 (Park 1973: 248–9).

[3] Bilateral trade has increased dramatically with the total value rising from $1 billion in 1972 to $211 billion in 2006. In addition, both private and public investments and capital flows have boomed. Aside from its investment in Hong Kong, the cumulative total of Japan's foreign direct investment (FDI) in China was $66.6 billion as of 2004. Until the fiscal year 2004, the cumulative total of Japanese loans, grants, and technical cooperation to China was ¥3,133.1 billion, ¥145.7 billion, and ¥150.5 billion, respectively, (Ministry of Foreign Affairs of Japan 2006).

M.G. Koo, *Island Disputes and Maritime Regime Building in East Asia*,
The Political Economy of the Asia Pacific,
DOI 10.1007/978-0-387-89670-0_5, © Springer Science+Business Media, LLC 2009

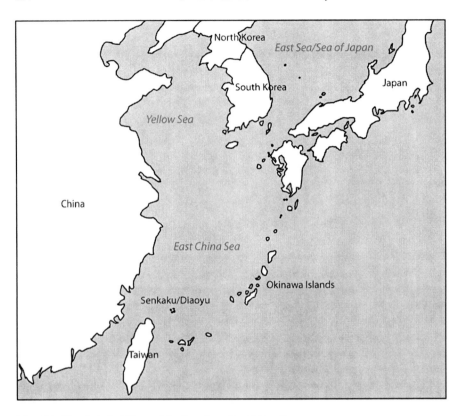

Map 5.1 The Senkaku/Diaoyu Islands and the East China Sea

As one commentator notes, however, "There is a huge disconnect between the economic and political relations of China and Japan...Japanese business enthusiasm for the China economic miracle continues. But at the political level, there is no talk of integration. Rather, there is a stiffening back of nationalism in both countries" (Gerald Curtis quoted in Marquand 2005). The so-called "cold politics and hot economics" (*seirei keinetsu* in Japanese or *zhengleng jingre* in Chinese) has thus become a defining feature of Sino–Japanese relations.

The reality in the East China Sea does not bode well for a shared effort to promote mutual cooperation, as the Senkaku dispute has served as the most persistent and explosive bone of contention between Japan and China. None of the claimants disputes the fact that Japan exercised control of the islands from 1895 until the end of World War II. Yet they differ on whether the islands were free for the taking in 1894, how Japan obtained control in that year, whether the islands were traditionally associated with Taiwan or Okinawa (Ryukyu), and what the implications of various peace treaties are.

The Chinese claim is that the islands were transferred with Taiwan to Japan by the Treaty of Shimonoseki, which ended the 1894–95 Sino–Japanese War, and should have been returned after World War II, under provisions of the 1943 Cairo Declaration, 1945 Potsdam Proclamation, and Article 2 of the San Francisco Peace Treaty (Inoue 1972; Cheng 1974; Ma 1984; Deans 1996; Austin 1998).[4] By contrast, Japan argues that the islands were *terra nullius* (unclaimed territory) and thus that they were legitimately incorporated as part of Okinawa Prefecture. In addition, Japan notes that the 1894 incorporation not only met with no Chinese protest, but also took place in the year before Japan defeated Imperial China. For Japan, therefore, the islands are not seen as spoils from its 1895 victory. Ultimately, Japan views the 1971 Okinawa Reversion Agreement with the U.S. as validating its sovereignty over the disputed islands (Prescott 1992: 31–2; Hara 2001: 275–80).

For both Japan and China, the Senkaku Islands – albeit diminutive in size above the sea level – have colossal significance, both tangible and intangible. Their tangible significance had been limited to fishing recourses until a high probability of oil and gas deposits in the continental shelf near the islands was discovered in the late 1960s. The global trend to adopt the UNCLOS further heightened the tangible values of these uninhabited islands. Their intangible dimension often centers on the enduring rivalry between Japan and China that can be traced back to the late nineteenth century at the latest. The competing claims to the islands have emotional content, presumably far beyond material significance, because giving way on the island issue to the other side would be considered as undermining their regional superpower status. To be sure, a return to the *status quo* that has left the islands in Japan's *de facto* control and that has left the *de jure* sovereignty undefined is satisfactory to neither Chinese nor Japanese nationalism. The disputed islands may lack the same degree of strategic and economic value as the Paracel and Spratly Islands for China and the Southern Kurile Islands for Japan. Yet the competitive elements in the Senkaku dispute, which has symbolic, political, economic, and historical significance, make it difficult for both Japan and China to give way on the territorial and maritime issues to the other side. Furthermore, a concession of sovereignty

---

[4] The 1951 San Francisco Peace Treaty included a renunciation of all Japanese rights, title, and claim to "Formosa (Taiwan) and the Pescadores (Penghu)" in Article 2. However, neither China nor Taiwan was seated at the San Francisco conference; neither signed the treaty. Yet the 1952 Treaty of Peace between Taiwan and Japan cited Article 2 of the 1951 San Francisco Treaty. It reiterated "Japan has renounced all right, title and claim to Taiwan and Penghu as well as the Spratly and Paracel Islands." It also recognized "all treaties, conventions and agreements concluded before December 9, 1941, between China and Japan have become null and void as a consequence of the war." The 1972 Joint Communiqué between China and Japan mentioned that Japan "adheres to its stand of complying with Article 8 of the Potsdam Proclamation" (Cheng 1974: 248–60; Li 1975: 151–3). The 1978 Peace and Friendship Treaty between China and Japan merely confirmed their Joint Communiqué.

over the Senkaku Islands and nearby maritime zone could possibly jeopardize their respective claims to the other disputed islands.

The postwar dispute over the Senkaku Islands has unfolded in multiple rounds. Neither China nor Taiwan had clearly challenged the Japanese claim to the islands until 1968 when it was first discovered that abundant oil and gas deposits might sit under the seabed near the islands. The diplomatic spat over the islands intensified when the U.S. agreed to return the Senkaku Islands to Japan in 1971 along with the Okinawa Islands. This very first round of dispute in 1968–71 was followed by four successive rounds of dispute in 1978, 1990–91, 1996–97, and 2004–05, most of which revolved around lighthouses that had been built by Japanese ultranationalists, first in 1978 and again in 1996.

Empirically, we see the Senkaku dispute persisting, neither reaching a peaceful settlement nor escalating into a full-scale militarized conflict. Conventional explanations for this phenomenon have largely focused on one or more of the following factors: the validity of contending historical evidence, domestic legitimization processes, competition for energy and marine resources, historical animosities, and the role of the U.S. as an architect of the postwar East Asian system. Despite their partial explanatory utility, these approaches cannot fully capture the continuing pattern of the rise and fall of conflict over the Senkaku Islands. This chapter argues that a liberal peace perspective offers a better account. I show that both Japan and China have found it in their interest to de-escalate conflicts because of concerns over damaging their economic relationship, thus supporting a liberal peace interpretation.

The rest of the chapter examines the transition between, and conclusion of, five different rounds of clash over the dispute islands. To summarize the main findings, the initial impetuses of the island dispute tend to come from ultranationalist activities in either Japan or China, or both. At first, both Beijing and Tokyo use them to mobilize political support for their regime or particular policy goals. Eventually, however, both governments seek to minimize diplomatic damages, fearing that contending Sino–Japanese nationalisms could snowball into a larger, possibly destabilizing movement that will undermine bilateral economic ties. The final section draws conclusions and policy implications.

5.2 The First Round of Dispute (1968–1971)

Before the Sino–Japanese diplomatic rapprochement of 1972, mutual economic dependence between China and Japan was insignificant at best, as indicated by the low levels of trade dependence scores less than 1% of their respective GDPs (See Table 5.1). Contending resource nationalisms, Chinese irredentism, and enduring rivalry aside, the liberal peace theory would predict a dispute initiation and escalation in the absence of the mitigating force of mutual gains from trade. The actual outcome in the late 1960s is in accordance with such a prediction. Yet by 1971, the

Table 5.1 GDP and trade statistics of China and Japan (1960–2005) (US$ million)

	China					Japan				
	GDP	Export to Japan	Import from Japan	Bilateral trade balance	TD on Japan (%)	GDP	Export to China	Import from China	Bilateral trade balance	TD on China (%)
1960	61,378	19	3	16	0.04	44,622	3	21	−18	0.05
1961	50,101	28	18	10	0.09	53,888	17	31	−14	0.09
1962	46,464	41	42	−1	0.18	61,154	39	46	−7	0.14
1963	50,280	67	69	−1	0.27	69,991	62	75	−13	0.20
1964	58,613	142	168	−26	0.53	82,329	153	158	−5	0.38
1965	69,709	202	269	−67	0.68	91,596	245	225	20	0.51
1966	75,879	278	347	−68	0.82	106,378	315	306	9	0.58
1967	72,057	245	317	−72	0.78	124,661	288	270	18	0.45
1968	69,994	203	358	−155	0.80	147,642	326	224	102	0.37
1969	78,719	213	430	−217	0.82	173,427	391	235	156	0.36
1970	91,506	231	626	−395	0.94	204,409	569	254	315	0.40
1971	98,562	293	636	−343	0.94	230,889	579	322	257	0.39
1972	112,160	454	681	−227	1.01	305,765	619	499	120	0.37
1973	136,770	884	1,147	−262	1.48	415,418	1,042	973	69	0.49
1974	142,255	1,186	2,182	−996	2.37	461,127	1,983	1,304	679	0.71
1975	161,163	1,390	2,484	−1,094	2.40	501,426	2,258	1,529	729	0.76
1976	151,628	1,248	1,833	−585	2.03	563,554	1,666	1,373	293	0.54
1977	172,349	1,418	2,150	−732	2.07	693,587	1,955	1,560	395	0.51
1978	147,321	1,719	3,105	−1,386	3.27	974,518	3,074	2,045	1,029	0.53
1979	175,574	2,764	3,944	−1,180	3.82	1,014,321	3,674	2,933	741	0.65
1980	188,242	4,032	5,169	−1,137	4.89	1,062,752	5,109	4,346	763	0.89
1981	192,952	4,747	6,183	−1,436	5.66	1,174,567	5,076	5,283	−207	0.88
1982	202,088	4,806	3,902	904	4.31	1,091,583	3,500	5,338	−1,838	0.81
1983	227,376	4,517	5,495	−978	4.40	1,190,692	4,918	5,089	−171	0.84

(continued)

Table 5.1 (continued)

	China					Japan				
	GDP	Export to Japan	Import from Japan	Bilateral trade balance	TD on Japan (%)	GDP	Export to China	Import from China	Bilateral trade balance	TD on China (%)
1984	256,107	5,155	8,057	-2,902	5.16	1,266,999	7,199	5,943	1,256	1.04
1985	304,912	6,091	15,178	-9,087	6.98	1,356,363	12,590	6,534	6,056	1.41
1986	295,716	5,079	12,463	-7,384	5.93	2,009,699	9,936	5,727	4,209	0.78
1987	268,218	6,392	10,087	-3,695	6.14	2,437,335	8,337	7,478	859	0.65
1988	307,167	8,046	11,062	-3,016	6.22	2,959,386	9,486	9,861	-375	0.65
1989	342,292	8,395	10,534	-2,139	5.53	2,961,160	8,477	11,083	-2,606	0.66
1990	354,644	9,210	7,656	1,554	4.76	3,039,693	6,145	12,057	-5,912	0.60
1991	376,617	10,252	10,032	220	5.39	3,475,955	8,605	14,248	-5,643	0.66
1992	418,181	11,699	13,686	-1,987	6.07	3,793,819	11,967	16,972	-5,005	0.76
1993	431,780	15,782	23,303	-7,521	9.05	4,354,707	17,353	20,651	-3,298	0.87
1994	542,534	21,490	26,319	-4,829	8.81	4,794,206	18,687	27,569	-8,882	0.96
1995	700,278	28,466	29,007	-541	8.21	5,283,057	21,934	35,922	-13,988	1.10
1996	816,490	30,888	29,190	1,698	7.36	4,688,254	21,827	40,405	-18,578	1.33
1997	898,244	31,820	28,990	2,830	6.77	4,305,591	21,692	41,827	-20,135	1.48
1998	946,301	29,718	28,307	1,411	6.13	3,931,051	20,182	37,079	-16,897	1.46
1999	991,356	32,399	33,768	-1,369	6.67	4,452,977	23,450	43,070	-19,620	1.49
2000	1,080,71	41,654	40,083	1,571	7.56	4,746,068	30,356	55,156	-24,800	1.80
2001	1,175,716	45,078	42,810	2,268	7.48	4,162,363	30,948	57,780	-26,832	2.13
2002	1,271,000	48,483	53,489	-5,006	8.02	3,972,485	39,958	61,792	-21,834	2.56
2003	1,417,000	59,423	74,151	-14,728	9.43	4,300,858	57,480	75,559	-18,079	3.09
2004	1,650,000	73,514	94,372	-20,858	10.17	4,668,420	73,818	94,227	-20,409	3.60
2005	1,843,120	84,027	100,412	-16,385	10.01	4,799,060	80,340	109,104	-28,764	3.95

Sources: Trade and GDP data are collected from a variety of sources including the International Monetary Fund's *Direction of Trade Statistics* (CD-ROM), the World Bank's *World Development Indicators* (CD-ROM), China General Administration of Customs, Japan External Trade Organization's *Japanese Trade and Investment Statistics*, and the World Trade Organization's *International Trade Statistics*

island issue eventually took a back seat with geopolitical and economic consideration becoming more pressing.

5.2.1   Initiation and Escalation Phase

The initial impetus of the first flare-up of the Senkaku dispute came in the late 1968. A geological survey, conducted by the Committee for Coordination of Joint Prospecting for Mineral Resources in Asian Offshore Areas (CCOP) under the auspices of the United Nations Economic Commission for Asia and the Far East (UNECAFE), suggested "a high probability exists that the continental shelf between Taiwan and Japan may be one of the most prolific oil reservoirs in the world, with potential estimated at between 10 and 100 billion barrels" UNECAFE 1968: 39–40).

The UNECAFE report caused a great sensation among the oil-hungry coastal states. In a preemptive move, the Taiwanese government and the Gulf Oil Corporation entered into a concession contract in July 1970 to develop oil from an area that included the disputed islands. Tokyo issued a grim warning to Taipei that the latter's bids to exploit the oil potential around the islands were not valid (Cheng 1974: 242–3). The competition for marine resources took an emotional and symbolic twist in September 1970 when a journalist from Taiwan hoisted the Taiwanese national flag on Uotsuri Island, the largest in the Senkaku chain, only to be removed by the Okinawa police of Japan. This incident served as the catalyst for a series of worldwide demonstrations and protest marches against "resurgent Japanese militarism" and the need to defend Chinese sovereignty on the Senkaku Islands. Hence the *Protect the Diaoyu Movement* started the trend of popular protests by Taiwanese, Hong Kongers, and overseas Chinese over the sovereignty question (Chung 2004: 26, 33–4).[5]

Japan reasserted its title to the islands themselves, but indicated that it was willing to collaborate with Taiwan to develop seabed resources in the adjacent continental shelf. This invitation was later extended to South Korea. Officials from Japan, Taiwan, and South Korea thus met in Tokyo in December 1970 to form the United Oceanic Development Company, while agreeing to freeze the sovereignty issue for later resolution (Park 1973: 227–9). However, Chinese intervention abruptly terminated the development boom. The sudden emergence of China placed

---

[5] The dispute was one of the first occasions when popular protest had been tolerated under Chiang Kai-shek's authoritarian regime in Taiwan. Although initially inspired by the Chiang government, the *Protect the Diaoyu Movement* soon gained a popular momentum of its own and developed into a major intellectual movement that addressed the broader questions of Taiwan's status and political circumstances (Long 1991; Deans 1996). This movement landed on mainland China in the late 1990s and has gained new political and organizational support since then.

the whole situation in a new perspective. The Beijing government claimed that the "Diaoyu Islands" (and Taiwan) were China's sacred territory and that exploitation of the area by foreign countries would not be tolerated (Park 1973: 222; Buzan 1978: 38–9; Chung 2004: 33).[6] The maritime interest of China had traditionally been confined to its coastline before the competing claims of Japan and Taiwan to the continental shelves of the East China Sea precipitated China's counter-claim. It was not a coincidence that China became an enthusiastic supporter of Latin American countries' claims to 200 nm zones of maritime jurisdiction (Park 1983: 107).

For Japan, because the Senkaku Islands had never been disputed before, it was a problem that emerged suddenly. Taiwan argued that Okinawa was not Japanese territory and opposed its reversion to Japan. China also criticized this reversion, but for a different reason, calling it a fraud because the U.S. military remained on the islands. The U.S. transferred all these islands to Japanese control in 1972, but these provisions were not predicated upon the transfer of sovereignty itself. At first the U.S. government appeared to support the Japanese claim. Yet because of the need to improve relations with China, the U.S. government then took a neutral stance over the dispute, which it has maintained ever since (Park 1973: 233; Hara 2001:376–80).

The conjunction of the UNECAFE report and the reversion of Okinawa turned the dispute over the islands into one of the major issues of the day in Japan. All political parties, even the left-wing parties which were traditionally highly critical of the ruling LDP's anti-China policy, supported the LDP's position on the islands. With nationalist sentiments worsening, the issue became highly emotive and dominated the Japanese media (Cheng 1974: 264; Chung 2004: 35). While not as significant in domestic politics as the dispute with the Soviet Union over the Southern Kurile Islands, the Senkaku issue was nevertheless one over which the Japanese government's negotiating position was severely restricted by public opinion (Deans 1996).

Geopolitical considerations were another reason for the conflict escalation. The location of the islands is strategically important for all of the claimant countries. Since the Senkaku Islands are located only 120 nm northeast of Taiwan, 200 nm

---

[6] On December 20, an editorial entitled "Resolutely Do Not Tolerate Attempts by American and Japanese Revisionists to Rob Our Country's Submarine Resources," suddenly made its appearance in Beijing's authoritative *People's Daily*. The editorial stressed "American and Japanese revisionists are now playing up this development cooperation through the United Oceanic Development Company to grab our country's submarine resources...Taiwan Province and the islets appertaining to it, which includes the Diaoyutai, constitute China's sacred territory. The oceans surrounding these islands and the Chinese coast and the submarine resources containing therein all belongs to China, which would resolutely not allow others to lay their dirty fingers on them. Only China has the right to explore and develop the submarine resources of this region" (Quoted in Chung 2004: 33).

west of Okinawa, and 250 nm west from mainland China, they constitute a potential strategic base from which one party might launch a threatening assault upon other parties. A Japanese military base on the Senkaku Islands would be as if the Japanese put their guns under the Chinese and Taiwanese noses. Presumably the opposite may also hold true (Suganuma 2000: 13).

At the heart of the dispute initiation and escalation were contending nationalisms of China and Japan with the unfortunate history of Sino–Japanese relations since the nineteenth century continuing to fuel the dispute on symbolic grounds. Specifically, the humiliations suffered by China at the hands of the Japanese during the wars in 1895 and in 1937 motivated the Chinese to contest the Japanese to express their dignity. Particularly for China, it was during this first round of the island dispute that irredentism became a prominent form of nationalism (Mack 1997; Deans 2000; Suganuma 2000; Bong 2002; Chung 2004).

Unsurprisingly, the initiation and escalation period lacked deterring economic forces. Before the Sino–Japanese diplomatic rapprochement of 1972, their mutual economic dependence was insignificant at best, as indicated by the low levels of trade dependence scores less than 1% of their respective GDPs (See Table 5.1). To some extent, Japan's decision to allow exports of plant equipment to China on a deferred-payment basis in August 1963, followed by a series of large-scale trade fairs in 1963 and 1964, represented a subtle Japanese gravitation towards rapprochement with China for economic reasons (Cha 1996: 151). Yet throughout the 1960s trade between China and Japan was conducted on a marginal scale between small and medium-sized trading companies, and thus the overall Sino–Japanese economic interdependence remained at low levels in absolute terms (Chung 2004: 52). Contending resource nationalisms aside, the liberal peace theory anticipates a dispute escalation in the absence of the mitigating force of mutual gains from trade. The actual outcome during this period is in accord with such a prediction.

5.2.2   De-escalation Phase

Despite a series of Chinese protests between late 1970 and early 1971, the island issue began to take a back seat from March 1971 in favor of getting on with more pressing geopolitical and economic affairs. Both Japan and the U.S. quickly responded to the Chinese protests. On March 11, Tokyo clearly signaled that, in order to avoid friction with Beijing, attempts to develop oil from the disputed area would be suspended and that return of Okinawa to Japan by the U.S. would be delayed until May 1972. In addition, Tokyo wanted to defuse the tension with Beijing in the middle of the Japan–Taiwan de-recognition crisis and the negotiations for the Sino–Japanese normalization (Park 1973: 233; Hara 2001: 376–80). At first, Washington supported the Japanese claim. But, it then decided to take a neutral stance over the dispute, which it has maintained ever since, claiming that America's involvement could "...in no way prejudice any underlying claims...

The United States…considers that any conflicting claims are a matter for resolution by the parties concerned" (Quoted in Park 1973: 255). The obvious intent was to prevent the oil dispute from affecting the détente between Washington and Beijing.

After the 1972 Sino–Japanese diplomatic rapprochement, the focus of the dispute shifted to a dispute between China and Japan rather than one between Taiwan and Japan (Deans 1996).[7] In 1972, at the state banquet to welcome Japanese Prime Minister Kakuei Tanaka who came to Beijing to sign the official document, Chinese Premier Zhou Enlai (1949–76) said: "There is no need to mention the Diaoyu Islands. It does not count as a problem of any sort compared to recovering normal diplomatic relations (with Japan)" (Quoted in He 2007: 4).

In hindsight, increasingly positive expectations about the Sino–Japanese economic relationships began to take the front seat at the turn of the 1970s, thereby shelving territorial issues as well as other thorny bilateral problems. During this period, the increase of bilateral trade was remarkable. According to Chinese statistics, its import from Japan expanded from $3 million in 1960 to $636 million in 1971, while its export to Japan increased from $19 to $293 million for the same period. China's trade dependence on Japan thus broke the 1% point in 1972 (See Table 5.1). It is quite plausible that a steady growth of commercial ties provided the backdrop for the 1972 normalization of quasi-enemy relationship, and the abrupt de-escalation of the first round of island dispute.

5.3   The Second Round of Dispute (1978)

The unresolved sovereignty question of the Senkaku Islands surfaced again in a more serious manner in the spring of 1978. The 1978 crisis was intimately related to the Peace and Friendship Treaty (PFT) negotiations between Japan and China. The island dispute had been a rumbling issue in the background, which both parties wished to leave out of the PFT negotiation agenda. In the wake of the second island flare-up, Deng Xiaoping, who seized power in 1978, proposed that China and Japan jointly explore the oil and gas deposits near the disputed islands without touching on the sovereignty issue. But national pride, yearning for energy supply, and ultra-nationalist public pressures pushed both the Chinese and Japanese governments to depart from such a conciliatory approach. Eventually, however, broader economic and geopolitical calculations took higher priority, thereby putting the territorial question on shelf again without causing further diplomatic damage. Mutual benefits in concluding the PFT and shelving the thorny sovereignty question over the

---

[7]Official pronouncements suggest that Taipei certainly wanted to stress its sovereign rights to explore and develop the continental shelf surrounding the Senkaku Islands, but they were conspicuously silent or evasive on the issue of the sovereignty of the islands itself. Faced with the imminent Sino–U.S. normalization of relations and the loss of its seat in the UN, Taiwan did its best to play down the island dispute, thus allowing the Japanese ownership claim to the islands itself to go unchallenged (Chung 2004: 35).

Senkaku Islands involved an increase in trade and investment between China and Japan, an expansion of the Chinese market to Japanese economic penetration, an external validation of Deng's open-door policy by a powerful neighboring country, and the creation of an informal common front against possible military moves from the Soviet Union.

5.3.1   Initiation and Escalation Phase

Following the normalization of relations in September 1972 the Japanese and Chinese governments negotiated a peace treaty. Yet the process was slow, delayed by a number of factors including the death of Mao Zedong in 1976, the post-Mao succession struggle, and the Japanese reluctance to agree to China's insistence on the inclusion of an "anti-hegemony" clause tacitly aimed at the Soviet Union.

The initial impetus for the 1978 flare-up came on April 7, 1978 when a group of anti-PFT Japanese politicians, consisting mostly of rightwing and pro-Taiwan LDP members, urged that the Senkaku matter be resolved as part of the PFT negotiations. During this period, the Soviet Union was negotiating a similar treaty with China's arch enemy, Vietnam. Those Japanese politicians believed that China would desperately need Japan's support for the anti-hegemony clause, thus motivating Beijing to compromise over the offshore islands (Tretiak 1978: 1241). However, raising the sovereignty issue at a very sensitive moment in the PFT negotiations caused a virtual collapse of the talks and the contending sovereignty issue soon became the focus of the day.

In China, the foremost proponent of the PFT Deng Xiaoping thus became trapped in a dilemma: confront Japan over the sovereignty question and risk losing the Sino–Japanese PFT, which would cement a *de facto* security alliance between China and Japan against a common threat from the Soviet Union; or not challenge Japan over the islands and risk alienating domestic power brokers who would criticize Deng's "open-door" policy as coming at the expense of China's territorial integrity (Chung 2004: 38–9). His immediate reaction was to escalate the island issue. On April 12, 1978, more than a hundred fishing trawlers bedecked with Chinese national flags reached the area and more than thirty of them entered into the islands' 12 nm territorial sea. Allegedly under the People's Liberation Army Navy (PLAN)'s command, the presence of Chinese vessels sharply increased the level of tension. It was in fact China's clear show of intent that it would not tolerate Japanese territorial claim even at the risk of jeopardizing PFT negotiations. Following the fishing expedition, the Chinese side ignored all Japanese demand for talks on the disputed islands (Tretiak 1978: 1242–3).

The 1978 clash demonstrated how Japanese ultranationalist groups could hijack Sino–Japanese relationship. In a rare demonstration of national solidarity on matters with respect to China, all major Japanese political groups rallied around the flag and endorsed the Japanese government's accusation of the Chinese fishing expedition (Tretiak 1978). In particular, a Japanese rightist group – *Seirankai* (Blue Storm Group) – exacerbated the island dispute in August 1978 by erecting a lighthouse on Uotsuri Island in the Senkaku group in an effort to reinforce Japan's territorial claim to the islands, apparently without government opposition (Mutsuko 1996).[8] Although, the construction of the lighthouse did not aggravate the situation any further, it would become a focal point of the island dispute a decade later. Following the construction of the lighthouse, Sino–Japanese hostility reached near-crisis proportions. The 1978 clash clearly demonstrates the emerging efforts by Japan's ultranationalist groups to keep the island dispute spinning out of control, thereby promoting their own nationalist agenda (Deans 1996; 2000).

5.3.2   De-escalation Phase

Despite the growing domestic pressures on both sides for a more aggressive, definitive territorial policy, neither Tokyo nor Beijing wished to exacerbate the already tense situation. Although greatly embarrassed by the fishing expedition and intense public outcry at home, the Japanese government appealed for calm, making it clear that it would not resort to military force to deal with the Chinese fishing operation. On May 27, 1978, in an attempt to defuse the tension built up for weeks, Japanese Prime Minister Takeo Fukuda announced that his government had decided to resume PFT talks with China (Tretiak 1978: 1243; Chung 2004: 40).

The Chinese government took a reciprocal step towards de-escalation as well. At a meeting with a group of journalists in May, Deng Xiaoping reiterated China's claim to the islands, but also promised that incidents like the April fishing expedition would not occur again. For Deng and his cohorts in the Chinese Communist Party (CCP), it was dangerous to press Japan too hard on the territorial front, as cooperation with Japan was critical not only for China's economic development, but also for their own domestic power position (Chung 2004: 38–41). The negotiations for the PFT finally resumed on July 18 and the 1978 flare-up ended abruptly when the two countries made a diplomatic breakthrough in Beijing on August 8, thus shelving the island issue (Tretiak 1978: 1246–7).

From one perspective, such a dramatic turn of events can be attributed to the unique geopolitical circumstances in East Asia towards the end of 1978. The Chinese mood was slightly more conciliatory by the end of summer 1978 than it had been in spring partly because of the severe security threat posed by a renewed Soviet–Vietnamese alliance. By working so hard on the anti-hegemony clause, Chinese leaders impressed their Japanese counterparts with Beijing's seriousness

---

[8]This first beacon was nothing more than a simple electric light bulb hanging from an iron pipe. Although *Seirankai*'s application to the Ministry of Transportation to have its proposed lighthouse registered in the navigational chart was approved, the Ministry of Foreign Affairs did not want to create another clash with China and vetoed the proposal, and the lighthouse was not authorized for construction. *Seirankai* nonetheless went ahead with its construction (Chung 2004: 41).

about containing Soviet expansionism by improving Sino–Japanese relations (Tretiak 1978: 1237–9). The U.S.–Japan alliance began to view the successful conclusion of the PFT as a vital element to contain Soviet expansionism in the region. U.S. President Jimmy Carter wished a successful conclusion of the PFT during Prime Minister Fukuda's May 1978 visit to the Carter's national security advisor Zbignew Brzezinski also spoke in favor of a speedy conclusion to the PFT in his meetings with Fukuda. That was all the political space that Fukuda needed to justify his conversion to a pro-PFT stance and calm the fear of Japanese socialists that the PFT might provoke the Soviets (Chung 2004: 40).

A closer look at the economic relations between China and Japan reveals that another pacifying force already began working. Although it was not until December 1978 that Deng officially announced a new open-door policy, the transformation of China's economy already started months earlier. His new initiatives fundamentally altered the context through which Chinese and Japanese elites calculated their strategies vis-à-vis the island dispute. Some numerical illustrations make the point clearer. After the 1972 Sino–Japanese diplomatic rapprochement, Sino–Japanese economic interdependence began to take off. Between 1972 and 1978, China's trade dependence on Japan as a share of GDP increased from 1.01 to 3.27% (an increase by 240% points), while Japan's trade dependence on China increased from 0.37 to 0.53% (an increase by 43% points). These trade dependence scores indicate that bilateral trade became more significant than before for both China and Japan. At the same time, Sino–Japanese bilateral economic relations took an asymmetric path. During the same period, China's trade deficit against Japan also increased dramatically from $227 million to $1.4 billion. As indicated by the widening gap between their respective trade dependence scores, China depended on Japan for trade more than Japan did on China (See Table 5.1).

On the whole, the positive influence of growing bilateral trade ties outweighed the negative impact of inequality. Within policy circles in both China and Japan, it was increasingly recognized that the sovereignty question could possibly jeopardize the PFT negotiations, thus undermining prospective economic gains. The Japanese business community was also strongly committed to the PFT treaty, generally convinced that it would ease implementation of the long-term (1978–85) bilateral trade agreement signed with Beijing in February 1978. It was believed that the PFT would ensure trade beyond the $20 billion bilateral trade floor that the agreement had set. The head of the Japanese Association of Business Organizations (*Keidanren*) said "the treaty conclusion signifies that both Japanese and Chinese are determined to build mutual, true friendship and prosperity that will last forever" – euphemisms for Japanese industry's desire for a clearer path towards greater trade with China in the coming years. After the 1978 clash, shelving territorial claims for economic development seemingly became the two countries' diplomatic leitmotif in their treatment of the island dispute (Tretiak 1978: 1236–48; Chung 2004: 38–9).

5.4   The Third Round of Dispute (1990–91)

Perhaps the passage of a dozen years was not enough to make political leaders both in China and Japan "wiser" to find common ground with respect to the island question.[9] Once again, contending sovereignty claims between Japan and China collided in September 1990 when the Japanese government accepted an application filed by *Nihon Seinensha* (Japan Youth Federation), which sought official lighthouse status for a beacon that *Seirankai* had built on the Uotsuri Island in 1978. *Nihon Seinensha* repaired the lighthouse in 1988 and 1989 to meet the Japanese Maritime Safety Agency (JMSA)'s technical standards and applied for official recognition. The 1990–91 flare-up shows how ultranationalist groups endeavored to keep the sovereignty issue spinning out of government's hands. Aside from contending territorial nationalisms, the geopolitical vacuum left by the collapse of the Soviet Union also contributed to the initiation and escalation of the 1990–91 clash. In contrast to their combative rhetoric and endorsement of public nationalistic sentiments, however, both Japanese and Chinese leaders eventually sought to defuse the dispute quickly and quietly, because they saw a far greater importance in keeping their bilateral economic relations intact than in standing up for nationalist values of territorial integrity.

5.4.1   Initiation and Escalation Phase

Initially, the 1990–91 flare-up concerned only Tokyo and Taipei, leaving Beijing outside the dispute arena. Taipei swiftly issued a statement that it would not tolerate Japanese invasion of Chinese territory (Chung 2004: 42). On October 21, 1990, a group of Taiwanese activists attempted to land on the disputed islands to place an Olympic torch as a symbol of Taiwanese sovereignty against the Japanese lighthouse. The JMSA kept their boats away from the islands, subsequently provoking a series of anti-Japanese demonstrations in Taiwan and Hong Kong with Japanese flags burnt and Japanese goods destroyed (*South China Morning Post*, October 29, 1990). This incident was one of the most serious diplomatic clashes between Japan and Taiwan after the termination of their diplomatic relations in 1972 (Iwano 1992: 211–20).

The failed landing attempt by rightwing activists dominated the news in Taiwan in late October. The Taipei government came under severe criticism for failing to properly represent Taiwan's national interest on the international stage. Riding on the nationalistic sentiment of an angry public, the opposition party – Democratic Progress Party (DPP) – immediately proposed a retaliatory plan to dispatch a 300-boat flotilla. The Taipei government rejected this political move as political showmanship and opposed the very idea of using the national military. Although, the

---

[9]In October 1978, Deng reaffirmed that both the Chinese and Japanese governments had agreed to shelve the islands issue in 1972 and that this was still the policy of both governments: "It is true that the two sides maintain different views on this question…It does not matter if this question is shelved for some time, say, ten years. Our generation is not wise enough to find common language on this question. Our next generation will certainly be wiser. They will certainly find a solution acceptable to all" (Quoted in Lo 1989: 171-2).

DPP's proposal never materialized for political and logistical reasons, the Taipei government was forced to set up a special seventh coast guard detachment to deal with such possible incidents in the future (Bong 2002: 29–30; Chung 2004: 43).

It was not until October 18 that Beijing began condemning Tokyo's intention to recognize the lighthouse and demanded that the Japanese government restrict the ultranationalist activities of its citizens (*Kyodo News*, October 22, 1990). During the early stage of the first lighthouse incident, Beijing did not take any immediate action against Japan, probably owing to its low international status after the Tiananmen incident of June 1989 and its reluctance to further antagonize Japan. The initial low-key response severely undermined the CCP's nationalist credentials. Citizens in Beijing who belatedly learned about the dispute vented their anger towards their leaders who they believed had failed to live up to their nationalist rhetoric in a desperate move of begging for Japanese loans (Downs and Saunders 1998/1999: 131–2).

Chinese public anger was an extension of anti-Japanese demonstrations that had taken place in the mid-1980s. Most notably in 1985 and 1986, university students demonstrated in cities across China in opposition to "the revival of Japanese militarism" and "Japanese economic imperialism." They protested Prime Minister Yasuhiro Nakasone's visit to the Yasukuni shrine, Japanese textbooks' distortions of Japan's war history, and the dumping of Japanese goods in Chinese market, while accusing some in the Chinese leadership of belonging to a "pro-Japanese faction" (Kelly 1987: 140–1). As Deans (2000: 122) notes, the attacks on Japanese economic imperialism were also a criticism of the reform process and the speed at which China was opening up to foreign investment and influence. In response to growing domestic pressure, the CCP government was forced to pressure Nakasone to cancel his visit to Yasukuni after 1985 and fire Education Minister Masayuki Fujio in the wake of the second textbook controversy in 1986.

The first lighthouse incident thus demonstrated again how domestic groups could use the sovereignty issue to embarrass their own and the other governments. Japanese nationalism, especially the activities of ultranationalist groups, has been fundamental to the way in which the dispute has manifested itself. These groups – most notably *Seirankai* in the 1970s and 80s and *Nihon Seinensha* since the 1990s – played a central role in driving the dispute beyond political leaders' control ever since they had contributed to the precipitation of the 1978 crisis. These ultranationalist groups may be a minor political force, but they are an indication of a more assertive nationalism emerging in Japan (Deans 2000: 124–6).[10]

---

[10] Although *Seirankai*'s membership was only about 3,000 at its peak, it certainly exerted an influence much beyond its limited size to the highest corridors of power, for in its heyday it counted fourteen members of the Fukuda faction and ten of the Nakasone faction in its ranks. By 1990, the political grouping with the strongest organizing and financial power was *Nihon Seinensha*. Its founder was Kusuo Kobayashi, a one-time vice president of the gangster group Sumiyoshikai. After Kobayashi's death in January 1990, leadership of *Nihon Seinensha* fell to Eto Toyohisa, a one-time *Seirankai* activist who had made Japan's claim to the Senkaku Islands his life-long cause. It was he who, along with half a dozen associates, erected the first lighthouse on Uotsuri Island in August 1978, and with another six colleagues built the second one on Kitakoji Island in July 1996. The Japanese government estimates that there are about 120,000 right-wing sympathizers in the country, although not all of them are involved with the Senkaku issue (Chung 2004: 45–6).

The 1990 flare-up demonstrated the aggravating effect of bilateral economic friction in the 1980s and the skeptical and pessimistic views of opposition groups in China about the gains from trade with Japan. China's trade deficit with Japan reached a record high level of $9.09 billion in 1985 and remained significant for the rest of the decade. In addition, the structure of mutual trade dependence was becoming increasingly asymmetric. For example, the gap between their respective trade dependence scores widened from the average of 3.86% during the period of 1979–84 to the average of 5.13% during the period of 1985–90, indicating that trade with Japan became more important for China's economy than the converse. As noted by realists, asymmetric economic interdependence can aggravate the sovereignty issue (See Table 5.1).

In addition, the geopolitical vacuum left by the sudden collapse of the Soviet Union made the Chinese political elites anxious about their political future. Furthermore, the latter half of 1990 witnessed the start of the Gulf War and heated debate in Japan about its doomed Gulf Cooperation Bill (GCB) that would have dispatched Japanese Self Defense Forces (SDF) to the Persian Gulf albeit in a noncombatant capacity. Viewing the GCB debate and JMSA action to recognize the lighthouse as more than a sheer coincidence, the Chinese leadership began mounting a major propaganda campaign against Japan to shore up its threatened legitimacy (Downs and Saunders 1998/1999: 127; Chung 2004: 42).

5.4.2   De-escalation Phase

After the initial and brief squabble, Japan and China both chose de-escalation as the norm to govern their differences in the East China Sea. On October 23, 1990, Japanese Prime Minister Toshiki Kaifu promised that Japan would adopt a cautious attitude in dealing with the lighthouse application. A week later, diplomats in Beijing and Tokyo announced that both countries had agreed to quietly drop the dispute and avoid further provocative actions. In April 1991, the 1990 lighthouse flare-up formally ended as the Japanese government rejected the lighthouse application by *Nihon Seinensha* (Shaw 1999: 17; Bong 2002: 30).[11]

As the *de facto* owner, Japan had more to lose by further escalating the territorial dispute with China – an action that might have served as an invitation to international legal intervention. In addition, having endured heated criticism from the

---

[11]In an attempt to downplay the issue, the Taiwanese government stated that it would not protect individuals going to the islands unless they applied for government permission in advance. To a large extent, Taipei was in no position to continue massive anti-Japan campaigns any longer because its diplomatic isolation deepened at the turn of the 1990s (Bong 2002: 33).

West when it had decided not to join the U.S.-led embargo against Beijing for the June 1989 massacre, Japan did not want to risk worsening its relations with China (Bong 2002: 34–5). Japan also wanted to reassure China that the GCB debate did not indicate a resurgence of Japanese militarism (Cheung and Smith 1990: 19).

In China, alarmed by the growing domestic discontent and criticism, the CCP began to tighten domestic control to prevent public anger towards the lighthouse incident from translating into regime disapproval. The Central Committee and the State Council issued a memorandum for local governments that explained why friendly relations with Japan should be given priority over the controversy about the "strategically and economically valueless islands" (Downs and Saunders 1998/1999: 131–2). For Chinese elites, however, weighing the risks and benefits of de-escalating the controversy about the disputed islands was a complex task. Because of their extremely strained power positions both domestically and internationally, pro-reform elites had to deal with the dual burden of balancing nationalist and pragmatic foreign policy goals. A clash of nationalism with Japan would have impeded China's diplomatic effort to break from the shadow of the Tiananmen incident. At the same time, greatly alarmed by the growing domestic discontent and criticism, Chinese leaders began tightening domestic control to prevent public anger towards the lighthouse incident from translating into regime disapproval (Downs and Saunders 1998/1999: 131–2; Bong 2002: 35–44).

As it turned out, the intricate dependence of China's economy upon Japan made Beijing take a more tempered approach to the Japanese claim to the disputed islands. As of 1990, Chinese economy hit rock bottom after it opened up its economy in 1978. Its real GNP grew at a rate of 1.8% during the first half of 1990, state enterprises posted losses of $3.2 billion (twice the 1989 total), and rural unemployment soared (Shambaugh 1991: 44). Inflows of foreign investments slowed to a trickle as the World Bank and the Asian Development Bank froze billions of dollars of loans in an effort to sanction Beijing's brutal massacre of prodemocracy advocates in 1989 (Downs and Saunders 1998/1999: 127–8).

Japan warmly received China's genuine effort to shelve territorial claims for economic development. In November 1990, Japan – China's only dependable source of capital at that time – formally signed a loan agreement which was first proposed at the July 1990 Group of Seven (G7) Summit. As a matter of fact, China has been the largest recipient of Japanese ODA since 1979 and Japan's ODA to China in 1990 alone amounted to $723 million in loans and grants (Downs and Saunders 1998/1999: 115–7; Chung 2004: 43). Indeed, the first half of the 1990s was an economic honeymoon between China and Japan. China's trade with Japan sharply increased with total values rising from $1.9 billion in 1990 to $5.7 billion in 1995 (See Table 5.1).

The island dispute seemingly subsided by the spring of 1991. Yet it was not until 1992 that the overall status of the Sino–Japanese relationship was restored to the predispute level (Shaw 1999: 17).[12] In April 1992, Chinese President Jiang Zemin visited Japan to assure the Japanese government of Beijing's commitment to more market-oriented economic development and to assuage the growing concern over the new signs of rising nationalism in China. He also advocated the so-called 1978 formula for the Senkaku issue as "a realistic approach that dodged the contradictions while preventing from hurting each other's feeling." Presumably in return for Jiang's efforts, Tokyo finally accepted his request of ¥700 billion in the form of financial assistance for its oil and coal development projects. Two months after Jiang's visit, Prime Minister Kiichi Miyazawa ushered in the signing of a memorandum between the Ex-Im Bank of Japan and the Bank of China regarding financial aid to projects, the core components of the eighth five-year plan which had begun in 1991. This financial package was to be separate from the ¥810 billion in the third package of loans that Japan agreed to grant to China from fiscal years 1990 to 1995. Given the fact that Financial Minster Hata had declined the same request to separate the two packages a year earlier, this decision signified that Japan had become more confident about the prospect of Chinese economic liberalization (Bong 2002: 45–50).[13]

5.5   The Fourth Round of Dispute (1996–97)

The long-running island dispute reared its ugly head again above the East China Sea in the summer of 1996. Coupled with the introduction of UNCLOS, the initial impetus for the 1996–97 flare-up was provided by another lighthouse built on one

---

[12]Between 1991 and 1992, unfriendly encounters between China and Japan continued near the Senkaku Islands, but both governments exercised a great deal of caution in dealing with such encounters. On December 6, 1991, for example, when Chinese vessels fired warning shots at a Japanese ship near the islands, the Chinese government immediately contacted the Japanese Foreign Ministry to deliver its regrets over the mistaken fire shots. It was the first official acknowledgment by Chinese authority of Japanese claims over at least 16 incidents alleged to have occurred since March of the same year in which Japanese vessels came under fire or were inspected by Chinese patrol boats (*Kyodo News*, July 21, 1992). In the meantime, the passage of China's new Territorial Waters Law in February 1992 posed an immediate challenge to the *status quo* of the island issue. Expanding the realm of China's sovereign waters, the Law categorically stipulated as indigenous Chinese territory those islands over which China had been consistently engaged in disputes with its neighbors. The Law also permitted the Chinese armed forces to engage in "hot pursuit" of foreign vessels intruding into its broadly defined "territorial waters." At the same time, however, political leaders in both China and Japan quickly marshaled efforts to maintain the fragile balance in the East China Sea (*Xinhua News*, February 25, 1992). For more details about the internal debate between the People's Liberation Army (PLA) and the Chinese Foreign Ministry regarding the adoption of the Territorial Waters Law, see Greenfield (1992).

[13]In a symbolic gesture to emphasize the pragmatic management of the island issue, the Japanese government granted approval of a joint-development plan with China near the islands in November 1992. Chinese patrol boats occasionally fired on Japanese fishing boats near Senkakus, but both governments remained low-key in their response (Bong 2002: 49–50).

of the Senkaku Islands by an ultranationalist Japanese group. The situation became much more complicated by fluid geopolitical and geoeconomic conditions in the mid-1990s. On the security front, China's assertive nuclear tests and intimidation of Taiwan heightened regional security tensions, thus motivating the U.S. and Japan to reinforce their bilateral security alliance in spite of China's protest. On the economic front, Japan's trade deficits with China widened by more than 300% between 1991 and 1996, thereby fueling relative gains concerns held by Japanese ultranationalists vis-à-vis the economic interdependence of Japan and China. With the confluence of unstable bargaining situations, the 1996 flare-up turned out to be far more serious in terms of its political salience and its level of hostility than were its predecessors. Yet both governments eventually sought to minimize the damage done to Sino–Japanese relations and to defuse the 1996 incident in favor of pursuing greater strategic and economic interests at stake.

5.5.1   Initiation and Escalation Phase

The mutual restraint that had shelved the first lighthouse incident did not last long as the island dispute reared its head again in the summer of 1996. On July 14, 1996, seven members of *Nihon Seinensha* erected a new lighthouse on Kita-kojima Island in the Senkaku group, and subsequently requested that the JMSA designate it an official navigational post (Mutsuko 1996). Having confirmed the landing of Japanese activists on the islands, China demanded that the Japanese government make clear its official stance on the ownership of the islands. The Japanese government immediately denied its involvement in the incident, but added fuel to China's suspicion by declaring its EEZ, which included the disputed islands as a part of Japanese territory (Chung 2004: 43–4). Japanese Prime Minister Ryutaro Hashimoto's visit to the Yasukuni shrine on July 29, 1996 further heightened tensions (*The Straits Times*, July 19, 1996; *Kyodo News*, July 29, 1996).[14]

On August 28, Japanese Foreign Minister Yukihiko Ikeda dropped a diplomatic bombshell during his visit to Hong Kong by asserting "Senkakus have always been Japanese territory; Japan already effectively governs the islands, so the territorial issue does not exist" (Quoted in Downs and Saunders 1998/1999: 133).[15] Ikeda's ill-timed

---

[14] Arguing that the building of the lighthouse violated Taiwan's rights over the islands, the Ministry of Foreign Affairs of Taiwan reiterated that Taipei would "continue to consult with Japan over the disputed islands" (*BBC Summary of World Broadcasts*, Asia-Pacific, July 18, 1996). In attempts to present itself as a "true" protector of China's territorial rights, Taipei invited Beijing to join its efforts to safeguard the islands. As long as China and Taiwan eyed each other with suspicion, however, it was impossible for them to coordinate a joint sovereignty other than by separately reaffirming Chinese sovereignty over the islands (Bong 2002: 71-2; Chung 2004: 52).

[15] Early that year, Ikeda had already created a diplomatic battlefield between South Korea and Japan over the Dokdo issue by stating that Takeshima is a part of Japanese territory from the view point of international law and history. See Chapter 4 of this book for more details.

statement galvanized Chinese nationalism everywhere: *Protect the Diaoyu Movement* in Hong Kong, Taiwan, and North American Chinese community, and the anti-Japanese activities in China once again went into full swing (Chung 2004: 46).[16] In particular, a rumor that the CCP leaders had decided not to provoke the Japanese government for fear that it might scrap its promise to rescind upcoming loans (which accounted for nearly 70% of total foreign economic aid to China) had been widely and persuasively held among the citizens, students, and the military in China (Bong 2002: 69).

Ikeda's provocative and preemptive statement, and growing discontent among the Chinese both on the mainland and abroad, forced Beijing to issue a stern warning to Japan. The Chinese Foreign Ministry condemned Ikeda's remarks as irresponsible, and stressed that the actions of ultranationalist Japanese groups were related to the Japanese government's attitude (*Kyodo News*, August 29, 1996). In addition, the Chinese Foreign Ministry denied the possibility that Japanese loans would alter China's sovereignty claims, while stating that Japanese yen loans were helpful for promoting Sino–Japanese economic cooperation and trade, but as far as the issue of sovereignty was concerned, the Chinese government could not make any compromise. The Chinese government also turned a blind eye to Chinese news media awash with anti-Japanese propaganda, presumably in order to counter criticism about its softness towards the sovereignty question because of its valuable trading ties with Japan (Chung 2004: 48).[17]

In September 1996, a series of abrasive behaviors in the East China Sea escalated the initial squabble to a serious diplomatic crisis. On September 4, the JMSA forcefully detained a Taiwanese fishing boat near the disputed islands. The Taiwanese Foreign Ministry protested at Japan's use of force. Two days later, the JMSA drove out Hong Kong TV crews near the islands. On September 9, members of *Nihon Seinensha* returned to the islands to repair the new lighthouse, which had been damaged by a typhoon. The next day they reapplied for official recognition of the lighthouse. On September 13–14, the PLAN practiced blockades and landings

---

[16] From August 28 to September 18, 1996, there were daily protests and demonstrations in Hong Kong. The biggest anti-Japanese protest march drew 20,000 people, and provided great opportunity for Hong Kongers of all political stripes to demonstrate their allegiance to the motherland in anticipation of Hong Kong's return to China in less than a year's time. These events were led by the same prodemocracy activists who had been campaigning against Chinese plans to replace the partially elected colonial legislature with a provisional one. These activists were apparently hoping not only to tap into a genuinely popular cause for political support, but also to prepare the ground for future demands that would be difficult for China to resist (Chung 2004: 46).

[17] In a commentary, the official *People's Daily* accused the Japanese government of "leading Sino-Japanese relations astray" by "conniving" with the right-wingers, and wondered whether their activities "have the government's tacit support and whether there are ulterior motives for stirring up these incident" (*People's Daily*, September 21, 1996). The *Liberation Army Daily* bellowed "it would rather sustain a heavy economic cost than lose an inch of soil" (*Time International Magazine*, October 7, 1996).

on islands off of Liaoning Province – acts that were allegedly intended to warn Tokyo against further incursions on the Senkaku Islands (Downs and Saunders 1998/1999: 135).[18] On September 26, anti-Japanese sentiment surged following the death of David Chan, a pro-China activist from Hong Kong who drowned after jumping in the water when the JMSA prevented his boat from landing on one of the Senkaku Islands. Chan's death inspired large-scale anti-Japanese protests and boycotts in Hong Kong, Taiwanand North America, and prompted a second and more successful attempt by Hong Kong and Taiwanese activists to plant their national flags on the islands in October (*Hong Kong Standard*, October 1, 1996; *South China Morning Post*, October 10, 1996).[19]

Aside from the long-running symbolic contests over the sovereignty issue, the material value of the disputed maritime area became particularly salient in 1996, as both countries engaged in the final process of ratifying the UNCLOS. The UNCLOS considerably expanded national maritime boundaries through the adoption of a wider definition of territorial waters, contiguous zones, continental shelves, and EEZs. Negotiating with each other over how to delimit the overlapping claims of their respective EEZs in the East China Sea quickly became the bone of contention, placing the Senkaku issue once again under the spotlight. In early 1996, both Beijing and Tokyo already began reinforcing their claims over this area, while indicating that they would not mind announcing their respective EEZs unilaterally. It was not a coincidence that an increasing number of controversial seabed resource surveys conducted by Chinese vessels met Japanese protests during this period (Bong 2002: 60–1).

Japan began to openly defend its sovereignty claim to the islands, while continuing to express a desire to separate the territorial issue from bilateral negotiations over fishery accord and EEZ delimitation. The Hashimoto cabinet became more inclined to appeal to its domestic constituents by using nationalist rhetoric than to maintain a friendly relationship with China by consciously sidestepping delicate bilateral issues. Gradually, Japanese state elites' increasing emphasis on protecting national pride and independent foreign policymaking

---

[18]The PLA conducted two large-scale military exercises, one naval exercise in the East China Sea and one air force exercise in the Gobi Desert. These military exercises, the goal of which was allegedly to "safeguard China's independence, sovereignty, and territorial integrity," were believed to be not only targeted at Japan but also at influencing CCP leaders and the Foreign Ministry to toughen their stances (Downs and Saunders 1998/1999: 138–42).

[19]On October 8, 1996, about 40 ships carrying approximately 300 protesters and media crews succeeded in entering the waters near the Senkaku Islands, with surprising ease. Seven Chinese activists from Hong Kong remained on Uotsuri Island for approximately 15 minutes, during which time they hoisted Chinese and Taiwanese national flags. Despite this disruption, reactions from the Japanese government remained noticeably restrained and Prime Minister Hashimoto pleaded for calm (Bong 2002: 84).

undermined the previous consensus on "good-neighbor" diplomacy with China (Bong 2002: 60–5).[20]

The unstable geopolitics also contributed to the escalation of the 1996 flare-up. China's assertive nuclear tests in the first half of the 1990s seriously strained Sino–Japanese diplomatic relations. After the test in October 1993, Tokyo became concerned with China's nuclear tests despite its anti-nuclear rhetoric in the past. Following another test conducted in June 1994, Tokyo immediately warned Beijing that the continuation of its nuclear weapons program would prompt Japan to use its economic aid program as an instrument of advancing Japan's strategic interests. Once Tokyo revealed its intention to tie economic aid to the suspension of China's nuclear testing, the whole issue of nuclear tests became a contest of power and will between the two regional rivals. Beijing conducted three additional rounds of nuclear tests from October 1994 to August 1995, showing that it had no intention to sacrifice sovereign rights in exchange for economic aid (Bong 2002: 54–5; Takamine 2005: 445–6).

The 1995–96 Taiwan Strait crisis further aggravated Beijing's relations with Tokyo as well as Taipei and Washington. The crisis reached the highest point in early 1996, shortly before the presidential election in Taiwan, as China continued its military bluffing to intimidate proindependence Taiwanese voters and the U.S. sent two aircraft carriers to the vicinity of the Taiwan Strait. China clearly influenced Taiwan's assessment of the costs of independence and succeeded in reassuring the "One China policy" to the U.S.[21] Yet, China's threat to use force greatly alarmed

---

[20]Because the EEZ delimitation was closely intertwined with the renewal of their bilateral fishery accord, neither China nor Japan was able to afford flexibility on the Senkaku issue. Preparing to ratify the UNCLOS, the Japanese government submitted in 1995 the preliminary version of its domestic laws, which deliberately exempted the area west of 135° eastern longitude from the 200 nm zone where the Senkaku Islands are located (*Kyodo News*, December 16, 1995). The preliminary proposal angered the Japanese fishery industry, which had been putting immense pressure on the Hashimoto cabinet to aggressively advocate its interests in negotiating for the EEZ in the East China Sea and led to a public rally in Tokyo in which approximately 6,000 Japanese fishermen participated – the largest demonstration in Tokyo in 20 years (*The Nikkei Weekly*, March 4, 1996). With the October 1996 Lower House election looming large, Japanese politicians quickly exhibited sympathetic gestures, criticizing the Foreign Ministry for the alleged exceptions in the delineation and ruled out the possibility that Japan would exclude the waters around the disputed Senkaku Islands in establishing the new EEZ (Bong 2002: 62–3). The election saw Hashimoto retain the premiership, more seats for the LDP, and the Japan Socialist Party being replaced as the main opposition party by the New Frontier Party (*Shinseito*), a new political party formed in 1993 whose main differences with the LDP were over domestic issues rather than foreign policy. Together, both conservative parties controlled 80% of the seats in the Japanese Diet after the 1996 general election, with the LDP and *Shinseito* winning 251 and 156 of the 500 seats, respectively, (Chung 2004: 44).

[21]From late January through February, 1996, the PLA mobilized more than 100,000 troops in Fujian province, a coastal area facing Taiwan. In the third round of exercises in March, the PLA conducted surface-to-surface missile tests, and air and naval exercises with live ammunition in waters near Taiwan. Taiwan held its own military maneuvers, strengthening its resistance to the mainland's "anti-Taiwan struggle" (Ross 2000: 107). Accusing China of being "reckless" and "provocative," Washington sent the Independence battle group from Okinawa to the waters east of Taiwan; the Nimitz carrier group was ordered from the Persian Gulf to the Philippine Sea (Bong 2002: 58–9).

Japan and the U.S., thus motivating them to further strengthen their mutual security ties in the form of a renewed defense guidelines of 1997 (Ross 2000: 87–123). As China gradually escaped from the shadow of the 1989 Tiananmen incident, prore- form political leaders also began to see the merits of projecting a nationalistic image in order to consolidate their weakening position in the face of the allegedly intensifying U.S.–Japan conspiracy (Sutter and Mitchener 1996: 1–14; Goldstein 1997/1998: 38).

In addition to the unstable geopolitics in the region, the shifting patterns of economic interdependence between China and Japan exacerbated the sovereignty problem. In the first half of the 1990s, bilateral trade between China and Japan boomed, rising from $20.3 billion to $57.5 billion. Furthermore, the Sino–Japanese trade balance turned favorably towards China. According to Chinese statistics, its trade deficits began to fall from $7.5 billion in 1993 to $541 million in 1995, and in fact turned to a surplus of $1.7 billion in 1996.[22] By contrast, Japan was feeling the pressure of a reversed trade balance. Yet the degrees of pressure seemed to have been much greater than what the Chinese figures would have suggested. According to Japanese statistics, its trade deficits against China widened from $5.6 billion in 1991 to $18.6 billion in 1996, as compared to $220 million and $1.7 billion for the same period according to Chinese statistics.[23] It is highly likely that growing rela- tive gains concerns held by Japanese ultranationalists vis-à-vis the economic inter- dependence of China and Japan fueled the 1996 flare-up.

---

[22] Nevertheless, Chinese mistrust of Japan in the economic realm persisted in the public's mind. In the *China Youth Daily* poll of 1996, for example, 96.3% of respondents believed that the aim of Japanese investment in China was to occupy the market and seek profit, 50.7% thought it was to control China economically, and 45.3% thought it was to dump outmoded facilities, with only 9.5% believing it was to help Chinese economic development (Quoted in He 2007: 11).

[23] Such a contradiction indicates that the official trade statistics of Japan and China have huge discrepancies. Of all the economic issues between Japan and China, none has the potential for greater confusion than the bilateral trade deficit. It is often assumed that corresponding export and import data between partner countries should be consistent. That is, the exports from Country A to B should be equal to the imports of Country B from A, after taking into account the insurance and freight costs under the generally observed case that Country B imports are valued on a c.i.f. (Cost, Insurance, and Freight) basis. Notwithstanding the inclusion of insurance and freight in imports c.i.f., there often exist several complications that can cause inconsistency between exports to a partner and the partner's recorded imports f.o.b (Freight on Board), or between imports f.o.b. from a partner and the partner's recorded exports. The principal reasons for the inconsistent statistics on destination and origin of a given shipment are differences in classification concepts and detail, time of recording, valuation, and coverage, as well as processing errors (IMF, *Direction of Trade Statistics Yearbook*, 2004: xi–xii). Yet the discrepancies of Sino–Japanese trade statistics appear much greater than the standard error terms might warrant. In fact, much of the difference is due to, among other things, the different treatment of Hong Kong's entrepôt trade by the two sides. Since 1993, the Chinese customs authorities have attempted to determine the final destination for goods exported to Hong Kong with greater accuracy, so as to improve its reported trade statistics. It is still the case, however, that many of the goods bound for either Japan or China via Hong Kong are not recorded as such. For a similar concern about the discrepancies in U.S.–China trade statistics, see Feenstra et al. (1998).

5.5.2 De-escalation Phase

Despite combative rhetoric, both governments became increasingly concerned that the level of their mutual hostility had reached one of its highest points since their diplomatic rapprochement in 1972. The death of David Chan prompted both Beijing and Tokyo to quickly bring the 1996 flare-up under control. The successive disruptions by Chinese activists near and on the islands in October saw remarkably restrained reactions from Tokyo. The burgeoning *Protect the Diaoyu Movement* also alarmed China's ruling elites. Although the government crackdown on this movement prompted accusations that the Chinese leadership was illegitimate and unpatriotic, Beijing wasted no time in minimizing the effects of the death of David Chan (Downs and Saunders 1998/1999: 137–8; Bong 2002: 83–4; Chung 2004: 49–50).

Both governments carefully prevented political activities from igniting antagonism on the other side. Japanese Prime Minister Hashimoto's visit to Beijing in September 1997 and Chinese Premier Li Peng's reciprocal friendly gesture in November manifested their mutual efforts to restore good Sino–Japanese ties.[24] The immediate payoff was a new bilateral fishery agreement signed on November 11, 1997. The new fishery agreement chose to shelve the thorny sovereignty issue, while the areas near the disputed islands became subject to tight and carefully coordinated management by both governments (Bong 2002: 90–1; Kim 2004: 273–6; Zou 2005: 99–100).[25]

Such a dramatic turn of events can be attributed to the combination of two components of a territorial bargaining game: one strategic and the other economic. In contrast to its more assertive actions in the South China Sea, military action has never been a feasible option for China to resolve the Senkaku dispute because of the balance of power politics in the East China Sea. Military actions to consolidate its physical possession of the islands would have triggered a direct response from

---

[24]During Hashimoto's visit, the Fiscal Year 1997 portion of a ¥580 billion loan package for 1996–98, to which Tokyo and Beijing initially agreed upon in December 1994, was finalized. The Ex-Im Bank of Japan, which had already provided ¥243 billion in "semi-commercial" financing to support trade and investment in China during 1996, endorsed another agreement with Chinese authorities in 1997 on a $220 million package of united loans for social infrastructure (Bong 2002: 90–1).

[25]Under the new pact, the two countries agreed on establishing a jointly controlled provisional zone in the East China Sea, between 30° 40' and 27° north latitude excluding areas up to 52 nm from both countries' shores, while continuing talks to establish their respective 200 nm EEZs. The two sides also agreed to mutually set fishing quotas in their future EEZs and apply the "coastal country" principle to control illegal fishing (Bong 2002: 90). Yet it was not until February 2000 that the two countries reached an agreement on fishing quotas and fishing conditions in each other's EEZ, and on the fishing order in the waters to the north of the provisional zone. Japan and Taiwan also reached an accord that would ensure the fishing activities of Taiwanese boats in a triangular zone between Taiwan, the Senkaku Islands, and Yoan, which had been traditionally recognized as a common fishing zone between the two since Japan's Sowa period (*BBC Summary of World Broadcasts*, Asia-Pacific, July 11, 1997).

Japan, thereby disrupting profitable economic ties with Japan and, most undesirably, inviting U.S. intervention of some kind (Goldstein 1997/1998: 52–4).[26] The pressure from the U.S. also mitigated Japan's responses. The U.S. State Department reiterated its official position as adopted on the eve of the reversion of Okinawa in 1972 that it would not side either with Japan or the two Chinas in their claims to the Senkaku Islands (*Central News Agency*, October 17, 1996). U.S. Ambassador to Japan Walter Mondale subsequently stated that the Senkaku Islands were not covered by the U.S.–Japan security alliance (*Sankei News*, November 5, 1996). By stressing its supposedly neutral stance with regard to the sovereignty question, the U.S. seemed to signal to the post-election LDP leaders that it was not the time to adopt an abrasive foreign policy (Chung 2004: 51–2).

A closer examination of the de-escalation process of the 1996 flare-up also reveals that economic considerations strongly motivated the adoption of a conciliatory policy despite strong nationalist pressures. Contending nationalisms were held at bay, while economics dictated prudence in the handling of the sovereignty dispute, particularly for China. As clearly expressed in President Jiang's speech at the Fifteenth Congress of the CCP in September 1997, the CCP leaders wished to avoid any further damage to Sino–Japanese economic ties during a time when economic reform in China was moving to another stage – namely the "building of a complete market system in the national economy." Challenging Japanese sovereign claims would have negatively affected China's efforts to secure Japan's support for its deepening economic modernization (Bong 2002: 77).

During this period, their bilateral trade continued to grow from $57.5 billion in 1995 to $60.8 billion in 1997, although the rate of increase slowed down, as compared to the early 1990s (See Table 5.1). In terms of financial flows, Japan's presence in China was also becoming significant. As of the mid-1990s, its cumulative investment in China amounted to $13 billion as compared to $6 billion in Taiwan and $14 billion in Hong Kong. Also, Japan became the largest development aid provider to China by contributing an estimated $19 billion between 1979 and 1995, and the third largest investor in China, behind the U.S. and Hong Kong. Total Japanese loans to and investment in China were valued at $3.2 billion in 1995 (Chung 2004: 52).

The 1996 dispute illustrated an interesting pattern similar to previous flare-ups. The initial impetuses came from Japanese ultranationalist activities. At first, both Beijing and Tokyo used them, either implicitly or explicitly, to mobilize political support for their regime. Eventually, however, they sought to minimize the damage done to Sino–Japanese relations, fearing that contending Sino–Japanese nationalisms could snowball into a larger destabilizing movement detrimental to their domestic and international reputations, and ultimately undermine bilateral economic ties (Deans 2000: 122–3). Despite strong demands for a tougher policy against the other claimants, political leaders in both Beijing and Tokyo again proved willing to undermine their nationalist credentials in pursuit of economic cooperation and strategic stability.

---

[26] For more details about China's military actions in the South China Sea, see Chapter 6 of this book.

5.6   The Fifth Round of Dispute (2004–05)

For a long period after the diplomatic normalization of 1972, the economic ties with Japan carried much more weight for China than did ties with China for Japan. Yet recently, their bilateral economic relationships are becoming equally important to each other. This latest development has both positive and negative implications for their bilateral relationships. On the one hand, rising interdependence provides greater economic incentives for both countries to avoid costly conflict. On the other hand, increasingly equal mutual dependence means that China's bargaining power vis-à-vis Japan has improved significantly such that China is now less constrained to challenge Japan than in the previous decades. Against the emerging balance of power and new interests, the 2004–05 flare-up serves as a window to the Sino–Japanese rivalry in the new millennium. In the context of Chinese economic success and military buildup and the resurgence of Japanese international assertiveness, territorial and resource competition in the East China Sea has become more than a serious bilateral irritant.

5.6.1   Initiation and Escalation Phase

In contrast to the previous clashes, where Japanese ultranationalist groups or Hong Kong-based Chinese activists served as principal initiators, the 2004–05 flare-up was catalyzed by a group of Chinese activists who landed on Uotsuri Island on March 24, 2004.[27] The Japan Coast Guard arrested them for violating the Japanese law, and deported them to Shanghai after two days of detention. Tokyo lodged a strong protest with Beijing only to find an even stronger accusation of arresting Chinese citizens (*Japan Times*, March 27, 2004). In response to the landing, *Nihon Seinensha* announced that it would visit the islands, which in turn further inflamed Chinese public opinion. The timing of the landing incident was particularly unpropitious for Sino–Japanese ties as it coincided with a high-profile murder trial that horrified Japan and gave rise to anti-Chinese sentiment.[28]

---

[27] Mainland activists first boarded Hong Kong protest boats to go the islands in 1998, and attempted their expeditions from 2000. The Chinese activists' landing on Uotsuri Island marked their fourth attempt in the previous nine months. Prior attempts had all failed, although they almost succeeded in mid-January 2004 when two boats carrying Chinese activists were deterred at the last moment by a water cannon shot by the Japan Coast Guard (*BBC News*, World Edition, January 16, 2004).

[28] Prior to the landing incident, the diplomatic temperature between Japan and China already dropped to near freezing levels, thanks to the 2002 Shenyang incident to which Japan reacted emotionally, accusing Chinese police of infringing on Japanese sovereignty by dragging out North Korean asylum seekers from the Japanese Consulate-General in Shenyang without permission (Wan 2003). On top of this, on the day before the 2004 island incident, a 24-year-old former Chinese student pleaded guilty to brutally murdering a family of four in June 2003 for about $350, subsequently dumping their bodies in the local bay. The callous nature of the murders shocked ordinary Japanese, creating intense anti-Chinese sentiments (*Asia Times Online*, March 26, 2004).

This incident indicates that the recent opening up of Chinese society has created more public space for bottom-up emotional venting and policy advocacy. Following the March landing incident, Chinese protesters ripped up and burned the Japanese national flags in front of the Japanese Embassy in Beijing. The group also criticized Japanese Prime Minister Junichiro Koizumi's recurring visits to the Yasukuni shrine and the dispatch of Japan's SDF to Iraq, while echoing the widely held view in China that Japan has not adequately apologized for its World War II occupation and wartime atrocities (*BBC Monitoring Asia Pacific*, March 25, 2004).

Under mounting public pressure, the Chinese government could no longer shelve or set aside the island dispute as it had done in the past, but had to assert Chinese sovereignty explicitly and exclude any options of compromise. The advent of the Internet and information technology has not only made the CCP leadership less capable of censuring the dissemination of news that might provoke anti-Japanese feelings, but also made it easier for otherwise small, poorly financed activist groups to mobilize support for their nationalist agenda (He 2007: 13–7).

Most notably, the *Protect the Diaoyu Movement* landed in mainland China with full force by the end of the 1990s, which suggests that Beijing is losing its firm grip on society vis-à-vis the Senkaku dispute. For the CCP leaders, popular nationalism is a double-edged sword. On the one hand, visceral nationalist sentiment may facilitate social mobilization and solidify popular allegiance to the CCP leadership that claims to best represent Chinese national interest. On the other hand, anti-foreign nationalism can quickly transform into an anti-government movement if the government is considered to be conciliatory in foreign policy. It can also undermine Beijing's diplomatic effort at securing a stable inflow of foreign investment and technology as well as cultivating China's image as a peaceful and responsible player in the international community (Chung 2004: 55–7).

In a chain reaction, ultranationalist activities have emboldened the Japanese sense of indignation against China. Japanese ultranationalists hold a radically chauvinistic view of history that refuses to admit the aggressive nature of the Pacific War and completely deny Japan's war responsibility. After the 1982 textbook controversy, they attacked the government for capitulating to foreign pressure to include accounts of Japanese war atrocities in history textbook, which, they believed, would hurt national pride. Although those ultranationalists are only a small fraction of Japanese population, the political disturbance they spark has been too boisterous for the Chinese nationalists to ignore (Yang 2003: 61–87; He 2007: 17–8; Suzuki 2007).[29]

---

[29] In Japan, the growing emotional tensions with China were crystallized in a survey conducted by Japan's Cabinet Office in October 2004. According to the survey, the percentage of respondents who said they felt friendly towards China fell by 10.3% from a year ago to 37.6%, the lowest level since the survey began in 1975. The percentage of respondents who said they did not feel friendliness towards China rose to 58.2% while those who thought that relations between Japan and China were good fell nearly 19 percentage points to 28.1% (*Kyodo News*, December 20, 2004). In a similar vein, a Chinese Academy of Social Sciences survey shows that only 5.9% of Chinese felt friendly towards the Japanese, compared to 43.3% who did not feel so (*The Straits Times*, August 14, 2004).

Such a stormy clash of rival nationalisms amplified intense resource competition from the spring through the summer of 2004. Controversy flared up on May 7, 2004 when a Chinese maritime research ship was detected operating in what Japan considers its own EEZ in the East China Sea. Japan's request to end the survey activities notwithstanding, China began the construction of a natural gas drilling facility in the disputed area. In response, Japan launched a survey of the disputed area and started exploring for natural gas (Pryzstup 2004). In July, the Chinese held a series of emotionally charged demonstrations outside the Japanese Embassy in Beijing to protest Japan's "illegal" oil exploration activities (*Kyodo News*, July 9, 2004).

China's discomfort with Japan's territorial and maritime claims in the East China Sea was also expressed during the Asian Cup soccer tournament held in Beijing in August 2004. Holding banners claiming that the Senkaku Islands are Chinese territory, Chinese fans booed throughout the Japanese national anthem and whenever Japanese players controlled the ball. After China lost the final match, they started a riot that could have hurt the Japanese team had riot police not outnumbered them. Despite their second straight Asian Cup, the Japanese were infuriated by Beijing's harassment of the Japanese soccer team (*The Associated Press*, August 7, 2004). For many commentators, therefore, the summer of 2004 marked one of the lowest points of Sino–Japanese relations in the post-normalization era.[30]

The 2004 flare-up demonstrates that major changes in East Asian energy patterns are creating additional dangers to the troubled Sino–Japanese relations chronically oriented towards the past. China is currently the second largest energy consumer after the U.S. Rising oil demand and imports have made China a significant factor in world oil markets. China also surpassed Japan as the world's second largest petroleum consumer in 2003. Japan is the world's fourth largest energy consumer and was the second largest energy importer after the U.S. (Kenny 2004). As Calder (1996) notes, East Asia's emerging energy problems cut subtly across the conventional boundary between economics and security, fueling the political and economic uncertainties in the region.

On the security front, the Sino–Japanese relationship continues to show a classic example of the security dilemma, reinforced by enduring rivalry and resource nationalism. They see each other as a threat to their search for political and energy security. On the one hand, the growing perception of the "China threat" has resulted in Tokyo's toughening China policy, which in turn has consolidated China's anti-Japanese prejudice.[31]

---

[30]Interview with Japan's Ministry of Foreign Affairs (MOFA) officials conducted in Tokyo in June 2004.

[31]Japan's chronic economic stagnation during the "lost decade" has promoted anti-foreign, particularly anti-Chinese, sentiments in Japan. Anxious to jettison postwar constraints on its remilitarization and international activism, Japanese nationalism has seriously collided with Chinese popular nationalism that tends to view Japan's current behaviors through the lens of bitter memories of its past aggression. For Japan, revising the guidelines for U.S.–Japan military cooperation, embracing joint research and development on missile defense, strengthening Japan–South Korea military coordination, planning for a more autonomous satellite reconnaissance capability, and initiating an open debate about Japan's military-security needs and international role, all of these efforts were directly linked to the troubling actions of the North Koreans during the 1990s. But these efforts simultaneously prepared Japan for an East Asian future in which its most worrisome military planning contingency may be China (Goldstein 2003: 188).

On the other hand, although Chinese analysts presently fear U.S. power much more than Japanese power, in terms of national intentions, they view Japan with less trust and, in many cases, with a loathing rarely found in their attitudes towards the U.S. (Christensen 1999: 52). Chinese attitudes and suspicions obviously factor into Japan's own anxieties about the rising power and intentions of its large neighbor (Mastanduno 2003: 153–4).

The year 2005 proved even worse. On February 9, in an unexpectedly bold move, the Japan Coast Guard took possession of the lighthouse built on Uotsuri Island because the private owner of the lighthouse had given up the ownership claim.[32] China strongly criticized the action, but Japan played down China's protest (Marquand 2005). The tension in the East China Sea came to a boiling point when a series of sometimes-violent anti-Japanese rallies broke out in the major cities of China in April 2005, damaging the Japanese Embassy in Beijing and consulates in other cities.[33] China acknowledged that diplomatic relations with Japan were at a three-decade low, but blamed the dispute on Tokyo for refusing to face up to its militaristic past. Unmistakably, China's reaction evoked Japanese anger over the former's lack of regret for violent anti-Japanese protests (*The Associated Press*, April 18, 2005).

5.6.2   De-escalation Phase

In the middle of rising public anger against each other, Beijing and Tokyo tried to mend their strained relationship. The CCP leadership began to pressure the demonstrators, expressing its particular concern about the use of mobile phones and the Internet to organize unauthorized demonstrations (*The Economist*, April 28, 2005). On April 17, 2005, Japanese Foreign Minister Nobutaka Machimura flew to Beijing to seek an apology for the anti-Japanese demonstrations and compensation for damage. His Chinese counterpart Li Zhaoxing declined, arguing that China had not wronged the Japanese. Li told Machimura that Tokyo must take "concrete action" to show that it is facing up to history. Despite the harsh rhetoric, however, both sides agreed to launch a joint study panel on their bilateral history (*The Associated Press*, April 18, 2005). At the Asian–African Summit in Jakarta, Indonesia on April 23, Chinese President Hu and Japanese Prime Minister Koizumi made a diplomatic breakthrough by agreeing to make sincere efforts to narrow their bilateral differences including the vexing territorial and historical issues (*People's Daily*,

---

[32] Japanese ownership claims over the island group are multilayered. Privately-held Kuba-jima Island and the Islands of Uotsuri, Kita-kojima, and Minami-kojima have allegedly been rented out to the Japanese government since 1972 and 2002, respectively, while Taisho-jima Island has always been owned by the Japanese government. For more details, see Urano (2005: 206–7).

[33] These Chinese protests were inflamed by the Japanese government's authorization of history textbooks in early April that have reinforced Japan's territorial claim to the islands as well as glossing over its wartime atrocities. The Japanese campaign for a permanent UN Security Council seat was also a target of Chinese public anger.

April 28, 2005). Although tentative, this agreement helped cool down the diplomatic temperature.

Currently, the haggling is over precisely which areas should be developed. In fall 2005, Japan proposed to China the joint development of four natural gas fields, which straddle the median line suggested by Japan and lie between the two areas proposed by China. Beijing does not recognize the median line, because the Japanese side of the median line includes China's continental shelf. After several official rounds of negotiations, however, the two countries tentatively reached an agreement on joint development in mid-June 2008. The expected agreement would likely sidestep the thorny sovereignty issues by simply leaving it unresolved for now. By allowing Japanese companies to invest in Chinese development of the gas fields, the agreement would allow Japan to share the profits from their development (Fackler 2008). This latest development supports the argument of this study: Economic considerations have repeatedly fostered the de-escalation of Sino–Japanese conflict over territorial and maritime rights.

5.6.3 Rising Resource Nationalism and Future Challenges

Is the complex partnership characterized as "cold politics and hot economics" sustainable? The structure of Sino–Japanese economic interdependence deserves special attention, as it is currently undergoing dramatic transformation. For a long period after the diplomatic normalization of 1972, the economic ties with Japan carried much more weight for China than did ties with China for Japan. More recently, however, their bilateral economic relationships are increasingly becoming important for Japan as well in both absolute and relative terms.

The changes in the structure of Sino–Japanese economic interdependence are represented by Japan's increasing reliance on China vis-à-vis its economic growth. Japan's trade dependence on China almost tripled from 1.48 to 4.32% during the period of 1997–2006 (See Table 5.1).[34] There is little doubt that Japan's recent

---

[34] It does not necessarily indicate that the Sino–Japanese commercial ties are becoming symmetric, however. Currently China's trade dependence on Japan, which reached double digits (10.17%) for the first time in 2004, tends to grow slightly faster than Japan's trade dependence on China. It should also be noted that the official trade statistics of Japan and China have huge discrepancies, as mentioned earlier in footnote 23 of this chapter. According to their respective official statistics, both countries have had trade deficits against each other and the gaps are widening. The gap has been widening since the early 1980s, reaching the widest in 2004. In 2004, according to the Japanese official statistics, Japan's trade deficit against China amounted to $20.4 billion, while according to the Chinese official statistics China's trade deficit against Japan reached $20.8 billion. Despite these huge discrepancies in individual import and export figures, each country's sum of exports and imports falls within similar range. The average discrepancy in total trade figures during the period of 1985–2004 is $492 million, which is marginal in comparison to the total trade volumes. Therefore, the trade dependence scores calculated from each country's export and import figures continue to serve their basic conceptual purposes.

economic recovery owes much to its soaring exports to China. In addition to the acceleration in the number of Japanese companies setting up business in the Chinese market, the expansion of Chinese domestic demand, and other factors, has caused Japan's dependence on trade with China to drift upwards. This new development has both positive and negative implications. On the one hand, rising interdependence provides greater economic incentives for both parties to avoid costly conflict. On the other hand, rapidly increasing Japan's dependence on China means that Japan's bargaining power vis-à-vis China has declined significantly.[35] China may thus feel less constrained to challenge Japan than any time before. Indeed, their bilateral relationship could get worse before it gets better.

5.7 Conclusion

In the East China Sea, the territorial *status quo* has been repeatedly challenged, while leaving both Japan and China unsatisfied. Since the potential of abundant oil and gas deposits in the East China Sea was found in the late 1960s, the Senkaku dispute has unfolded in five rounds of distinct clashes. As the *de facto* owner, Japan is unwilling to negotiate the settlement of the territorial issue. To the Chinese, the Senkaku dispute represents an attempt by Japan to keep from the Chinese what it stole from them during half a century of invasion and occupation.

According to the conventional wisdom, the Senkaku problem arose both directly and indirectly as a consequence of U.S. Cold War policy in East Asia. As the architect of the island dispute during the San Francisco Peace Treaty negotiations, the U.S. has officially remained neutral on the sovereignty issue, but its hegemonic position has helped to ensure that the dispute takes place within certain confines. Yet, the growing perception of the "China threat" has resulted in Tokyo's toughening China policy, which in turn has consolidated China's anti-Japanese (and anti-U.S.) prejudice. Further fueled by energy competition, the Senkaku incident has indeed the potential to inflict substantial damage not only on already strained Sino–Japanese relations but also on the fragile balance of power in East Asia.

The combination of fluid geopolitics and competitive domestic politics fueled by contending territorial and resource nationalisms has repeatedly hijacked Sino–Japanese bilateral relations. Ultranationalist groups on both sides have exerted considerable pressures for more assertive territorial and maritime policies.

---

[35] According to Japanese statistics, FDI from Japan increased between 2000 and 2003 by an average of 41%, but China has absorbed FDI from elsewhere faster than that. As a result, Japanese capital does not secure its share in the total FDI inflows to China. Only 7.9% of foreign capital actually used by China was from Japan in 2002, compared to 14.4% in 1990. Also, Japan slashed its government aid to China. Yen loans, a pillar of this package, amounted to ¥214.4 billion in 2000. But the sharp reduction squeezed the figure to ¥96.7 billion, only 45.1% of that in 2000, in 2001 (*People's Daily*, July 15, 2004). All this may point to the erosion of Japan's economic influence on China.

The Senkaku dispute might not trigger any major conflicts immediately. Yet, the accumulation of grievances could escalate minor quarrels, such as those involving energy developments near the islands, into major conflicts.

Nevertheless, conventional explanations alone cannot fully capture the dualistic nature of the Senkaku dispute: Notwithstanding the destabilizing influence of resource competition, fluid geopolitics, and contending nationalisms, the two countries have successfully managed to contain their respective territorial and maritime claims thus far. This chapter has argued that the two countries have been deterred from pushing for a more definitive political showdown with respect to the island dispute in the interest of maintaining the lucrative trade and investment relations that both countries have enjoyed since 1972. In spite of the fact that the island dispute remains unresolved, both parties have found it a convenient strategy to shelve final resolution attempts rather than to risk the rupture of vastly consequential, common strategic and economic interests.

In conclusion, the relationship between the Senkaku dispute and Sino–Japanese economic interdependence could be explosive, particularly if Chinese economic success allows Beijing to be more aggressive towards Japan either economically or strategically. Yet, as long as profitable economic opportunities continue for both sides, it is likely that a system of control and restraint will become a stable feature of the Senkaku dispute.

References

Austin G (1998) China's ocean frontier: International law, military force and national development. Allen and Unwin, Canberra

Bong YD (2002) Flashpoints at sea? Legitimization strategy and East Asian island disputes. PhD Dissertation in Political Science, University of Pennsylvania, Philadelphia

Buzan B (1978) A sea of trouble? Sources of dispute in the new ocean regime. Adelphi Paper 143, International Institute for Strategic Studies, London

Calder KE (1996) Pacific defense: Arms, energy, and America's future in Asia. William Morrow, New York

Cha VD (1996) Bridging the gap: The strategic context of the 1965 Korea–Japan normalization treaty. Korean Studies 20:123–160

Cheng T (1974) The Sino–Japanese dispute over the Tiao-yu-tai (Senkaku) islands and the law of territorial acquisition. Virginia Journal of International Law 14(2):221–266

Cheung TM, Smith C (1990) Rocks of contention. Far Eastern Economic Review, November 1

Christensen TJ (1999) China, the U.S.–Japan alliance, and the security dilemma in East Asia. International Security 23(4):49–80

Christensen TJ (2006) Fostering stability or creating a monster? The rise of China and U.S. policy toward East Asia. International Security 31(1):81–126

Chung C (2004) Domestic politics, international bargaining and China's territorial disputes. Routledge, New York

Deans P (1996) The Diaoyutai/Senkaku dispute: The unwanted controversy. Kent Papers in Politics and International Relations 6

Deans P (2000) Contending nationalisms and the Diaoyutai/Senkaku dispute. Security Dialogue 31(1):119–131

Donaldson J, Williams A (2005) Understanding maritime jurisdictional disputes: The East China Sea and beyond. Journal of International Affairs 59(1):135–156

Downs ES, Saunders PC (1998/1999) Legitimacy and the limits of nationalism: China and the Diaoyu islands. International Security 23(3):114–146

Fackler M (2008) Japan and China near agreement on offshore gas fields. The New York Times, June 18

Feenstra RC, Hai W, Woo WT, Yao S (1998) The U.S.–China bilateral trade balance: Its size and determinants. NBER Working Paper 6598

Fravel MT (2005) Regime insecurity and international cooperation: explaining China's compromises in territorial disputes. International Security 30(2):46–83

Friedberg AL (2005) The future of U.S.–China relations: Is conflict inevitable? International Security 30(2):7–45

Goldstein A (1997/1998) Great expectations: Interpreting China's arrival. International Security 22(3):36–73

Goldstein A (2003) Balance-of-power politics: Consequences for Asian security order. In: Alagappa M (ed) Asian security order: Instrumental and normative features. Stanford University Press, Stanford

Greenfield J (1992) China's practice in the law of the sea. Clarendon Press, Oxford

Hara K (2001) 50 Years from San Francisco: Re-examining the peace treaty and Japan's territorial problems. Pacific Affairs 74(3):361–382

He Y (2007) History, Chinese nationalism and the emerging Sino–Japanese conflict. Journal of Contemporary China 16(50):1–24

Inoue K (1972) The Tiaoyu islands and other islands are China's territory. Peking Review 15(19):18–22

Iwano H (1992) True Face of Taiwan: The choice of the third way. Keibunsha (in Japanese), Tokyo

Kelly DA (1987) The Chinese student movement of December 1986 and its intellectual antecedents. Australian Journal of Chinese Affairs 17:127–142

Kenny HJ (2004) China and the competition for oil and gas in Asia. Asia Pacific Review 11(2):36–47

Kim SP (2004) Maritime delimitation and interim arrangements in Northeast Asia. Martinus Nijhoff Publishers, The Hague/London/New York

Li VH (1975) China and off-shore oil: The Tiao-yu tai dispute. Stanford Journal of International Studies 10:151

Lind J (2004) Pacifism or passing the buck? Testing theories of Japanese security policy. International Security 29(1):92–121

Lo C (1989) China's policy towards territorial disputes: The case of the South China Sea Islands. Routledge, New York

Long S (1991) Taiwan: China's island frontier. Macmillan, London

Ma Y (1984) Legal problems of seabed boundary delimitation in the East China Sea. Occasional Papers/Reprints Series in Contemporary Asian Studies 62(3), University of Maryland School of Law, Baltimore

Mack A (1997) Island disputes in Northeast Asia. Working Paper No. 1997/2. Australian National University, Canberra, http://rspas.anu.edu.au/ir/pubs/work_papers/97-2.pdf, Accessed 10 February 2009

Marquand R (2005) Japan–China tensions rise over tiny islands: Japan took possession of disputed Senkakus. The Christian Science Monitor, February 11

Mastanduno M (2003) Incomplete hegemony: The United States and security order in Asia. In: Alagappa M (ed) Asian security order: Instrumental and normative features. Stanford University Press, Stanford

Ministry of Foreign Affairs of Japan (2006) Japan's regional diplomacy. In: Diplomatic bluebook 2006, Ministry of Foreign Affairs of Japan, Tokyo

Mutsuko M (1996) Center of the storm: Japan's rightists shed light on the issue. Asiaweek, September 20

Park C (1973) Oil under troubled waters: The Northeast Asia Sea-Bed controversy. Harvard International Law Journal 14(2):212–260

Park C (1983) The Sino–Japanese–Korea Sea resources controversy and the hypothesis of a 200-mile economic zone. In: Park C (ed) East Asia and the law of the sea. Seoul National University Press, Seoul

Prescott JRV (1992) Maritime jurisdiction. In: Morgan J, Valencia MJ (eds) Atlas for marine policy in East Asian seas. University of California Press, Berkeley

Pryzstup JJ (2004) Not the best of times. Comparative Connections 6(3):117–128

Ross RS (2000) The 1995–96 Taiwan Strait confrontation: Coercion, credibility, and the use of force. International Security 25(2):87–123

Shambaugh D (1991) China in 1990. Asian Survey 31(1):36–49

Shaw H (1999) The Diaoyutai/Senkaku islands dispute: Its history and an analysis of the ownership claims of the PRC, ROC and Japan. Occasional Papers/Reprints Series in Contemporary Asian Studies 152, University of Maryland School of Law, Baltimore

Suganuma U (2000) Sovereign rights and territorial space in Sino–Japanese relations: Irredentism and the Diaoyu/Senkaku islands. University of Hawaii Press, Honolulu

Sutter RG, Mitchener P (1996) China's rising military power and influence: Issues and options for the U.S., Congressional Research Service, Washington, DC

Suzuki S (2007) The importance of 'othering' in China's national identity: Sino–Japanese relations as a stage of identity conflicts. The Pacific Review 20(1):23–47

Takamine T (2005) A new dynamism in Sino-Japanese security relations: Japan's strategic use of foreign aid. The Pacific Review 18(4):439–461

Tretiak D (1978) The Sino–Japanese treaty of 1978: The Senkaku incident prelude. Asian Survey 18(12):1235–1249

United Nations Economic Commission for Asia and the Far East (UNECAFE) (1968). Geological structure and some water characteristics of the East China Sea and the Yellow Sea. 2 TECH. BULL. Technical Advisory Group Report

Urano T (2005) Senkaku islands, Okinawa islands, and China, Sanwa Shoseki (in Japanese), Tokyo

Wan M (2003) Tensions in recent Sino–Japanese relations. Asian Survey 43(5):826–844

Yang D (2003) Reconciliation between Japan and China: Problems and prospect. In: Funabashi Y (ed) Reconciliation in the Asia-Pacific. United States Institute of Peace Press, Washington, DC

Zou K (2005) Law of the sea in East Asia: Issues and prospects. Routledge, London, New York

Chapter 6
The Island and Maritime Disputes in the South China Sea

6.1 Introduction

The South China Sea, which stretches from the Karimata Strait between the Islands of Sumatra and Borneo in Indonesia to the Strait of Taiwan, encompasses hundreds of rocks, reefs, and small islands. The majority of them are located in the Paracel and Spratly archipelagos (See Map 6.1). The question of who owns these islands has become one of the most fundamental barriers to closer interstate relations in the region, particularly since potentially huge oil and gas deposits were found in the area in the late 1960s.[1] By the 1980s, seven East Asian countries became involved in disputes over the territory, and all of the claimants – except for Brunei and Indonesia – have established some kind of physical presence on at least one of those islands. Currently, Vietnam occupies more than twenty islands and reefs, China eight, Taiwan one, the Philippines eight, and Malaysia one (Lo 1989; Manning 2000; Burgess 2003; Tønnesson 2003).[2]

---

[1] Prewar claims and counterclaims to these islands can be traced to the late nineteenth century. The United Kingdom was the first European power to establish its control in the area. Yet the economic and strategic value of those dispersed islands had remained outside of colonial competition until France formally notified the world of its possession of those islands in July 1933. Japan immediately raised a formal protest against the French occupation and succeeded in occupying the entire archipelago by force by 1939. For Japanese militarists, the island groups had enormous economic and strategic values as Japan was entering the Pacific War. After Japanese troops withdrew from the area at the end of the war, both the Nationalist Chinese government and the French colonial administration in Vietnam immediately attempted to restore their prewar claims to the islands. When the People's Republic of China and the Republic of Vietnam were established in 1949 and 1955, respectively, both governments endorsed those claims (Luu 1996: 49–61; Peng Er 1996: 997–8; Catley and Keliat 1997: 24–30; Tønnesson 2006).

[2] Indonesia claims none of the contested islands but a zone northeast of Natuna Island that overlaps the outer limits of China's and Vietnam's traditional claims. Brunei claims a huge maritime zone running through the Spratly area, based on a straight-line projection of its EEZ as stipulated by the UNCLOS.

M.G. Koo, *Island Disputes and Maritime Regime Building in East Asia*,
The Political Economy of the Asia Pacific,
DOI 10.1007/978-0-387-89670-0_6, © Springer Science+Business Media, LLC 2009

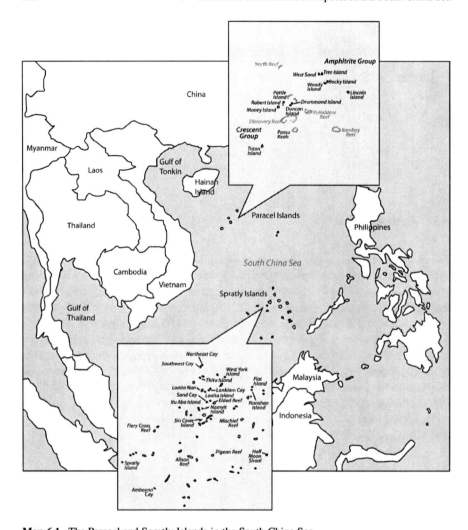

Map 6.1 The Paracel and Spratly Islands in the South China Sea

The significance of the South China Sea as a strategic passageway is unquestioned. It is the second busiest international sea-lane, and well over half of the world's petroleum-bearing traffic passes through this area. For outsiders, the military value of those contested islands may seem to be limited to serving as an observation post. Yet in practice, they can also serve as bargaining chips for maritime rights under the UNCLOS that can exclude naval forces from other countries. While the prohibitive cost of drilling in the deep waters of the South China Sea remains a significant barrier to the utilization of hydrocarbon potentials, the scramble for those islands looms large during a period of sharply rising energy consumptions in East Asia, particularly in China (Snyder 1996; Valencia et al. 1997; Townsend-Gault 1998; Rosenberg 2002).

This chapter focuses on the Sino–Vietnam dyad vis-à-vis the dispute over the Paracels and Spratlys. Aside from the dispute with Taiwan, China's most important bilateral disputes in the South China Sea are with Vietnam. Although Vietnam is not the only party to the many territorial disputes with China in the South China Sea, it has had the sharpest differences with Beijing until recently. The other countries also have claims that overlap either China's or Vietnam's, but they have been less salient except in a few cases.[3] In the South China Sea (and the Gulf of Tonkin), Vietnam's claims have become a hurdle as well as a possible means by which the relations with its archenemy, China, whose interests and policies Vietnam must always take into account can be improved.

With the inauguration of Deng Xiaoping's coastal development strategy in 1979, a high level of economic activity began to be concentrated along the eastern seaboard, thereby heightening the significance of maritime security and resources for economic prosperity. These strategic and economic concerns have been embodied in and reinforced by the modernization and expansion of the Chinese PLAN. China's assertive actions in the South China Sea have also been closely related to the power disparity in the region. With its power advantage, China seems to find it easy to take offensive military actions to back up its territorial claims. China might also believe that its aggressive territorial policy would not trigger a dangerous escalation, because buck-passing would likely be the dominant strategy among other Southeast Asian countries. In turn, such developments have increased Southeast Asian countries' concerns about the rising presence of China in the South China Sea. Many of them have begun to take limited but significant military modernization steps of their own, creating the potential for a regional arms race. Like other Southeast Asian claimants, Vietnam currently lacks the military might to fully defend its claims. Its navy is primarily a coastal-defense force that has also been delegated the responsibility of the surveillance of EEZ in the South China Sea and the Gulfs of Thailand and Tonkin. Nevertheless, Chinese leaders may have strong incentives to delay the settlements of these offshore island disputes, while slowly but steadily reinforcing their physical and symbolic footholds in the area (Valencia 1995: 30–1; Goldstein 1997/1998: 52–4; Cole 2000; Fravel 2003).[4]

In the eyes of China and Vietnam, the disputes over the Paracel and Spratly Islands have not been an isolated issue from the very beginning. The official posi-

---

[3]For the other countries' entanglement in the South China Sea, see Lin (1997), Castro (1998), Nordhaug (2001), and Austin (2003).

[4]Snyder (1996) points to Chinese "salami tactics," in which China tests the other claimants through aggressive actions and then backs off when it meets significant resistance. China's ambiguity on the extent and nature of its claims is regarded as a tactical ploy to stall or defer any attempt to achieve a negotiated settlement until it is prepared to get what it wants through military strength. In a similar vein, Fravel (2003: 73–80) argues that only severe international shocks that threaten China's strategic interests and overall position in the international system would likely create incentives to compromise over the disputed islands.

tion of Beijing on the sovereignty matter was first stated publicly in 1951. Commenting on the 1951 San Francisco Peace Treaty, China's then Foreign Minister Zhou Enlai argued "the Draft Peace Treaty stipulates that Japan should renounce all rights to (the Paracel and Spratly Islands), but again deliberately makes no mention of the problem of restoring sovereignty over them. As a matter of fact, just like all (the Spratly, Macclesfield, and Pratas Islands, the Paracel Islands) have always been China's territory" (Quoted in Lo 1989: 27–8).

At the San Francisco conference, the South Vietnamese delegation also delivered its claim to the Paracel and Spratly Islands. In addition, the South Vietnamese government followed the practice of the French colonial administration in sending regular patrols to the Crescent group of the western Paracels. China tolerated Vietnam's presence in the Crescent group, while setting permanent settlements in the Amphitrite group of the eastern Paracels in late 1950. Chinese tolerance never meant that South Vietnam's position in the Paracel Islands was acceptable to China. China's protest to Vietnam's provocation continued throughout the 1950s. In the summer of 1956, the South Vietnamese government sent naval units to some of the Spratly Islands as well, planting flags and setting up landmarks to symbolize its occupation. In response, China lodged a strong protest in September 1958 that the Spratlys were a part of Chinese territory to be used as a baseline from which to draw the 12 nm territorial sea. South Vietnam vehemently opposed this claim, repeating Vietnam's sovereignty over those islands. On the whole, however, the Paracel and Spratly Islands remained insignificant specks on the geopolitical map of East Asia in the first two decades of the postwar era (Luu 1996: 19–60; Catley and Keliat 1997: 29; Fravel 2003: 371).

In the 1970s, Sino–Vietnamese relations began to change dramatically with a series of military skirmishes in the South China Sea. Repeated clashes have left an enduring legacy of bitterness and suspicion on both sides. The most serious one was China's invasion and capture of the Crescent group from South Vietnam in 1974. After losing the battle for the Paracels, the South Vietnamese government immediately sent troops to occupy six islands of the Spratly archipelago. These were taken over by the Socialist Republic of Vietnam (SRV) in 1975 after the Vietnam War. In 1978–79, combined with fluid geopolitics in Indochina, bilateral differences over the Spratly Islands resulted in a large-scale border dispute between China and Vietnam. In early 1988, Chinese and Vietnamese naval forces violently clashed again over the occupation of several reefs in the Spratly chain. A number of minor confrontations continued in the 1990s, but none of them escalated beyond accusations, claims, counterclaims, minor displays of military force, and seizures of civilians.[5]

---

[5]By contrast, violent actions and reactions marked the other dispute dyads in the 1990s. Most notably, China occupied the aptly named Mischief Reef in the Spratly group, a circular reef well within the EEZ of the Philippines, leading to encounters between military vessels from the Philippines and China in spring 1995. In the same year, Taiwanese artillery opened fire on a Vietnamese supply ship. In January 1996, three alleged Chinese vessels engaged in a 90-minute gun battle with a Philippine navy gunboat. In 1998, Vietnamese soldiers opened fire on a Philippine fishing boat. The dispute over structures built on Mischief Reef reemerged in 1999 as a security flashpoint between China and the Philippines (Gurtov and Hwang 1998: 259–66; Burgess 2003: 9).

In what follows, I show that the territorial bargaining game approach can explain the transition between, and conclusion of, three different rounds of Sino–Vietnamese dispute over the Paracel and Spratly Islands. Coupled with growing resource competition and unstable geopolitics in the South China Sea, the clash of rival nationalisms between China and Vietnam has had an enduring influence on the initiation and escalation of the recurring rounds of island dispute. The lack of deterring economic forces during the Cold War period further exacerbated the situation. By contrast, there is strong evidence that the pacific influence of increasingly salient economic interdependence between China and Vietnam has begun to work, thus preventing the island issues from spinning out of control, particularly since the two sides normalized their diplomatic relations in 1991. The evidence found in this chapter suggests that in recent years both the Chinese and Vietnamese governments have recognized it as a convenient strategy to shelve the final resolution of the island dispute, while deepening bilateral economic ties and hammering out joint development of the South China Sea.

6.2   The First Round of Dispute (1974)

Despite the consistency and firmness of the competing claims of China and South Vietnam vis-à-vis the offshore islands in the South China Sea, no military action had been taken until January 1974, when China suddenly asserted its claim to the Crescent group of the western Paracel Islands in a forceful manner. The growing strategic and economic value of the offshore islands and the decline in U.S. presence created a golden opportunity for China to act. Unsurprisingly, this period lacked mitigating economic forces between China and South Vietnam. But further escalation was averted due to the complex geopolitical and strategic atmosphere in Indochina in the mid-1970s.

6.2.1   Initiation and Escalation Phase

For most of the 1960s, the Paracel dispute between South Vietnam and China remained relatively dormant. Naval patrols did not confront each other directly. The last reported clash between Chinese fishing vessels and the South Vietnamese Navy occurred in early 1961. The principal sources of stability were twofold. First, the continued weakness of the PLAN placed logistical limitations on China in conducting naval patrols and operations beyond the Amphitrite group in the eastern Paracels. Second, the *status quo* in the South China Sea was a byproduct of the deteriorating domestic situation in South Vietnam. South Vietnamese forces consolidated their position on Pattle Island, one of the largest in the Crescent group, but, at some point in the 1960s, began to withdraw from other smaller ones including Duncan, Drummond, and Palm Islands. While China continued to upgrade its position in the Amphitrite group, South Vietnam apparently did not establish permanent military presence on any of the Crescent group (Fravel 2003: 373).

Set against this backdrop, the battle for the Paracels was catalyzed by the South Vietnamese government's administrative decision in September 1973 to incorporate the Spratly Islands into Phuoc Tuy Province, a move designed to strengthen its maritime rights in support of its offshore oil contracts with Western companies (Samuels 1982: 99). Four months later, China responded with a statement that "The decision of the Saigon authorities to incorporate [Rifleman, Itu Aba], and other islands in the [Spratly chain] into South Vietnam is illegal, null, and void...The Chinese government will never tolerate any infringement on China's territorial integrity and sovereignty by the Saigon authorities" (Quoted in Lo 1989: 55). In a statement released a few days later, the Foreign Minister of South Vietnam strongly rejected China's claim. Subsequently, South Vietnam dispatched destroyer escort HQ-4 to patrol the Paracels. The South Vietnamese ship arrived on January 15 and discovered that Chinese fishermen had been sent to three islands of the Paracels, hitherto claimed by South Vietnam, to set up huts, display Chinese flags, and dig tombs. The South Vietnamese Foreign Minister described these activities as a threat to the security of the region. The South Vietnamese government sent more vessels and troops to the Paracels, where they were soon to be confronted by Chinese gunboats (Do and Kane 1988: 175).

During January 16–18, 1974, skirmishes took place between Chinese and South Vietnamese vessels, which played a game of hide and seek in between the islands and reefs. These skirmishes finally led to serious armed clash on January 19. The South Vietnamese ships approached China's position around Duncan, Drummond, and Palm Islands from two sides, squaring off against the four PLAN boats. Approximately 40 South Vietnamese troops landed on Duncan and Palm Islands. The troops on Duncan Island retreated, but the two sides engaged each other on Palm Island before the South Vietnamese force withdrew after suffering three casualties. The South Vietnamese ships attacked the PLAN vessels, which immediately returned fire. When the smoke cleared within a few days, South Vietnamese forces were clearly defeated and forced to withdraw from the Paracel Islands (Fravel 2003: 381–2).

In hindsight, South Vietnamese forces were not only unprepared to fight, but also miscalculated the situation. For China, the Paracel operation was an allegedly self-defensive measure against South Vietnamese provocations. Yet China might have recognized that Saigon's 1973 declaration of sovereignty over the offshore islands in the South China Sea was nothing more than a symbolic claim, lacking the substantial will and capability with which to defend its claim. Nevertheless, the Chinese did counterattack, thus feeding a conspiracy theory that the South Vietnamese had been set up (Muller 1983: 154).[6]

---

[6]Fravel (2003: 382–5) disagrees with the strategic set-up argument. He argues that China's behavior was shaped by *ad-hoc* incentives created by the changing strategic context of the dispute, rather than by well-planned military scenarios. As evidence for his argument, he points out that there were no PLAN vessels on patrol in the Crescent or Amphitrite groups when China issued the January 11th statement; the only ships were fishing boats, which usually monitored South Vietnamese activities for the PLAN.

The South Vietnamese government launched diplomatic efforts to defend its position over the Paracel Islands. It solicited the attention of the UN Security Council. Yet its efforts went nowhere. Even South Vietnam's closest ally, the U.S., remained neutral throughout the battle. The U.S. Seventh Fleet, which had been ordered to keep out of the vicinity of the Paracel Islands, ignored the South Vietnamese government's appeal for the rescue of its troops who had been missing in action (Lo 1989: 57). As such, South Vietnam could not help but accept the new grim reality of China's sovereignty right over the entire Paracel archipelago.

For China, the seizure of the Paracel Islands was presumably a preemptive move to control marine resources in the South China Sea with the advent of active debate about the UNCLOS. In 1973, the UN Seabed Committee just completed its work, followed by the opening session of UNCLOS III. Although the UNCLOS was not concluded until 1982, by the mid-1970s it became clear that a number of littoral states would seek to expand significantly their maritime and territorial rights in adjacent sea areas. The semi-enclosed nature of the South China Sea meant that an intense contest for maritime rights was imminent for Southeast Asian countries (Park 1978; Polomka 1978; Siddayao 1978; Valencia 1995).[7]

Geopolitical interests have also influenced China's policies in the South China Sea. It was easier for China to settle the Paracel dispute by force before the impending collapse of South Vietnam, which would minimize objections from the Soviet Union and prevent any further deterioration of ties with North Vietnam (Segal 1985: 197–210). In the couple of years before the 1974 clash, Sino–Vietnamese relations were already deteriorating, which in turn gave Beijing a free pass to launch the Paracel operation. A study by Fravel (2003: 366–7; 385–7) shows that China has used force over offshore islands when the decline of superpower influence in the region removes constraints on China's behavior. From this viewpoint, China's assertiveness in 1974 resulted from U.S. and then Soviet naval disengagement from the South China Sea. With the U.S. decision to withdraw from Indochina, concern began to grow over a shift in the strategic balance of power in the region and its potentially destabilizing effect

---

[7]In 1970, the Philippines completed a seismic survey of the energy resources in the South China Sea and began drilling test wells in 1971. To bolster its maritime rights, the Philippine government occupied five islands and reefs in the Spratly group in 1970–71. Philippine forces challenged through a show of force Taiwan's garrison on Itu Aba, the largest in the Spratly chain. Other claimants to the area, including China and South Vietnam, issued formal diplomatic notes of protest, asserting their own claims. Around the same time, South Vietnam also launched a program to exploit offshore petroleum resources. With its entry into the UN in 1971, China began to participate in the work of the UN Committee on the Peaceful Uses of the Seabed and the Ocean Floor beyond the Limits of National Jurisdiction. China also became an enthusiastic supporter of convening the UNCLOS. Accordingly, China extended its claims to include nearby waters of the islands and the resources thereof (Park 1978; Fravel 2003: 375).

on the security of critical sea-lanes in the South China Sea.[8] As the U.S. decreased its presence in the South China Sea, the Soviet Union began to signal its interest in the area.[9] In the middle of shifting geopolitics, China became more anxious, but less constrained, to publicly denounce Vietnam's claim to sovereignty over the Paracel and Spratly Islands (Leifer 1978, 1984; Catley and Keliat 1997: 75–7).[10]

Finally, from a liberal peace perspective, the 1974 flare-up was not a big surprise given that China and South Vietnam had few economic ties at the dawn of the armed clash. According to Chinese statistics, the cumulative bilateral trade between the two countries during the period of 1969–74 amounted to only $275 million, accounting for less than 1% of China's total trade during the same period (See Table 6.1). Such a low level of bilateral economic ties indicates that there was no economic deterrence to prevent China from escalating the Paracel dispute.

6.2.2   Settlement and Beyond

Having lost the 1974 Paracel battle, South Vietnam began to worry about its position in the Spratly Islands. In a preemptive move, Saigon sent troops to six of them to consolidate its sovereignty claim. This initiative was followed by a flurry of protests from China, as well as from Taiwan and the Philippines. Yet, due to the complex nature of the Spratly issue as well as the limitations in its naval projection capability, China did not really implement its warning into action (Lo 1989: 57–8).

It is not difficult to explain why China directed its attention to the Paracel Islands but not to the Spratly Islands in 1974. The Paracel Islands are geographically closer to the Chinese mainland, thus making them more essential for national security than the Spratly Islands. At the same time, China found it more difficult to undertake

---

[8] With the 1973 Paris Peace Agreement between North Vietnam and the U.S., U.S. forces withdrew not only from Vietnam but also from the surrounding Asian mainland area. Hanoi looked upon the Peace Agreement as a major victory because it enabled the North to continue the war in the South against only the South Vietnamese troops at a time of their own choosing (http://www.ehistory.com/vietnam/essays/theend/0001.cfm, Accessed 10 February 2009).

[9] In 1971, the Soviet Union signed a treaty with India that provided access to the Indian Ocean, edging closer to Southeast Asia. In 1972–73, the Soviet Union issued diplomatic notes concerning access to the Straits of Malacca, which would link its Pacific Fleet to the Indian Ocean, further indicating its interest in the South China Sea (Fravel 2003: 376–7).

[10] By contrast, China's attitude towards the other two claimants, the Philippines and Malaysia, were much more restrained, as they assumed a new, positive role in China's anti-Soviet and anti-Vietnamese united front. During 1974–84, China sought to contain the disputes with the Philippines and Malaysia over the Spratly Islands, stressing the importance of peaceful solutions (Lo 1989: 38–9, 137–8, 147–57).

Table 6.1 GDP and trade statistics of China and Vietnam (1960–2003) (US$ million)

	China					Vietnam[a]				
	GDP	Export to Vietnam	Import from Vietnam	Bilateral trade balance	TD on Vietnam (%)	GDP	Export to China	Import from China	Bilateral trade balance	TD on China (%)
1960	61,378	0	0	0	0.00	78	0	0	0	0.00
1961	50,101	0	0	0	0.00	82	0	0	0	0.00
1962	46,464	0	0	0	0.00	90	0	0	0	0.00
1963	50,280	0	0	0	0.00	96	0	0	0	0.00
1964	58,613	0	0	0	0.00	94	0	0	0	0.00
1965	69,709	0	0	0	0.00	103	0	0	0	0.00
1966	75,879	0	0	0	0.00	90	0	0	0	0.00
1967	72,057	0	0	0	0.00	877	0	0	0	0.00
1968	69,994	0	0	0	0.00	857	0	0	0	0.00
1969	78,719	55	0	55	0.07	914	0	36	-36	3.90
1970	91,506	45	1	44	0.05	771	0	29	-29	3.77
1971	98,562	54	2	52	0.06	934	0	47	-47	5.07
1972	112,160	40	3	38	0.04	1,055	0	51	-50	4.81
1973	136,770	29	6	23	0.03	1,165	2	23	-21	2.13
1974	142,255	34	5	29	0.03	1,065	5	38	-33	3.97
1975	161,163	10	2	8	0.01	922	2	14	-12	1.71
1976	151,628	0	0	0	0.00	4,975	0	0	0	0.00
1977	172,349	0	0	0	0.00	5,076	0	0	0	0.00
1978	147,321	16	41	-24	0.04	5,185	37	18	19	1.06
1979	175,574	0	0	0	0.00	4,891	0	0	0	0.00
1980	188,242	0	0	0	0.00	4,255	0	0	0	0.00
1981	192,952	0	0	0	0.00	4,358	0	0	0	0.00
1982	202,088	0	0	0	0.00	4,756	0	0	0	0.00
1983	227,376	0	0	0	0.00	5,088	0	0	0	0.00

(continued)

Table 6.1 (continued)

	China					Vietnam[a]				
	GDP	Export to Vietnam	Import from Vietnam	Bilateral trade balance	TD on Vietnam (%)	GDP	Export to China	Import from China	Bilateral trade balance	TD on China (%)
1984	256,107	0	0	0	0.00	4,508	0	0	0	0.00
1985	304,912	0	0	0	0.00	5,857	0	0	0	0.00
1986	295,716	0	0	0	0.00	5,990	0	0	0	0.00
1987	268,218	0	0	0	0.00	6,212	0	0	0	0.00
1988	307,167	0	0	0	0.00	6,584	0	0	0	0.00
1989	342,292	2	6	−3	0.00	7,112	0	0	0	0.00
1990	354,644	2	1	1	0.00	6,472	8	5	3	0.19
1991	376,617	21	11	11	0.01	7,642	19	18	1	0.49
1992	418,181	106	73	34	0.04	9,867	96	32	64	1.29
1993	431,780	277	123	154	0.09	13,181	136	86	50	1.68
1994	542,534	342	191	151	0.10	16,286	296	144	151	2.70
1995	700,278	722	332	390	0.15	20,736	362	330	32	3.34
1996	816,490	842	308	534	0.14	24,657	340	329	11	2.71
1997	898,244	1,079	357	721	0.16	26,844	474	404	70	3.27
1998	946,301	1,024	217	806	0.13	27,210	440	515	−75	3.51
1999	991,356	964	354	610	0.13	28,684	746	673	73	4.95
2000	1,080,741	1,537	929	609	0.23	31,173	1,536	1,401	135	9.42
2001	1,175,716	1,805	1,010	796	0.24	32,685	1,417	1,606	−189	9.25
2002	1,271,000	2,150	1,115	1035	0.26	35,058	1,518	2,159	−641	10.49
2003	1,417,000	3,179	1,456	1723	0.33	39,164	1,323	3,496	−2173	12.31

[a]For 1960–74, figures are for South Vietnam alone

Sources: The International Monetary Fund, *The Direction of Trade Statistics* (CD-Rom); The World Bank, *World Development Indicators* (CD-Rom); The World Trade Organization, *International Trade Statistics*; United Nations Department of Economic and Social Affairs, *Monthly Bulletin of Statistics*, Asian Development Bank, *Key Indicators of Developing Asian and Pacific Countries*; Socialist Republic of Vietnam, General Statistical Office, *Statistical Data of the Socialist Republic of Vietnam 1979*; South Vietnam's GDP for the period of 1960–75 is author's estimates based on various sources

military action in the Spratlys due to the sheer distance from its coast. In addition, the situation of the Spratly Islands was far more complicated, as multiple parties were concerned. Aside from Vietnam, Taiwanese and Philippine troops were already stationed there as of 1974. It was most likely that another military confrontation with South Vietnam could have easily escalated into a region-wide, multiparty conflict, which China could not afford to handle. Relations with Taiwan and the Philippines were more sensitive, and therefore much higher political risks for China would have been involved. Hence, although China was greatly annoyed by South Vietnam's unilateral occupation of several features in the Spratlys, it chose not to escalate the Spratly dispute (Lo 1989: 72–3; Catley and Keliat 1997: 76; Fravel 2003: 370).

Finally, it is important to recognize North Vietnam's ambivalent position. Throughout the 1974 flare-up between China and South Vietnam, North Vietnam remained tolerant, if not supportive, of China's claim to the Paracel Islands. When the PLAN invaded the western Paracels and the South Vietnamese troops fled, the Hanoi government made no public protest, although it deeply resented the Chinese move. For Hanoi, the war in Indochina required support from China. Hence, it contained any indication of resentment towards Chinese assertiveness on the offshore islands. During talks on the division of the Gulf of Tonkin between North Vietnam and China from August to November 1974, the sovereignty dispute over the South China Sea islands was completely shelved (Lo 1989: 86).[11]

Aside from the unification of the country, the most important issue that concerned Hanoi leadership throughout the 1950s and 1960s was the economic reconstruction of North Vietnam. During the period of 1955–60, China assisted North Vietnam with 900 million yuan in grants and 300 million yuan in long-term loans. From 1954 to 1978, China also funded 450 projects, of which 339 were completed by March 1978.[12] However, from 1958 to 1960, as the Sino–Soviet rift began to develop, Moscow's interest in preempting Chinese influence in Vietnam increased, and Soviet aid to North Vietnam surpassed aid from China.[13]

---

[11] In 1887, just after Vietnam became a French colony, a treaty was signed in Beijing stipulating that longitude 108°3'18'E formed the boundary between China and Tonkin (French Vietnam). The boundary regime had remained stable until the 1970s. But with the end of the Vietnam War and burgeoning Vietnamese-Soviet relations, the issue of boundary delimitation in the Gulf of Tonkin became a major irritant between Beijing and Hanoi. Vietnam insisted that the 1887 treaty line delimited not only land borders but also the sea boundary in the Gulf. For China, this interpretation was not acceptable because such a line would give two thirds of the Gulf to Vietnam. Not surprisingly, two rounds of talks in 1974 and 1977–78 did not produce any solution (Valencia 1995: 33–7).

[12] These included rice-husking factories, sugar refineries, paper mills, match factories, chemical plants, shipyards, iron and steel complexes, railroads, and radio networks. China also assisted North Vietnam with 700 million yuan in commodity aid during the war years and reconstruction period (1965–75), while sending about 20,000 advisers, specialists, and technicians. According to Chinese sources, the total value of China's aid to Vietnam exceeded $20 billion (Vo 1990: 42).

[13] In the first five-year plan period (1961–65), the Soviet Union assisted North Vietnam with a grant of 20 million rubles and a loan of 430 million rubles. The Soviet Union also promised to fund nearly 100 projects, about half of which were considered major. During the war years and reconstruction period, the Soviet Union provided North Vietnam with 1.5 billion rubles in aid (Vo 1990: 41).

Indeed, the aid to Hanoi played an important role in determining the course of Sino–Vietnamese and Soviet–Vietnamese relations alike.

After the intense debate at the turn of the 1970s, the Chinese leadership saw the Soviet Union as the principal threat to China's security and began to seek rapprochement with the U.S. An irreparable damage to Sino–Vietnamese relations was thus done in 1971 when Chairman Mao Zedong invited U.S. President Richard Nixon to China. The Vietnamese leadership felt a deep sense of betrayal. From 1972 onwards, Mao's pictures disappeared in Hanoi. The ethnic Chinese in Vietnam began to be ill-treated. The activities of the Sino–Vietnamese Friendship Association and the publication of Hanoi's only Chinese language newspaper were suspended in early 1974. Clearly and unmistakably, the Sino–U.S. *détente* deepened the mutual distrust between Beijing and Hanoi and transformed Hanoi's role from Beijing's ally to its archrival backed by Moscow. Concurrent with the potential improvement in Sino–American relations, those between Moscow and Washington entered a period of *détente* following President Nixon's trip to Moscow in May 1972. These shifts in international relations led to a certain balance of influences among the U.S., the Soviet Union, and China. But Washington's growing rapprochement with Beijing and its *détente* with Moscow did not mean that the three powers stood equidistant from each other. The advent of a strategic triangle surrounding Indochina was unstable at best from the very beginning (Gottleib 1977; McGregor 1988: 9–13; Kimura 1989: 67; Lo 1989: 68–9; Amer 1994: 359–63).

In sum, both Beijing and Hanoi managed to conceal their mutual suspicion and resentment before the end of the Vietnam War in 1975. When China launched the Paracel operation, it sent a message to Hanoi that it saw the issues of division of the Gulf of Tonkin and sovereignty over the South China Sea islands in a different light. For China, the division of the Gulf was an unsettled issue, and it was willing to hold talks with North Vietnam to find a solution. By contrast, China's sovereignty over the Paracel and Spratly Islands was regarded as indisputable and non-negotiable. As long as Hanoi did not make any noise about the islands, China had no reason to make a preemptive move against North Vietnam (Lo 1989: 86–8; Valencia 1995: 33–7). However, it was only a matter of time that their "marriage of convenience" would turn into a "nightmare of divorce," as their relationship went from bad to worse in the mid-1970s.

6.3   The Second Round of Dispute (1978–79)

The second half of the 1970s marked turbulent Sino–Vietnamese relations. From a geopolitical perspective, Vietnamese reunification after the fall of Saigon to North Vietnam on April 30, 1975 largely resulted from massive Soviet aid to the North in the absence of U.S. aid to the South. With the substantial decrease in the Chinese aid after the reunification of Vietnam, Hanoi became even closer to the Soviet Union. Deepening ties between Hanoi and Moscow and their hegemonic ambition in Indochina was far from acceptable to Beijing. The competition for influence in Laos and Cambodia further intensified the mutual distrust between Hanoi and Beijing. Against this stormy backdrop, Hanoi took over the maritime policies of South Vietnam, claiming both the Paracels and Spratlys as inherent Vietnamese territory. It was clear that in the immediate aftermath of the 1974 battle for the Paracels, Hanoi departed from its previous position of recognizing China's sovereignty over the Paracel and Spratly Islands. Hanoi and Beijing eventually collided over the island issues, contributing to the outbreak of the 1979 Sino–Vietnamese border war. Combined with the rise of contending territorial nationalisms, unstable geopolitics surrounding Indochina and the lack of mitigating economic forces drove the once "lips-and-teeth" relationship between Hanoi and Beijing on a collision course.

6.3.1   Initiation and Escalation Phase

In April 1975, North Vietnam took over six islands in the Spratly group, which had been controlled by South Vietnam. A month later, Hanoi's military newspaper, *Quan Doi Nham Dan*, published a map depicting the Spratly Islands as part of Vietnam's territory. China did not confront Hanoi's provocative actions immediately. Rather, it closely watched and carefully assessed Hanoi's new territorial policy. Even when Vietnamese Communist Party (VCP) leader Le Duan officially raised the sovereignty issue during his visit to Beijing in September 1975, China remained cautious and low-key. Yet China's excessive patience did not last longer. Once Hanoi raised the bilateral differences over the Paracel and Spratly Islands at the official level, Beijing no longer felt inhibited from producing intensive propaganda about these issues (Lo 1989: 96–8).[14] At the same time, Beijing began to take a number of diplomatic measures to undermine Hanoi's influence in the region. First, it started negotiations to normalize its relations with ASEAN countries, towards which Hanoi was still antagonistic. To Hanoi's embarrassment, Beijing also developed particularly close relations with the new Khmer Rouge government in Cambodia, which was fiercely anti-Soviet and anti-Vietnamese as well. China cultivated the Khmer Rouge government as a potential client for containing Hanoi's influence in the region (McGregor 1988: 33–8; Kimura 1989: 78–82).

Throughout 1976, Vietnam managed to take a relatively low-key approach to the sovereignty matter. In early 1977, however, Hanoi became increasingly anxious

---

[14]For instance, China issued a statement on June 14, 1976 asserting "[the Spratly Islands as well as the Paracel, Macclesfield, and Pratas Islands] have always been part of China's territory... China has indisputable sovereignty over these islands and their adjacent sea areas...[T]he resources there belong to China...Any foreign country's armed invasion and occupation of any of [the Spratly Islands] or exploration and exploitation of oil and other resources in [the Spratly Islands] area constitute encroachments on China's territorial integrity and sovereignty and are impermissible. Any foreign country's claim to sovereignty over any of [the Spratly Islands] is illegal and null and void" (Quoted in Lo 1989: 98–9).

about Beijing's assertiveness and began to adopt a more aggressive approach. The situation was set for a serious confrontation. In December 1976, the VCP purged Hoang Van Hoan, a founding member of the Indochinese Communist Party and once a close associate of Ho Chi Minh, for his allegedly pro-China political background. The purge cleared the way for a tougher response to China's regional policy and its significance became obvious in 1979, when the Sino–Vietnamese conflict intensified and Hoang defected to China (Lo 1989: 99–100).

When its request for talks on the Paracel and Spratly Islands was turned down by China in April 1977, Hanoi finally decided to play tough with China. Its first warning shot came in May 1977. Adding to Beijing's discomfort, Hanoi made extensive claims to maritime space in the South China Sea, including a 12 nm territorial sea, a 23 nm contiguous zone, a 200 nm EEZ, and a 200 nm continental shelf of the Paracel and Spratly Islands. In less than a month, Vietnam's Defense Minister Vo Nguyen Giap ordered a taskforce team consisting of 29 vessels to carry out a combined sea–air exercise near the Paracel Islands. China was clearly tempted to launch a preemptive strike during the summer of 1977.[15] For the rest of 1977, the two countries continued to exchange hostile rhetoric (Lo 1989: 100–4; Luu 1996: 111).

The year 1978 featured major geopolitical events that resulted in public breakdown of Sino–Vietnamese relations: (1) China signed a peace treaty with Japan in October and normalized diplomatic relationship with the U.S. in December; and (2) Vietnam signed a Treaty of Friendship and Cooperation with the Soviet Union in November. Sino–Vietnamese relations rapidly deteriorated and the dispute over the Paracel and Spratly Islands became a more serious bone of contention. Growing Vietnamese nationalism further fueled the distrust between Hanoi and Beijing. In particular, the ethnic Chinese in Vietnam felt growing pressures. As was the case in most of the other countries in Southeast Asia, the ethnic Chinese had a strong economic position in Vietnam. Yet many of them began to suspect that Hanoi had deliberately been trying to undermine their economic influence. Beijing protested Hanoi's treatment of the ethnic Chinese. In the aftermath of the row over their status and position in spring 1978, Beijing completely stopped providing economic aid to

---

[15] In July 1977, Chinese Foreign Minister Huang Hua gave a speech to a closed meeting of senior cadres in which he clearly defended China's claims to the South China Sea: "Another important question is the problem of the jurisdiction of the islands of the South China Sea...The jurisdiction of the Paracel and Spratly Islands has been in dispute since oil-exporting Arab countries, following the fourth Middle East War, initiated oil warfare which triggered the energy crisis in the capitalist world...Since the Paracel Islands are under our control, we do not mind whether Vietnam keeps saying that they are theirs...But the crux of the problem is the Spratly Islands. Although we refrain from dealing with the problem of the Spratly Islands for the time being, their jurisdiction is still ours. No exploitation of resources on the Spratly Islands and their surrounding seabeds is valid without China's consent. You may exploit them as you like; but we will confiscate all of them in due time...When we will recover these islands depends upon opportunity" (Quoted in McGregor 1988: 15–6).

Hanoi (McGregor 1988: 19; Amer 1994: 359–363; Duiker 1995: 207). By the end of the year, it became clear that diplomatic maneuver and subtle signaling were then replaced by propaganda exchanges and a measure of military confrontation.

The widening rift between China and Vietnam was manifested in their worsening economic relations. During both Indochina Wars – the first with the French and the second with the South Vietnamese and Americans – China was a major supplier of arms to North Vietnam, and they also supplied significant amounts of economic aid. Industrialization in Vietnam would have been impossible without a substantial amount of aid from China. Yet in the wake of a series of Sino–Vietnamese disputes, Chinese economic aid to Vietnam came to a halt (Sharpe 2005: 158). Official bilateral trade ties had already been severed since 1976 (See Table 6.1). Given the low level of economic ties, neither China nor Vietnam felt constrained to pursue maximal territorial demands backed by the threat or use of force.[16]

In a dramatic turn of event, the island dispute ignited a large-scale militarized conflict in a Sino–Vietnamese border area in early 1979.[17] From one perspective, the island dispute probably did not play a primary role in the 1979 Sino–Vietnamese War. Admittedly, other issues had dominated their bilateral relations before the island dispute drew headlines. But there is no denying that diplomatic skirmishes over the islands caused serious secondary effects on Sino–Vietnamese relations. Given the small patch of borderland in dispute, it is likely that both sides saw the border dispute as a convenient cover under which to express their dissatisfaction with the other side's position on the more important island dispute in the South China Sea (McGregor 1988: 19–20). Hence it can be argued that Sino–Vietnamese disputes over the offshore islands interacted with disputes at other levels to create a vicious cycle that eventually led to the 1979 border war.

---

[16] Vietnam's second five-year plan (1976–80) was a complete failure, with economic growth reaching only 0.4% per year. Compounding the postwar hardships, Vietnam's intervention in Cambodia resulted in diplomatic and economic isolation, further straining its resources (Alpert and Sanders 2005: 35). Hanoi was in desperate situation. After the termination of Chinese aid (and the U.S. refusal to help in Vietnam's rehabilitation), Vietnam's ties with the Soviet Union grew rapidly. During the period of 1976–80, the Soviet Union provided Vietnam with economic and technical assistance for the 94 important economic projects, while supplying Vietnam with 46.2% of its needs in machinery and equipment, 8.2% in oil products, 16.6% in wheat and flour, 6.4% in cotton fiber. It is estimated that the Soviet Union provided $3.8 billion in economic assistance during the same period (Vo 1990: 98–101).

[17] In April 1977, Cambodian forces launched a large-scale military operation along the Vietnam–Cambodia border. Hanoi long suspected that Phnom Penh had been collaborating with Beijing in a plot to contain Vietnam. The intransigence of Phnom Penh in the border dispute exacerbated Hanoi's suspicions and eventually led Vietnam to invade Cambodia on December 25, 1978 with the support from the Soviet Union. In February 1979, China decided to "teach Vietnam a lesson" and launched a military attack on Vietnam. In the short but bloody three-week Sino–Vietnamese border war, 85,000 Chinese troops penetrated into Vietnam, leaving behind them a trail of destruction in a 30-mile belt south of the eastern sector of the Sino–Vietnamese border. For more details about the war, see Leifer (1979), Tretiak (1979), Heder (1981), Segal (1985), McGregor (1988), Kimura (1989), Duiker (1995) and Amer (1994).

6.3.2 Stalemate

The Sino–Vietnamese border war did not clearly resolve the territorial issues, and the offshore islands dispute was no exception. Although bilateral talks on a wide range of issues followed after the war, there appeared to be little room for the negotiated settlement of the island dispute. The tension was most salient in certain areas of the bordering provinces, where mutual accusations about military incursions and shelling became part of everyday life. Before long, both sides took the debate away from the negotiation table, but neither side was in a position to use force again in the aftermath of the 1978–79 clash.

China's growing offshore oil interests in the South China Sea added a complication to the island dispute. The year 1979 marked the turning point for China's offshore oil exploration program, thanks to a combination of three key factors: (1) the formal adoption of Deng Xiaoping's open door policy; (2) the advent of second oil crisis; and (3) major oil discoveries in the South China Sea. To Vietnam's great dismay, the Chinese government granted seismic survey blocks in the Gulf of Tonkin to a number of Western oil corporations. China also signed contracts with 48 foreign oil companies to conduct maritime surveys far beyond China's coast, signaling its intention to expand its territorial and maritime claims deep into the South China Sea (Lo 1989: 126–8).

Hanoi strongly protested against Beijing's oil exploration activities and issued stern warnings against Western oil companies. In July 1979, Vietnamese gunboats fired shots at two oil-rig supply vessels of an American oil corporation, Amoco, in the Gulf of Tonkin, subsequently postponing the seismic survey plans in the area (Lauriat and Liu 1979). In face of Hanoi's hostility, Beijing increased its military presence in the Gulf of Tonkin and the Paracel Islands to defend its oil exploration program. It also took a variety of symbolic actions. In July 1979, the Civil Aviation Administration of China designated four "danger zones" near the southern part of Hainan Island and the northern part of the Paracel Islands. The danger zones covered parts of the high seas and cut across the important busy air corridor, Amber One. The proclamation was presumably intended to create trouble for Vietnam in the disputed area (Luu 1996: 72).

While Beijing was willing to damage its relations with Vietnam, it was aware of its possible side effects on China's relations with the other claimant countries. China's assertive behavior was therefore limited to its claim of sovereignty over the islands, and the sensitive issue of other maritime rights was avoided. A number of minor military incidents did occur in the South China Sea in the early 1980s.[18] Yet neither Beijing nor Hanoi let those incidents slip out of control.

---

[18] In March 1982, for instance, Vietnam arrested a number of Chinese armed vessels allegedly operating under the disguise of fishing boats on the Vietnamese side of the Gulf of Tonkin. China condemned the deliberate act as having aggravated Sino–Vietnamese tensions. Several days later, China retaliated by capturing a Vietnamese vessel in the vicinity of the Paracel Islands (Lo 1989: 119–20).

6.4   The Third Round of Dispute (1987–88)

After a decade of relative calm since the second round of dispute, the two sides
violently clashed again on Johnson Reef in the Spratly chain in March 1988.
China's controversial establishment of a physical presence on Fiery Cross Reef in
January preceded the March incident. This clash, which cost three Vietnamese
ships and 74 Vietnamese lives, was China's first armed conflict in the Spratlys.
From January to March, China occupied six submerged reefs by force. China's
surprise move clearly demonstrated its growing assertiveness and ambition in
dealing with the disputed islands. The virtual absence of commercial ties
between China and Vietnam provided little deterrence for the violent clash. The
third round of dispute could have been much worse, but did not escalate to a
larger military confrontation as seen in 1978–79. At the turn of the 1990s,
Sino–Vietnamese relations began to improve dramatically, primarily thanks to
Vietnam's loss of Soviet aid and its dire need for an alternative source of economic support. Official trade between China and Vietnam resumed in 1989 and
an agreement was reached in November 1991 to normalize their diplomatic
relationships.

6.4.1   Initiation and Escalation Phase

In the late 1970s and early 80s, the presence of Soviet naval forces based at Cam
Ranh Bay in Vietnam severely constrained China's strategic space in the South
China Sea. Yet with Soviet President Mikhail Gorbachev's retrenchment policy
from 1986, China became more assertive in the area.[19] Chinese decision in early
1987 to establish a permanent foothold on Fiery Cross Reef in the Spratlys was one

---

[19]The Soviet Union's serious domestic economic crises from the early 1980s made it even more
important for Moscow to improve Sino–Soviet relations. However, Sino–Soviet negotiation over
rapprochement during the Andropov and Chernenko periods had been unsuccessful due to China's
three preconditions for diplomatic rapprochement: (1) disengagement from the Vietnamese occupation of Cambodia; (2) Soviet withdrawal from Afghanistan; and (3) a reduction of troops along
the Sino-Soviet border. Beijing offered Moscow a choice between improved Sino–Soviet relations
(and thus weakened Soviet–Vietnamese relations) and the *status quo* in the Cambodian crisis.
Faced with economic collapse and political rebellion in the Communist regimes of Eastern Europe
and the Soviet Union, Gorbachev rose to the top leadership position in the Communist Party. His
response was *perestroika*, or democratic liberalization, a process that ultimately led to independence in the former Soviet bloc in Europe and the dissolution of the Soviet Union itself. Moscow's
hands-off policy in the March 1988 Sino–Vietnamese naval clash raised questions about the real
value of the 1978 Soviet–Vietnamese Treaty of Friendship and Cooperation (Ross 1991: 1174;
Austin 1998: 84; Sloreby 2002: 43).

of early indications of China's aggressive maritime and territorial policy during the waning Cold War years. At the fourteenth meeting of United Nations Educational, Scientific and Cultural Organization (UNESCO)'s Intergovernmental Oceanographic Commission (IOC), China agreed to establish five observation posts as part of a worldwide ocean survey, including one post in the Spratly Islands. The UNESCO project provided diplomatic cover for China's move into the South China Sea. In March 1987, UNESCO's IOC entrusted China with the task of building an observation post in the Spratlys. China began to conduct a series of surveys and naval patrols to prepare for the establishment of the post accordingly. In April, China chose Fiery Cross Reef as the prime candidate for the observation post not only because the size of the reef was large enough but also because the unoccupied reef was isolated from those features occupied by other claimant countries. China might have believed that the isolated location of Fiery Cross Reef and its UNESCO mandate would mitigate other claimants' concerns. China was proven utterly wrong as its move immediately increased tensions and created the conditions for the deadly clash with Vietnam. Between January and February, Vietnamese forces occupied several vacant reefs and began closely monitoring China's moves, which inevitably led to a series of confrontations as PLAN units sought to defend its new position (Fravel 2003: 388–95).

The first confrontation occurred on January 31, 1988 when two armed Vietnamese cargo ships with construction materials approached Fiery Cross Reef, apparently seeking to build some structures to symbolize Vietnamese claim. PLAN forces immediately intercepted those boats and turned them away. The second confrontation occurred on February 17 over Cuarteron Reef, which is located between Fiery Cross Reef and Vietnam's main operational base in the area, Spratly Island. A PLAN destroyer, escort, and transport ships were surveying the area when a Vietnamese mine-sweeper and armed freighter approached. Both sides dispatched landing parties, but the Vietnamese were forced to withdraw by their Chinese counterparts. The third and violent confrontation occurred on March 13–14. The clash focused on Johnson Reef to the east of Fiery Cross Reef. A PLAN guided missile escort ship was surveying the reef, when three Vietnamese ships entered the area. Seamen from both sides landed on the reef, while their ships confronting each other at sea. Once shots were fired on the reef, ships from both sides opened fire against each other. PLAN ships clearly overpowered Vietnamese forces, sinking all Vietnamese ships within half an hour and killing 74 Vietnamese lives. As a result of the victory, China occupied six reefs and atolls in the Spratly group by the end of 1988 (McGregor 1988: 16–8; Sheng 1995: 26; Chen 2000: 100–2; Fravel 2003: 395–6).

It became apparent that China was more assertive in its claims to the energy-rich South China Sea than ever before. For China, a growing sense of economic necessity as well as lost opportunity increased the value of establishing a physical presence in the Spratly Islands. With Deng's reform policy, China's economic center of gravity shifted from the hinterland back to the coastal provinces in the 1980s. In addition to increasing the importance of maritime defense, the reform policy also increased the value of securing access to maritime resources, especially hydrocarbon energy, to sustain economic development. It is no coincidence that offshore oil and gas exploration was one of the first projects that China opened to foreign participation in early 1979 (Lo 1989: 126; Chung 2004: 5–6).

Unlike in the 1970s, the rise of PLAN and the improvement of its long-range naval capabilities in the 1980s motivated Beijing to act more aggressively in the South China Sea. The factional interests of maritimists within the Chinese leadership also played a key role in defending claims to these islands. Indeed Chinese perceptions about the importance of naval strategy underwent a marked change in the 1980s, and Beijing was becoming increasingly committed to developing a bluewater navy. Most notably, Chief Naval Commander, Liu Huaqing used the mission of defending China's territory in the Spratlys to justify and fund PLAN's own modernization efforts, particularly the development of offshore, noncoastal capability. Liu oversaw changes in naval doctrine that stressed first the Soviet threat, and then the need to defend China's territorial claims offshore (McGregor 1988: 16–8; Garver 1992).[20]

The development of Hainan Island provided the combustible addition to the issue of the South China Sea. The island is only some 160 nm from Vietnam across the Gulf of Tonkin. In April 1988, the Chinese government passed a legislation turning Hainan into a separate province and also into a special economic zone. Concerned about the strategic vulnerability of Hainan in the event of a resumption of large-scale hostilities with Vietnam, Beijing increased the military presence on the island. Hanoi hoped that the Soviet naval presence in the region, and Soviet participation in Vietnam's search for oil in the South China Sea, would increase the risk for China of involving the Soviet Union in any fighting over the Spratlys. But the lack of Soviet support during the events of early 1988 gave little comfort to Hanoi, while encouraging Beijing to increase the pressure on Vietnam over the islands (McGregor 1988: 17–9; Catley and Keliat 1997: 79–82).[21]

---

[20]After Mao's death in 1976, the PLAN was instrumental in bringing reformist leaders into power and keeping them there. From 1977 to 1993, Deng Xiaoping was engaged in an exhausting struggle with his own army leadership and chose to strengthen the PLAN's power base in Beijing to counterbalance the army. It was no coincidence that Deng brought Liu Huaqing into the Central Military Commission (CMC) as a personal adviser in 1979. As hoped by Deng, Liu and his PLAN cohorts provided core support for all aspects of reform and opening, including the subordination of military strengthening to the larger task of economic reconstruction (Heginbotham 2002: 112–3).

[21]It was almost impossible for Hanoi to physically challenge Beijing given the former's limited military capability and enormous economic problems at home. Between 1979 and 1988 there had been a substantial shift in the relative power of the two countries. In the 1980s Vietnam was no match at all in fighting a naval war against China that had reportedly deployed 25 submarines, five destroyers, and 200 coastal attack crafts near the disputed area. Moreover, Vietnam had demobilized half of its armed forces since 1987, from about 1.2 million to 600,000 soldiers. Thus China's 260,000 PLAN far outranked that of Vietnam which had mere 31,000 personnel in the navy and naval infantry (Catley and Keliat 1997: 96).

Finally, the years from the late 1970s to late 1980s during which Vietnam closely followed the Soviet economic model had the detrimental effect on Vietnam's international trade. Biased towards autarky, it was an inward-looking system that tended to limit Vietnam's economic relations with the world outside the Soviet bloc. Unsurprisingly, the official bilateral trade between China and Vietnam dwindled to nil, although border trade did begin to resume on an informal basis, mostly by barter and on the backs of porters who walked across the border (Sharpe 2005: 150–8; see also Table 6.1). From a liberal peace perspective, the virtual absence of commercial ties between China and Vietnam provided little deterrence to the violent clash in 1988. Hence a certain pattern of conflict behavior can be detected: neither China nor Vietnam was constrained to escalate the island dispute to a higher level of hostility, as in the previous cases.

6.4.2 The Advent of Sino–Vietnamese Rapprochement

An outburst of mutual accusations followed the 1988 naval clash. Vietnam feared that China would continue to invade the Vietnamese–held Spratlys as it had invaded the Paracels. Yet this did not happen. If China had invaded the Vietnamese-held Spratlys, it would have met with stronger resistance than in 1974. At the same time, Beijing had been enjoying the benefits of being on good relations with Washington for over a decade and did not want to risk the fragile relationship breaking down at the edges of the South China Sea (Tønnesson 2003: 60–1).

The crackdown in Tiananmen Square in 1989 severely weakened China's position in the South China Sea. In particular, the PLAN was in no position to maintain its assertive maritime policy in the South China Sea. After conservative reactions in early 1989 threatened the viability of the reform effort, Deng Xiaoping re-enlisted Liu Huaqing and other naval officers to protect the reform agenda. Yet later that year, the Tiananmen Square demonstrations and the ensuing military crackdown gave the political initiative to the conservatives, while edging reformists and maritimists out of key positions. The Tiananmen incident indeed brought into question the loyalty of the PLAN when called on to suppress liberal dissents (Heginbotham 2002: 114–5).

In addition to, and probably more important than, the political unrest, the macroeconomic stability of China came under heavy pressure. Reform measures initiated in 1978–79 raised national income, but also unleashed pent-up demand among the population. By 1989, there emerged a growing criticism of the reform process and the speed at which China was opening to foreign investment and influence. Fearing social unrest, the Beijing authorities deferred or reversed market-oriented decisions. But their efforts to soft-land the economy soon resulted in falling output, deflationary pressures, and rising inventories. The state owned enterprises (SOEs) were hard hit, suffering a severe decline in revenues as people deferred purchases. All these provided the socio-economic backdrop for the conservative backlash at the turn of the 1990s (Deans 2000: 122; Pham 2003: 160–1).

Deng, seeing his reform legacy in danger, came out of retirement in 1992 and exerted all of his leverage to stack the CMC with sympathetic figures. He first promoted Liu (aged 76) to the top uniformed position within the CMC, and, in an effort to bring in the PLAN as a counterpoise to the army, appointed six naval officers as full or alternate members of the party's Central Committee – more than any other branch of the military.[22] In his famous 1992 southern China tour, Deng reaffirmed the government's commitment to deepening and expanding economic reforms with full speed even at the price of occasional macroeconomic instability. The Chinese Constitution was amended in 1993, stating that the government's goal was to establish a "socialist market economy," and that the nonstate sector was an essential part of the economy, along with the state sector. The constitutional amendment thus made it official that the government no longer views the market system as incompatible with socialism (Pham 2003: 161).

Under these circumstances, Hanoi had neither intention nor capability to escalate the Spratly dispute. From the start of the 1980s, the failure of Vietnam's first post-Vietnam War five-year plan (1976–80) forced its leadership to consider alternative approaches to improving Vietnam's economic performance. The VCP adopted reforms in 1979 to allow private production and trading of goods. Despite incentive measures partially implemented to spur production in the agricultural and industrial sectors, the heavily regulated economy was quickly beset by spiraling inflation. The annual inflation rate reached 34.9% in 1981 and 82.6% in 1982, while grain and food prices increased by 96% in 1982. The hyperinflation quickly wiped out the effect of wage increases in the public sector and produced a continuing drop in the standard of living of government officials, whose support was critical to the regime. In 1982, a backlash by conservative factions in the party resuscitated Communist orthodoxy. But again, by 1986, the economic crisis reached its breaking point, forcing the party authorities to embrace reform. With General Secretary Le Duan's death in July 1986 and the VCP's Sixth Party Congress in December 1986, the painful and slow process of socio-economic reform resumed. At the December VCP Congress, the party leadership underwent the largest shake-up in its history. The resignation of three senior politburo members inevitably resulted in leadership instability (Alpert and Sanders 2005: 36).

Nevertheless, the embrace of *Doi Moi* (meaning renovation, renewal, or reform) marked a dramatic departure from an orthodox communist ideology to a more pragmatic socialist market economy. *Doi Moi* allowed currency and some commodity prices to float freely and gave more autonomy to state-operated enterprises. What Hanoi needed at the end of the 1980s was peace and stability so that it could focus on its economic reform (Easterline 1988: 89; Williams 1992: 25; Catley and Keliat 1997: 96; Sloreby 2002: 42). Bold and thorough steps of *Doi Moi* began to bear fruits from 1992 when the economy grew rapidly and the hyperinflation was finally curbed.

---

[22] While the PLAN was useful in staving off a final surge by conservative revolutionary figures in 1992–93, the death or retirement of those figures in the mid-1990s eliminated one political motivation for naval promotion (Heginbotham 2002: 115).

Trade and foreign investment dramatically increased, especially after the U.S. lifted its economic embargo in February 1994. During the period of 1976–91, GDP grew at 4.1%, which was equal to the growth rate of the 1955–75 period. By contrast, the GDP growth rate jumped to 8.8% during 1991–95 (Tran 2003: 15–21). During 1991–95, Vietnam's total exports increased from $2.2 billion to $5.6 billion, while its total imports from $2.5 billion to $8.4 billion. For the same period, the ratio of disbursed FDI to GDP rose from 2.4 to 12.9%.

At the turn of the 1990s, Sino–Vietnamese relations began to improve dramatically (Amer 1994; Thayer 1994, 1995). The immediate reason why this process of rapprochement started was Vietnam's loss of Soviet aid and support. Despite great economic difficulties after its invasion of Cambodia in 1978, Vietnam had been able to survive its isolation mainly because of Soviet aid. Yet, when Gorbachev scaled down Soviet aid and curtailed the deployments of the Soviet Navy, Vietnam found itself without any powerful allies.[23] Hanoi had no other choice but to withdraw forces from Cambodia.[24] With the aid from and trade with Eastern Europe dwindling, Hanoi sought a resumption of official trade with China as well. Resolving the Cambodian conflict facilitated the contacts between China and Vietnam. Roads and paths in the border area were cleared off mines. The normalization process began with low-level contacts in the mid-1980s and expanded to high-level meetings from early 1989. In November 1991, Beijing and Hanoi finally signed a normalization treaty, paving the way for closer economic ties between the two countries (Amer 1994: 365–6; Sharpe 2005: 158).

Once China and Vietnam normalized both state-to-state and party-to-party relations, their relationship began to improve with increasing economic and political ties. Neither Beijing nor Hanoi allowed its foreign policies to be dictated by ideological concerns any longer. Chinese leaders were more interested in economic growth and development than anything else. Vietnamese leaders had no alternative but to follow China's footsteps.

---

[23] As noted previously, Soviet aid in loans and various other forms was of great importance to Vietnam. Furthermore, the bulk of Vietnam's foreign trade was carried out within the Soviet bloc. Yet the network of economic relationships within the Soviet bloc began to unravel in 1989, and by the end of 1991 Soviet aid had almost disappeared. Barter trade agreements with Eastern European countries were in many cases cancelled, and many others simply became inactive. Soviet and Eastern European technical advisers were recalled as well (Sharpe 2005: 151–2).

[24] The costly venture in Cambodia had become a major cause of Vietnam's diplomatic isolation for a decade. On May 26, 1988, a joint statement by Hanoi and Phnom Penh announced a proposed withdrawal of 50,000 Vietnamese troops from Cambodia. In addition, Vietnam promised to dismantle its military high command in Cambodia, while leaving the reassignment of the remaining troops to Cambodian command. The joint announcement reflected a compromising attitude from Vietnam towards China. At the same time, its timing marked only 11 days after Moscow started withdrawal of troops from Afghanistan, and three days prior to the U.S.–Soviet summit meeting in Moscow (Sloreby 2002: 46).

6.5 Deepening Sino–Vietnamese Rapprochement and Its Prospects

In the early post-normalization era, China and Vietnam continued to engage in heated polemics over the disputed islands. Yet none of the confrontations escalated beyond accusations, claims, counterclaims, and minor displays of military force.

Most notably, tensions heated up close to the boiling point in 1992. In March, less than a month after the Territorial Sea Law's declaration, China continued its expansionist activities in the Spratlys by occupying Da Lac Reef. Vietnam promptly protested China's move, demanding that the Chinese remove their forces from the disputed reef. In May, China issued a concession for oil exploration within the Vietnamese claimed western part of the Spratly area to an American oil company, Crestone. In June, China sent a drill ship into Vietnamese territorial waters. In July, Vietnam claimed to have seized three Chinese fishing boats that had violated its territorial waters near Bach Long Vi Island. In response, two Chinese ships fired on a Vietnamese border-patrol boat as it approached for inspection. In October, Vietnam rejected a Chinese claim to traditional fishing rights in waters outside each other's 12 nm territorial sea. At the same time, Vietnam gave notice of an invitation to bid on Gulf of Tonkin oil acreage at conferences in London and Houston, including areas in the vicinity of China's Hainan Island. The resolution of South China Sea issues was set high on the agenda for the December 1992 talks in Vietnam between Premiers Li Peng and Vo Van Kiet. Regarding the Crestone concession, China proposed that Vietnam take the continental shelf area between China's traditional claim line and the western edge of the concession and that China retain the Crestone area. Yet Vietnam rejected China's proposal as unfair and inequitable. Tensions continued to rise even just before Chinese President Jiang Zemin's November 1994 visit to Vietnam. Hanoi angrily accused Beijing of a number of transgressions into its claimed waters in the Gulf of Tonkin. Eventually, however, both sides showed flexibility with Jiang and VCP leader Do Muoi both agreeing to shelve their differences and to negotiate a long-term solution to the Spratly dispute (Amer 1994: 367; Valencia 1995: 31–8; Kim 2000: 71).

The common Sino–Vietnamese interest in the existence and future success of the socialist market economy has united the two countries in a shared destiny. Both countries would most likely want to secure a peaceful management of their territorial disputes because of their broader negative consequences: a regional conflict would divert foreign investors to other countries, block international trade, and slow down economic growth, thus risking the internal stability of each country. Both parties have made economic growth the basis of regime legitimacy. Neither side can thus stop or reverse the economic reforms that have led to rapid economic growth. A reduction in the pace of economic reforms would most likely to lead to economic decline, which could in turn eliminate the basis of the regime legitimacy.

Indeed, the pacific influence of economic interdependence has recently become more visible in the South China Sea. Sino–Vietnamese economic ties are improving, although the total volume remains low in absolute terms.

Bilateral trade tripled from $1.1 billion in 1996 to $3 billion in 2001 and reached $4.6 billion in 2003. Vietnam exports mainly farm and marine products and oil and gas to China, while imports from China include machinery, fertilizers, and consumer durables. China also provides low-interest loans to upgrade factories built by the Chinese in Vietnam (mainly iron and steel plants). Altogether, China has invested $330 million in 320 joint venture projects in Vietnam.[25] Even though China is far from being Vietnam's largest trading partner and overall trade with Vietnam means relatively little for China, the cross-border trade is of special significance for the border provinces (Thayer 1995: 197; Ma 1999: 57; Shambaugh 2004/05: 81).[26]

Not surprisingly, tensions surrounding the Spratly Islands have eased considerably in recent years. In February 1999, Beijing and Hanoi signed the Agreement on Friendship, Good Neighborliness, and Longstanding Stability. The signing of the Land Border Treaty in December 1999, as well as the two treaties (one on fishery cooperation and the other on maritime delimitation) of the Gulf of Tonkin in December 2000, is a strong manifestation of improved relations (Sloreby 2002: 5).[27] Furthermore, during a state visit to Hanoi by Jiang Zemin in February 2002, the two countries agreed to a framework that consists of the following four objectives: (1) to build political exchanges at a variety of levels; (2) to share their experiences regarding economic development; (3) to encourage youth exchanges; and (4) to strengthen bilateral cooperation in international and regional forums (Shambaugh 2004/05: 81).

Sino–Vietnamese rapprochement reflects a broader trend in the region. Vietnam has sought to build alliance ties with its Southeast Asian neighbors in order to compensate for the security deficit in the post-Cold War era. In July 1992, Vietnam

---

[25]In 1988 the Soviet Union accounted for 40% of Vietnam's exports and 65% of imports. The collapse of those economies forced Vietnam to quickly move into other markets. By 1999, Vietnam's dealings with countries in the Asia–Pacific region accounted for 60% of trade, including ASEAN countries, which represented about 18% of the total. As of 2002 about 35% of Vietnam's export trade was with East Asian countries, of which the top partners were Japan (14.9%), Australia (7.6%), China (6.6%), and Singapore (5.5%). Vietnam's leading importers are also from Asia: South Korea (12.7%), China (12.2%), Japan (12.1%), Singapore (11.8%), and Thailand (5.4%) (Sharpe 2005: 144–57).

[26]The border trade has done much to meet consumer demand in Northern Vietnam. It is of considerable political importance for China as well. Development in the provinces of Guangxi and Yunnan, due to the increased Sino–Vietnamese border trade, supports Beijing's claim and propaganda that interior provinces as well as coastal areas are benefiting from economic reforms (Sutter 1993: 35).

[27]When the work to delimit the border according to the 1999 border treaty began in December 2001, the Vietnamese public discovered that some villages considered Vietnamese seemed to be ending up on the Chinese side. This led to widespread protests among overseas Vietnamese, arrests and trials of the most active Vietnamese dissidents, and problems inside the VCP. Dissidents and overseas Vietnamese also criticized the Gulf of Tonkin treaties, claiming that the government had given over to China thousands of square kilometers of Vietnamese maritime territory (Tønnesson 2003: 62–5).

signed the ASEAN Treaty of Amity and Cooperation and was granted observer status within the organization. Vietnam normalized relations with Japan in 1993 and with the U.S. in 1995. It took part in founding the ASEAN Regional Forum (ARF) in 1994 and obtained full membership of ASEAN in 1995 (Womack 1996; 1997; Nguyen 2002; Sloreby 2002). At the turn of the new millennium, engagement between China and ASEAN has also been truly impressive. Negotiations for a code of conduct in the region began in 1999, following a proposal by the Philippines. At their summit in Phnom Penh, Cambodia in November 2002, ASEAN and China signed a Declaration on the Conduct of Parties in the South China Sea, with the aim of preventing conflict and promoting cooperation in the region. During the negotiations for the code of conduct, ASEAN wished to prohibit all occupation of new islands and improvements to existing structures. In the face of strong Chinese opposition, however, the negotiating parties simply agreed to exercise self-restraint in the conduct of activities such as inhabiting presently uninhabited islands, reefs, shoals, cays, and other features. Although this declaration did not establish a legally binding code of conduct, it represents a significant step forward (Tønnesson 2003: 55–62).[28]

On the one hand, overlapping maritime claims still overshadow the improved Sino–Vietnamese relations, as the recent dispute over Hanoi-tendered, multinational-led naturalgas project in the Nam Con Son Basin showed. The distant basin near the Spratly archipelago became a bone of contention between China and Vietnam in 2007.[29] The flare-up strongly indicates that Beijing's soft-power overtures towards Southeast Asia can be hardening when it comes to energy-security concerns. China's insistence on resolving the territorial and maritime issues on a bilateral basis – rather than in a multilateral manner – has highlighted the difficult position in which Vietnam as well as other Southeast Asian countries are placed.

On the other hand, despite the high stakes, the 2007 flare-up between Beijing and Hanoi did not escalate into full blown diplomatic skirmishes as past contested claims have. Instead of exchanging hostile rhetoric and taking physical action

---

[28] At the same summit, China and ASEAN also signed three other landmark agreements: (1) the Joint Declaration on Cooperation in the Field of Nontraditional Security Issues; (2) the Framework Agreement on Comprehensive Economic Cooperation; and (3) the Memorandum of Understanding on Agricultural Cooperation. At their 2003 summit in Bali, Indonesia, China formally became the first nonASEAN state to sign the ASEAN's Treaty of Amity and Cooperation and subsequently signed the Joint Declaration on Strategic Partnership for Peace and Prosperity with ASEAN, which addresses a wide range of political, social, economic, and security issues. At their 2004 summit, Chinese Premier Wen Jiabao proposed two further initiatives: (1) to build upon the 2001 Framework Agreement on Economic Cooperation and Establishment of the China-ASEAN Free Trade Area to create a similar free trade area in East Asia; and (2) to establish an East Asian community to discuss political and other issues (Shambaugh 2004/05: 75–6).

[29] The contested gas fields in the Nam Con Son Basin about 370 km off Vietnam's southeast coast, are both run by British energy giant BP through a production sharing contract with state-owned PetroVietnam and in partnership with American oil firm ConocoPhillips (Symon 2007).

against each other, the two sides discussed the issue at a regular annual meeting between senior foreign ministry officials from ASEAN countries and China in light of the 2002 Declaration on the Conduct of Parties in the South China Sea. Indeed, over the past several years, China's soft-power strategy has remarkably lessened the uncertainties in dealing separately with China. In line with China's regional economic charm offensive, Beijing and Hanoi have recent years launched "friendship and cooperation" meetings, including regular reciprocal visits from each country's top government leaders. Improved political ties have paved the way for Vietnam to develop new transport infrastructure in its northern regions, designed to better connect its manufacturing base with China's booming southern provinces (Symon 2007).

6.6   Conclusion

This chapter focused on the Sino–Vietnam dyad vis-à-vis the dispute over the Paracel and Spratly Islands. The Sino–Vietnamese relationship has been imbued with widespread suspicion, painful memories, and lingering tensions. Much of this has been related to the sovereignty question in the South China Sea. In the eyes of China and Vietnam, the dispute over the Paracel and Spratly Islands has not been an isolated issue from the very beginning. Since the early 1970s, the South China Sea has been marked as a battlefield for a series of military skirmishes between the two longtime rivals. The most serious incident took place in 1974 when China invaded and captured the western Paracel Islands from South Vietnam. In 1978–79, combined with fluid geopolitics, bilateral differences over the Spratly Islands resulted in a large-scale border dispute between the pair. In early 1988, Chinese and Vietnamese naval forces violently clashed again over the occupation of several reefs in the Spratly chain. A number of minor confrontations continued in the 1990s, but none of them escalated beyond accusations, claims, counterclaims, minor displays of military force, and seizures of civilians.

  For China, the Paracel and Spratly Islands provide strategic foothold and a maritime buffer through which the mainland can be protected. The maritime resources, particularly hydrocarbon energy, in the vicinity of these offshore islands have also become essential for China's economic prosperity. For Vietnam, its top natural resources are oil and gas. Despite a bloated bureaucracy and corruption, foreign investors from all over the world have rushed to Vietnam in recent years to explore its continental shelf. Oil and gas sales have been one of the engines powering Vietnam's growth and high export sales. For both China and Vietnam, the strategic and economic value of the South China Sea thus looms particularly large during a global energy shortage.

  Set against the backdrop of growing resource competition, I showed that the territorial bargaining game approach can explain the transition between, and conclusion of, three different rounds of the Paracel and Spratly dispute. Unstable geopolitical situations often contributed to the clash of rival nationalisms between China and Vietnam, thereby leading to the recurring rounds of island dispute. The lack of deterring economic forces during the Cold War period further disturbed the already troubled water in the South China Sea. Yet the abrupt collapse of the Cold War fundamentally changed the ways in which Chinese and Vietnamese elites devise their strategies vis-à-vis the territorial and maritime disputes. Most importantly, the pacific influence of increasingly salient economic interdependence between China and Vietnam has prevented the island issues from spinning out of control since the two sides normalized their diplomatic relations in 1991.

The main reason why Beijing has seemingly stopped pursuing its sovereignty claims more aggressively is probably that its eyes are now fixed on bigger goals. China wants continued economic growth, access to the world's major export markets, and reunification with Taiwan. This means that Beijing has to avoid conflict with its neighbors, particularly its longtime archrival Vietnam. Within this context, China has recognized that it is not in its national interest to confront Vietnam and other ASEAN countries directly. In line with Beijing's regional economic charm offensive, diplomatic relations have warmed and economic ties have blossomed in the once conflict-ridden area.

For Vietnam and other ASEAN countries alike, China's rise is inevitable and the best strategy by which to hedge against potentially disruptive or domineering behavior is to engage China in as many ways as possible. Yet it remains to be seen whether China's efforts to improve its ties with Vietnam and other ASEAN countries truly reflect fundamental compromises that China has chosen to make in limiting its own hegemonic ambition for the sake of greater regional interdependence and cooperation.

Throughout much of the 1970s and 1980s the Soviet Navy, based at Vietnam's Cam Ranh Bay, and the U.S. Navy at Subic Bay in the Philippines kept the balance of power in the region. But with Soviet military might now defunct and the U.S. naval presence in the region significantly reduced, an increasingly assertive and self-confident China poses both a challenge to and an opportunity for its neighbors. With China continuing to build up its armed forces faster than any other countries in East Asia, it is unlikely that Beijing is in any mood to give up its unresolved territorial claims. Yet Beijing has apparently shown a willingness to discuss joint development of the resources near the offshore islands. Now it appears that the ball is in ASEAN's court as it is struggling to form a united front vis-à-vis joint resource development.

To conclude, overlapping territorial and maritime claims still overshadow the improved relations among the littoral states in the South China Sea. Yet within the context of a shifting regional balance of power with rising China at its heart, deepening economic ties have paved the way for those countries to lay a bridge over the troubled South China Sea.

References

Alpert WT, Sanders S (2005) Recent economic history: A stalled expansion. In: Alpert WT (ed) The Vietnamese economy and its transformation to an open market system. M.E. Sharpe, New York
Amer R (1994) Sino-Vietnamese normalization in the light of the crisis of the late 1970s. Pacific Affairs 67(3):357–383

Austin G (1998) China's ocean frontier: International law, military force and national development. Allen and Unwin, Canberra

Austin G (2003) Unwanted entanglement: the Philippines' Spratly policy as a case study in conflict enhancement? Security Dialogue 34(1):41–54

Burgess PJ (2003) The politics of the South China Sea: Territoriality and international law. Security Dialogue 34(1):7–10

Castro RCD (1998) The controversy in the Spratlys: Exploring the limits to ASEAN's engagement policy. Issues and Studies 34(9):95–123

Catley R, Keliat M (1997) Spratlys: The dispute in the South China Sea. Ashgate, Brookfield

Chen H (2000) The PRC's South China Sea policy and strategies of occupation in the Paracel and Spratly islands. Issues and Studies 36(4):95–131

Cole BD (2000) China's maritime strategy. In: Puska SM (ed) People's liberation army after next. Strategic Studies Institute, Carlisle

Do K, Kane J (1988) Counterpart: A South Vietnamese naval officer's war. Naval Institute Press, Annapolis

Duiker WJ (1995) Vietnam, revolution in transition. Westview Press, Boulder

Easterline JH (1988) Vietnam in 1987: Steps towards rejuvenation. Asian Survey 28(1):86–94

Fravel MT (2003) The long march to peace: Explaining China's settlement of territorial disputes. PhD Dissertation in Political Science, Stanford University, Stanford

Garver JW (1992) China's push through the South China Sea: The Interaction of bureaucratic and national interests. China Quarterly 132:999–1028

Goldstein A (1997/1998) Great expectations: Interpreting China's arrival. International Security 22(3):36–73

Gottleib TM (1977) Chinese foreign policy, factionalism and the origins of the strategic triangle. Rand Corporation, Santa Monica

Gurtov M, Hwang B (1998) China's security: The new roles of the military. Lynne Rienner Publishers, Boulder

Heder SP (1981) The Kampuchean-Vietnamese conflict. In: Elliott DWP (ed) The third Indochina conflict. Westview Press, Boulder

Heginbotham E (2002) The fall and rise of navies in East Asia: Military organizations, domestic politics, and grand strategy. International Security 27(2):86–125

Kim D (2000) Naval strategy in Northeast Asia: Geo-strategic goals, policies, and prospects. Frank Cass, London

Kimura T (1989) The Vietnamese economy 1975–86: Reforms and international relations. Institute of Developing Economies, Tokyo

Lauriat G, Liu M (1979) Pouring trouble on oily waters. Far Eastern Economic Review 28:19–21

Leifer M (1978) International straits of the world: Malacca, Singapore, and Indonesia. Sitjhoff and Noordhorf, The Netherlands

Leifer M (1979) Post mortem on the third Indochina war. The World Today 249–258

Leifer M (1984) The security of sea-lanes in Southeast Asia. In: O'Neil R (ed) Security in East Asia. International Institute of Strategic Studies, London

Lin C (1997) Taiwan's South China Sea policy. Asian Survey 37(4):323–339

Lo C (1989) China's policy towards territorial disputes: The case of the South China Sea islands. Routledge, New York

Luu VL (1996) The Sino-Vietnamese difference on the Hoang Sa and Truong Sa archipelagoes. Gioi Publishers, Hanoi

Ma L (1999) China and Vietnam: Coping with the threat of peaceful evolution. In: Thayer CA, Amer R (eds) Vietnamese foreign policy in transition. Seng Lee Press, Singapore

Manning RA (2000) The Asian energy factor: Myths and dilemmas of energy, security, and the pacific future. Palgrave, New York

McGregor C (1988) The Sino-Vietnamese relationship and the Soviet Union. Adelphi Paper 232, International Institute for Strategic Studies, London

Muller DG (1983) China as a maritime power. Westview Press, Boulder

Nguyen VT (2002) Vietnam-ASEAN cooperation after the Cold War and the continued search for a theoretical framework. Contemporary Southeast Asia 24(1):106–120

Nordhaug K (2001) Explaining Taiwan's policies in the South China Sea, 1988–99. The Pacific Review 14(4):487–508

Park C (1978) The South China Sea disputes: Who owns the islands and the natural resources. Ocean Development and International Law Journal 1:27–59

Peng Er L (1996) Japan and the Spratlys dispute. Asian Survey 36(1):995–1010

Pham T (2003) The Chinese economic model: Some tentative conclusions for Vietnam. In: Binh T, Pham CD (eds) The Vietnamese economy: Awakening the dormant dragon. RoutledgeCurzon, London

Polomka P (1978) Ocean politics in Southeast Asia. Institute of Southeast Asian Studies, Singapore

Rosenberg D (2002) The rise of China: Implications for security flashpoint and resource politics in the South China Sea. In: Humphrey C (ed) The rise of China in Asia: The security implications. U.S. Army War College Press, Carlisle

Ross RS (1991) China and the Cambodian peace process: The value of coercive diplomacy. Asian Survey 31(12):1170–1185

Samuels MS (1982) Contest for the South China Sea. Methuen, New York

Segal G (1985) Defending China. Oxford University Press, London

Shambaugh D (2004/2005) China engages Asia: Reshaping the regional order. International Security 29(3):64–99

Sharpe W (2005) Foreign investment and trade. In: Alpert WT (ed) The Vietnamese economy and its transformation to an open market system. M.E. Sharpe, New York

Sheng L (1995) Beijing and the Spratlys. Issues and Studies 31(7):18–45

Siddayao CM (1978) The offshore petroleum resources of Southeast Asia: Potential conflict situations and related economic considerations. Oxford University Press, Kuala Lumpur

Sloreby SJ (2002) Explaining improvement of bilateral relations: The case of Vietnam's relations with China, 19852001. Mater's Thesis in Political Science, University of Oslo

Snyder S (1996) The South China Sea dispute prospects for preventive diplomacy. Special Report, 18, United Sates Institute of Peace, Washington, DC

Sutter KM (1993) China's Vietnam policy: The road to normalization and prospects for the Sino-Vietnamese relationship. Journal of Northeast Asian Studies 12(2):21–47

Symon A (2007) China, Vietnam spar over gas. Asian Times Online, http://www.atimes.com/atimes/Southeast_Asia/IE01Ae01.html, Accessed 10 February 2009

Thayer CA (1994) Sino-Vietnamese relations: The interplay of ideology and national interest. Asian Survey 34(6):513–528

Thayer CA (1995) Vietnam's strategic readjustment. In: Harris S, Klinthworth G (eds) China as a great power: Myths, realities and challenges in the Asia-Pacific region. St. Martin's Press, New York

Tønnesson S (2003) Sino-Vietnamese rapprochement and the South China Sea irritant. Security Dialogue 34(1):55–70

Tønnesson S (2006) The South China Sea in the age of European decline. Modern Asian Studies 40(1):1–57

Townsend-Gault I (1998) Preventive diplomacy and pro-activity in the South China Sea. Contemporary Southeast Asia 20(2):171–191

Tran VT (2003) Economic development in Vietnam during the second half of the twentieth century: How to avoid the danger of lagging behind. In: Binh T, Pham CD (eds) The Vietnamese economy: Awakening the dormant dragon. Routledge Curzon, London

Tretiak D (1979) China's Vietnam war and its consequences. China Quarterly 80:740–767

Valencia MJ (1995) China and the South China Sea disputes: Conflicting claims and potential solutions in the South China Sea. Adelphi Paper 298, The International Institute for Strategic Studies, London

Valencia MJ, Van Dyke JM, Ludwig NA (1997) Sharing the resources of the South China Sea.
    University of Hawaii Press, Honolulu
Vo NT (1990) Vietnam's economic policy since 1975. Institute of Southeast Asian Studies,
    Singapore
Williams MC (1992) Vietnam at the crossroads. Chatham House Papers, Pinter Publisher,
    London
Womack B (1996) Vietnam in 1995, Successes in peace. Asian Survey 36(1):73–82
Womack B (1997) Vietnam in 1996, Reform immobilism. Asian Survey 37(1):79–87

Chapter 7
Maritime Regime Building in East Asia

7.1 Introduction

From an institutionalist point of view, boundary arrangements can increase certainty, reduce transactions costs, and thus facilitate international cooperation. Yet the task of delimiting national boundaries, whether land or maritime, is often time consuming, requiring strong political will and tireless diplomatic efforts of all neighboring states with conflicting claims. In the process of boundary delimitation, some important political decisions have to be made in each stage. Bernard H. Oxman (1994/1995: 255) identifies four important political decisions to be made in relation to boundaries, unless military options are brought to table: (1) the decision to negotiate; (2) the decision to propose a particular boundary; (3) the decision to make concessions with a view to reaching agreement; and (4) the decision to agree on a particular boundary. At the same time, all negotiating parties must take into account the effect of any proposal they make on their relations with their neighbors. Though selfish and conflictual unless given appropriate conditions under which to cooperate, states, both small and large, are often concerned about the reputation costs that would be incurred should they fail to comply with international rules and norms. Unless they are willing to use unrelated resources (either as carrots or as sticks) to obtain a favorable boundary, their proposal must be based upon more than unrestrained self-interest. The search for a proposal that has a plausible legal and equitable foundation will thus entail (Oxman 1994/1995: 261).

Not all of these conditions are currently present in littoral East Asian states. The maritime boundary delimitation is further complicated by the existence of islands in the disputed area. As we have seen in the previous chapters, "sovereignty" over disputed islands, if granted to the challenger country, would possibly enable the challenger country to claim "sovereign rights" over the continental shelf and/or the EEZ around the islands. This would likely give the challenger country exclusive economic rights to a significant portion of the area if the area is an enclosed or semi-enclosed sea such as the East Sea/Sea of Japan, the East

M.G. Koo, *Island Disputes and Maritime Regime Building in East Asia*,
The Political Economy of the Asia Pacific,
DOI 10.1007/978-0-387-89670-0_7, © Springer Science+Business Media, LLC 2009

China Sea, and the South China Sea.[1] In contrast, from the target country's perspective, the disputed islands under its sovereignty would likewise entitle the target country to an EEZ that would extend the country's sovereign rights, substantially encroaching on the challenger country's continental shelf and/or EEZ.

Although a host of measures have been utilized to deal with delimitation of the territorial sea, EEZ, and continental shelf between states with opposite or adjacent coasts the issues in contention are very much interwoven, and the positions of the contestant parties remain widely apart in East Asia. Under these circumstances, the chances of mutually agreeable boundary delimitation seem slim at best. To better explain the context in which these conflicting claims are taking place, we need to understand the key legal regimes of maritime jurisdiction established by the 1982 UNCLOS. In addition, we need to consider various methods of boundary delimitation such as the median- or equidistance-line approach and the equitable principle. This discussion forms the legal groundwork on which to design an institutional mechanism for a more stable and prosperous regional maritime order.

In the meantime, East Asian maritime issues have become multilateral, rather than purely bilateral, issues. They are interconnected with each other, possibly making bilateral solutions contradictory and conflicting with one another. For instance, interplay occurs between various bilateral fishery relations in East Asia. Korea–Japan fishery relations have implications for Sino–Korean and Sino–Japanese fishery relations because the three countries share the same maritime area and marine resources. It is no wonder that South Korea has expressed its deep concerns about the 1997 Sino–Japanese fishery agreement, particularly the northern-limit line of their joint fishing area, which overlaps with the Korea–Japan joint fishing zone in the East China Sea. By the same token, China has lodged a strong protest against the new fishery agreement concluded between South Korea and Japan in 1998 for illegally undermining China's sovereign rights in the border areas allegedly subject to trilateral consultations.

As a result, many states have found the regional level of organization to be an appropriate response to the challenges of delimiting maritime boundaries and managing ocean resources (Andresen 1989; Chircop 1989; Haas 1992, 2000; Vander Zwaag and Johnston 1998). Some arrangements have been independent in the sense of being created within a region, while others have operated under the auspices of broader global regimes. The list of substantive issues has been extended to include living and nonliving resource management, scientific research, maritime transport, military activities, environmental protection, and more broadly defined regional economic cooperation (Saunders 2001: 3–4). Yet seen in comparative regional perspective,

---

[1]The terms "enclosed or semi-enclosed seas" is defined in Article 121 of UNCLOS as "a gulf, basin or sea surrounded by two or more States and connected to another sea or the ocean by a narrow outlet or consisting entirely or primarily of the territorial seas and exclusive economic zone of two or more coastal States."

East Asia has the most pronounced "organization gap" in the area of regional maritime cooperation.

In this chapter, I explore key legal issues under the UNCLOS regime with which East Asian countries are currently grappling. Then I critically review some prominent modes of institutional cooperation with a focus on joint development regimes. From this conceptual basis, I assess the past bilateral dispute resolution between East Asian countries. Finally, I outline the ways in which effective provisional measures can be extended beyond bilateral boundaries and harmonious regional and multilateral solutions can be devised.

7.2   Maritime Zones and Delimitation: A Legal Perspective

7.2.1   UNCLOS Revisited: EEZ and Continental Shelf

As discussed in the previous chapters, the already complex maritime space in East Asia has become much more complicated since the claimant countries began ratifying the UNCLOS in the mid-1990s and then subsequently claimed their respective EEZs and continental shelves. In addition, the adoption of straight baselines for territorial seas and other maritime zones has made the already daunting task of delimiting maritime boundaries much more difficult.

The major innovation in the UNCLOS was the creation of EEZ, which combines sovereign rights with the continental shelf with sovereign rights over the water column beyond the territorial sea. It resulted from a compromise between those who wanted more control over offshore areas and those who wanted to retain as large an area as possible as high seas. According to UNCLOS Article 57, a coastal state can claim an EEZ extending up to 200 nm from the baseline. Within this zone, the coastal state has "sovereign rights" – as compared to "sovereignty" – to explore, exploit, conserve, and manage the natural resources, whether living or nonliving, of the water column, sea floor, and the seabed. A coastal state also has jurisdiction in the EEZ with regard to building and maintaining artificial islands, conducting scientific research, and protecting the marine environment (Article 56(1)). However, a coastal state cannot restrict the freedom of navigation within the EEZ, flight above it, or the laying of submarine pipelines or cables through it (Article 58(1)).

Article 76(1) of UNCLOS defines a coastal state's continental shelf as "the seabed and subsoil of the submarine areas that extend beyond its territorial sea throughout the natural prolongation of its land territory to the outer edge of the continental margin, or to a distance of 200 nautical miles from the baselines from which the breadth of the territorial sea is measured and where the outer edge of the continental margin does not extend up to that distance." Regardless of the physical extent of the margin, state jurisdiction "shall not exceed 350 nautical miles from the baselines from which the breadth of the territorial sea is measured or shall not exceed 100 nautical miles from the 2,500 meter isobath, which is a line connecting the depth of 2,500 meters" (Article 76(5)). The rights of the coastal state over the continental shelf are inherently the same as in the EEZ: "sovereign rights for the purpose of exploring it and exploiting its natural resources" (Article 77(1)). Yet these rights "do not affect the legal status of the superjacent waters or of the air space above those waters" (Article 78(1)). Unlike the EEZ, which must be claimed, rights over the continental shelf exist *ipso facto* and do not need to be declared (Article 77(3)).

In the history of the law of the sea, the UNCLOS sprang from longtime battles between the concepts of *mare liberum* and *mare clausum*. Sometimes it appeared that *mare liberum* had won the battle. However, the 1945 Truman Proclamation on the Continental Shelf tilted the subtle balance towards *mare clausum*, as the most powerful state in the early postwar period claimed the jurisdiction over the natural resources of the subsoil and seabed of the continental shelf extending from its traditional coastline. In the wake of this development and in light of the growing interest in offshore exploration of hydrocarbon resources, the 1958 Geneva Conventions provided legal foundations for the territorial sea and contiguous zone, the high seas, fishing and conservation of the living resources of the high seas, and the continental shelf. The concept of *mare clausum* culminated in the adoption of UNCLOS in November 1994, significantly reducing the space of high seas (Kim 2004: 17; Donaldson and Williams 2005: 137).

7.2.2   Baselines and Maritime Boundaries

As stipulated in the UNCLOS, maritime boundaries are measured from two types of baselines. UNCLOS Article 5 defines "Except where otherwise provided in this Convention, the normal baseline for measuring the breadth of the territorial sea is the low-water line along the coast as marked on large-scale charts officially recognized by the coastal State." However, states with the coastline being "deeply indented and cut into or if there is a fringe of islands along the coast in its immediate vicinity" are allowed to employ "straight baselines" as long as the drawing of straight baselines does "not depart to any appreciable extent from the general direction of the coast" (Article 7 (1) and (3)). These guidelines notwithstanding, the letter, if not the spirit, of the provisions for straight baselines is ambiguous at best. This ambiguity has in turn encouraged many states to adopt straight baselines, even where the basic conditions are not met.

On top of this, there has been a constant tension between the "equidistance" approach and the "equitable" principle in the history of the law of the sea. The UNCLOS chose to avoid any clear reference to either principle, thus providing insufficient guidance for delimiting maritime boundaries. UNCLOS Article 15 specifies that in the absence of "historic title or other special circumstances," a maritime boundary between adjacent states will follow "the median line every point of which is equidistant from the nearest points on the baselines from which the breadth of the territorial seas of each of the two states is measured." However, this equidistance principle only applies to the delimitation of the 12 nm territorial sea. The equidistance line is not referred to at all in either Articles 74 or 83, which define the delimitation of EEZ and continental shelf, respectively. Instead, they simply state that delimitation "shall be effected by agreement on the basis of international law, as referred to in Article 38 of the Statute of the International Court of Justice, in order to achieve an equitable solution." This is a significant departure from Article 6 of the 1958 Geneva Convention, which used the same terminology as UNCLOS Article 15 for maritime boundary delimitation.[2] However, the UNCLOS fails to clearly define what constitutes an "equitable solution" in determining maritime boundaries (Kim 2007: 73–6).

7.2.3   Key East Asian States' Baselines and Boundaries

7.2.3.1   South Korea

The Territorial Sea Act of 1977 adopted straight baselines as well as normal baselines for measuring the breadth of the territorial sea of South Korea. With regard to the validity of the straight baselines of South Korea, none of its neighbors have challenged them except for the area between the mainland Korea and Jeju Island, which lies between the Korea Strait and the northern East China Sea (Park 1983a: 139–42). In August 1996, the South Korean government promulgated the Exclusive Economic Zone Act in accordance with the UNCLOS. The 1996 Act provides "the EEZ boundary shall be established by agreement with the relevant States on the basis of international law." However, Article 5(2) of the Act indicates that the South Korean government would use a "median line" as a geographical limit in exercising its sovereign rights in the absence of delimitation agreed on with its neighbors. As will be discussed again in the following sections, it is not clear whether and to what extent a unilateral median line pending an ultimate delimitation of the EEZ or continental shelf boundary is consistent with the UNCLOS provision of Article 74(3), which remains silent in this regard (Kim 2004: 171–6).

---

[2]In many cases, the equidistance line has proven to be inappropriate for establishing a fair and equitable maritime boundary. In the 1969 North Sea Continental Shelf cases, the ICJ discovered that the concave nature of the coastlines of the Netherlands, Germany, and Denmark would leave Germany with only a small patch of maritime space if equidistance lines drawn from the coastlines were applied. In this and other cases, the ICJ found that strict equidistance lines might have distorting effects on delimiting maritime boundaries unless special circumstances such as history, geography, culture, and so forth were not properly considered (Donaldson and Williams 2005: 142).

7.2.3.2   Japan

The Japanese Law on the Territorial Sea of 1977 adopted the method of straight baselines along with normal baselines for measuring the breadth of the territorial sea. This practice was further extended by the 1996 Law on the Exclusive Economic Zone and the Continental Shelf of Japan amending the territorial sea and EEZ under the 1977 Act. Although the 1996 Law is nested within the UNCLOS, the provisions for straight baselines and median lines for boundary delimitation remain highly controversial. Immediately, South Korea lodged a strong protest that Japan's newly adopted straight baselines could not be applied to fishery relations based on the 1965 bilateral agreement. For South Korea, the Japanese delimitation of EEZ boundaries was not acceptable, either. The new Japanese legislation upholds a uni- laterally drawn equidistance line when there is no agreement (Kim 2004: 181–4; Kim 2007: 62–5).[3] Unmistakably, it sparked off a diplomatic spat with South Korea to which prior notice had not been given. Although the 1965 fishery agreement contained a compulsory arbitration clause, neither side asked for third-party arbitra- tion. As discussed in Chapter 4, the Japanese authorities began arresting South Korean fishing vessels by applying the newly adopted straight baselines and median lines. The dispute had thus gone from bad to worse until the two parties finally concluded a new fishery deal in late 1998.

7.2.3.3   China

Through the 1992 Law on the Territorial Sea and the Contiguous Zone, China con- firmed its position on a 12 nm territorial sea, while establishing a contiguous zone. The 1992 legislation employed the method of straight baselines for measuring the breadth of the territorial sea. However, it was not until 1996 that the Chinese gov- ernment specified its straight baselines by issuing the Declaration on the Baselines of the Territorial Sea of the People's Republic of China. The Chinese declaration sparked off protest from neighboring countries. Vietnam has strongly protested against the Chinese straight baselines around Hainan Island and the disputed Paracel Islands. South Korea challenged the legality of some of the Chinese base- lines drawn in the Yellow Sea and the East China Sea where South Korea is also a coastal state. Due to local concerns about a potentially negative impact on the

---

[3]With regard to the delimitation of EEZ, it provides "... where any part of that line (i.e., 200 nm line from the baseline) as measured from the baseline of Japan lies beyond the median line..., the median line (or the line which may be agreed upon between Japan and a foreign country as a substitute for the median lines) shall be substituted for that part of the line" (Quoted in Kim 2004: 183). An identical provision is found in Article 2 of the law on the delimitation of the continental shelf. In the meantime, the provisions of Articles 74(3) and 83 of UNCLOS place primary empha- sis on the cooperation and mutual restraints between relevant states in the absence of an agreed boundary.

Chinese fisheries industries, the Chinese government delayed the promulgation of the Act on the EEZ and the Continental Shelf until June 1998 (Kim 2004: 184–8). With regard to the delimitation, the Act provides equitable principles "…Conflicting claims regarding the exclusive economic zone and the continental shelf by the People's Republic of China and States with opposite and adjacent coasts shall be settled, on the basis of international law and in accordance with the principle of equity, by an agreement delimitating the areas so claimed" (Quoted in Kim 2004: 187).

7.2.3.4   Vietnam

In response to China's proclamation of straight baselines, Vietnam promulgated a straight baseline system, but has not yet claimed any baselines for its coast on the Gulf of Tonkin. Presumably, the Gulf of Tonkin, which is close to the Vietnamese side is considered Vietnam's historic waters, and there was thus no need for a baseline for its allegedly internal water. However, China does not recognize the Vietnamese claim of historic waters in the Gulf, requiring clear baselines and delimitation lines as well. With respect to delimitation of EEZ in the Gulf of Tonkin, the critical island is Bach Long Vi Island, which lies approximately in the middle line of the gulf. If both China and Vietnam prefer to apply the equidistance principle to the delimitation of the Gulf, then the problem of whether this island should be given a full or partial consideration requires careful management (Zou 2005: 82–3).

7.3   Reconciling Multiple Ocean Management Regimes

7.3.1   Institutional Designs and Policy Choices

As sketched out in Chapter 2, from a territorial bargaining game perspective, the process of a shift from a prevailing territorial *status quo* to a new one generally comes about with an initial impetus, which occurs through significant changes either at the international, regional, or domestic level. The initial impetus may create some type of externalities that affect the availability of goods that territory, whether land or maritime, can provide. When combined with a perception of enduring rivalry harbored by territorial disputants, the initial impetus and subsequent changes in the value of territory may result in contending territorial nationalisms, often manifested in the form of either resource nationalism (focused on tangible values) or irredentism (focused on intangible values), or both. States respond to the pressure of territorial nationalism in various ways based on their individual bargaining situations, defined by their economic interdependence, geopolitical postures, domestic power dynamics, and institutional contexts at the regional and global level.

If claimant states choose not to risk a large-scale conflict, they may enter into talks to defuse the tension. If they are committed to resolve their differences in a peaceful manner, talks will continue in a negotiations stage. During this stage, claimant states must decide whether and to what extent to offer any concessions over the contested territory. If a settlement is reached through mutually agreeable concessions, the dispute will end; otherwise, the dispute will persist in a stalemate stage and the challenger country will consider its policy options, either diplomatic or military, in another round of challenge-the-status-quo stage.

With respect to outcomes, if states decide to create a new arrangement or modify an existing one, they must decide on its characteristics including the participants, geography, scope, and degree of institutionalization. From a theoretical perspective, Aggarwal (1998) defines four types of connections among institutions: (1) nested links, whereby narrow arrangements conform to broader accords; (2) horizontal connections, whereby arrangements reflect a division of labor without any hierarchy among institutions; (3) overlapping agreements, which may create tension among participants' obligations under each arrangement; and (4) independent institutions, which govern distinct fields and thus have little or no interaction in functional terms. If institutions already exist and could potentially overlap with each other, actors contemplating institutional innovation must decide how important it is to reconcile institutions through "nested" connections that promote a division of labor. If one is developing narrow issue-area or regional-based maritime accords, and the issue's salience is low relative to broader issue-area or regional arrangements, actors will make strong efforts to nest the new institution within the broader one – even if there is no clear substantive connection among issues. An alternative mode of reconciling institutions would be to simply create "horizontal" institutions that would create an institutional division of labor. "Overlapping" arrangements can create conflict because of the potential for task competition (Aggarwal 1998).

In the area of maritime jurisdiction and boundary delimitation, unilateral approaches might have become more feasible with the incorporation of vast new areas within national control. In reality, a geographically focused regional approach has been adopted widely, albeit unevenly, and such a trend seems to accelerate as states have expanded their maritime jurisdiction for the past six decades. As Saunders (2001: 4) notes, it is likely that states are turning to the region because many ocean resources are inherently transboundary in nature, and that not all of these are functionally manageable at a global level. To be sure, the global level serves an indispensable function in creating blueprints for action, and in defining general principles, but in many cases it requires gigantic collective energy to smoothly run global multilateral institutions. Such difficulty is the most evident in the case of ambitious, multisectoral law-making efforts such as the UNCLOS. In response to this problem, the region can play an important mediating role between broadly defined global regimes and narrowly implemented national responses.

In the UNCLOS, the call for regionalization of various functions is clearly expressed in Article 123: "States bordering an enclosed or semi-enclosed sea should cooperate with each other in the exercise of their rights and in the performance of their duties under this Convention. To this end they shall endeavor, directly or through an appropriate regional organization: (a) to coordinate the management, conservation, exploration, and exploitation of the living resources of the sea; (b) to coordinate the implementation of their rights and duties with respect to the protection and preservation of the marine environment; (c) to coordinate their scientific research policies and undertake where appropriate joint programs of scientific research in the area; (d) to invite, as appropriate, other interested States or international organizations to cooperate with them in furtherance of the provisions of this article."

The creation or expansion of regional institutions itself would also be an expensive experiment requiring significant amounts of energy and time from individual member states.[4] Therefore, the relationship between the UNCLOS and regional maritime institutions would better be a nested one rather than horizontal or overlapping one.

7.3.2 Joint Development Regimes

UNCLOS Articles 74(3) and 83(3) call for neighboring states to "make every effort to enter into provisional arrangements of a practical nature and, during this transitional period, not to jeopardize or hamper the reaching of the final agreement." Joint development zone (JDZ) either of the continental shelf or for fishing purposes is a popular form of interim measure throughout the world. In many cases, JDZs are established along sections of a boundary in order to bypass disputed areas. The principles of joint development appear straightforward, but its implementation can be quite complicated, especially when the area in question has not been previously developed. There are significant variations in today's JDZs, but most fall into one of the three basic models identified by the British Institute of International and Comparative Law (BIICL) (Quoted in Groves 2005: 84):

Model I: each state retains authority to license its own nationals (or other licensees selected by the state) to operate within the joint development zone, with provision for compulsory joint ventures between these licensees;
Model II: a joint authority with licensing and regulatory powers manages development of the resources on behalf of both states;

---

[4] Saunders (2001: 10–11) enlists key elements that would make possible the development of durable regional ocean management regime: (1) pre-existing habits of cooperation and institutional development; (2) clearly defined benefits to be gained through regional cooperation; (3) the need for capacity-building, whether at the national level or through regional sharing of management capabilities; (4) the presence of external threats which may consolidate the regional position; (5) intraregional maritime disputes which threaten security generally, and which motivate a regime for conflict resolution; (6) cultural and political homogeneity; (7) the existence of significant transnational networks of epistemic communities; (8) public awareness and concern with a given issue or range of issue; and (9) levels of economic development and availability of funding source.

Model III: one state manages development of the resources on behalf of both with the other state's participation limited to revenue sharing and monitoring.[5]

Many states with conflicting maritime boundary claims have thus far chosen to defer delimitation of their maritime boundaries by forming cooperative arrangements in which they jointly develop natural resources in the disputed area. These arrangements have significantly reduced political tensions in the disputed areas, if not resolving the sovereignty question *per se* (Groves 2005: 83).[6]

Albeit rare in practice, states can still negotiate a JDZ agreement including *de facto* boundary clauses, either implicitly or explicitly, when there is a very strong *de facto* boundary held by one state and when there is an urgent need for another state to fish or explore in the area beyond the *de facto* boundary. In hindsight, this option led the Soviet Union and Japan to successfully conclude the 1977 provisional fishery agreement tacitly recognizing the presence of the *de facto* boundary but at the same time saving Japan's official position on the disputed Southern Kurile Islands (Kim 2004: 128–129).[7]

---

[5]The so-called unitization agreement is different from JDZ in that an agreed maritime boundary already exists and the unitization will only apply to the identified straddling field. A unitization agreement first defines the extent of the field in question. The parties concerned then decide the way in which exploration shall be conducted and how the revenue from the exploration shall be shared. Notably, most maritime boundary agreements since the mid-1970s have included provisions committing the signatory states to friendly consultation in the event of a new discovery of deposits straddling the existing boundary. For example, Article 7 of the 2000 Sino-Vietnamese agreement on maritime boundary delimitation states: "in case that any single geophysical structure of oil and gas or other mineral deposit should straddle the delimitation line as provided in Article 2 of this Agreement, the Parties shall, through friendly consultation, reach an agreement on the development of the structure or deposit in a most effective way as well as on equal sharing of the profits resulting from the development" (Quoted in Donaldson and Williams 2005: 146). The prevalence of these clauses in boundary treaties have set a precedent for states to cooperate over straddling deposits when a boundary has already been established. But obligations in case of no agreed boundary are less clear. Some scholars like Miyoshi (1999: 3–5) contend that neighboring countries should abstain from exploring in disputed areas until boundaries are concluded. Yet this view does not seem to have garnered unanimous support among East Asian countries.

[6]In this regard, the ICJ held "the Court cannot admit that such an agreed common fishery zone in these waters would involve a regime of common use of the land territory of the islets and rocks, since the Articles relied on refer to fishery only and not to any kind of use of land. Nor can the Court admit that such an agreed common fishery zone should necessarily have the effects of precluding the Parties from relying on subsequent acts involving a manifestation of sovereignty in respect of the islets" (Quoted in Kim 2004: 110).

[7]In March 1977, Moscow and Tokyo started negotiating the delimitation of their maritime boundaries. In the presence of the disputed islands, the negotiation process was rocky at best. The main obstacle was the definition of the geographical scope of the Soviet fishing zone as the Soviet Union insisted upon making it clear in the fishery treaty that the disputed islands belong to the Soviet Union. For Japan, however, a fishery treaty was urgently needed as its fishermen had been heavily fishing in the waters, which had been the high seas and then were claimed as part of the fishing zone by the Soviet Union in December 1976. In implementing the agreements, Japan has thus acted upon the reality that the Soviet Union exercised jurisdiction in the disputed islands, and recognized the equidistance line between the disputed islands and the Japanese islands as *de facto* maritime boundaries (Kim 2004: 129–30).

7.4   Current Practices of Delimiting Maritime Space in East Asia

7.4.1   Provisional Measures between South Korea and Japan

With the adoption of the 1958 Geneva Conventions, the special interest of the coastal state in the exploration of the resources near its coast was officially recognized. As of the early 1960s, however, such a new development was satisfactory neither to South Korea, because it was not strong enough to justify the Peace Line, nor to Japan, because it was not weak enough to completely reject South Korean claims. Notwithstanding, the Geneva Conventions were meaningful enough to suggest reference points for the peaceful settlement of bilateral disagreement at sea (Park 1983b: 62–5).

Since its inception, the delimitation of maritime zones between South Korea and Japan has revolved around two separate areas: the East China Sea with hydrocarbon potentials and the East Sea/Sea of Japan with thorny fishing and territorial issues.

In 1974, South Korea and Japan signed an agreement between the Republic of Korea and Japan concerning the establishment of boundary in the northern part of the continental shelf adjacent to the two countries. The two parties thus agreed on the delimitation in the western channel of Korea Strait/Tsushima Channel, i.e., the north of the East China Sea, and the south of the East Sea/Sea of Japan on the basis of the equidistant line. More notably, the two countries agreed on a JDZ in the northern continental shelf of the East China Sea. Without much diplomatic wordplay, they could agree on applying the equidistance principle in drawing the boundary in the East China Sea. As illustrated in Map 7.1, however, the boundary line stops at Point 35 leaving vast areas of the East Sea or Sea of Japan undelimited. Presumably, the Dokdo issue was the main reason for the incomplete delimitation (Park 1983c: 131–3; Kim 2004: 190–2).

The fishing issues in the East Sea/Sea of Japan have been much more complicated than the joint development in the East China Sea. The 1965 fishery agreement between South Korea and Japan defined 3 nm territorial waters around the Dokdo Islands, the 12 nm exclusive fishing zone, and jointly controlled waters. Yet neither the Peace Line nor the sovereignty over Dokdo was clearly mentioned in the treaty documents. Therefore, it became a strange form of establishing duplicate fishing rights over the same area and an unofficial, tacit agreement was reached to allow the Japanese fishing on occasion within the 12 nm limit of South Korea (Kajimura 1997: 466–73).

In the 1970s, however, the new global trend towards *mare clausum* outdated the practice under the 1965 fishery agreement that allowed foreign fishing immediately outside a coastal country's 12 nm exclusive fishing zone. As of 1965, few distant-water fishermen of South Korea were technically capable of operating within the coastal and offshore waters of Japan, but in the 1970s the South Korean fishing vessels became much more active in the waters off the Japanese coast with improved power and fishing equipment. The proclamation of 200 nm fishing zone

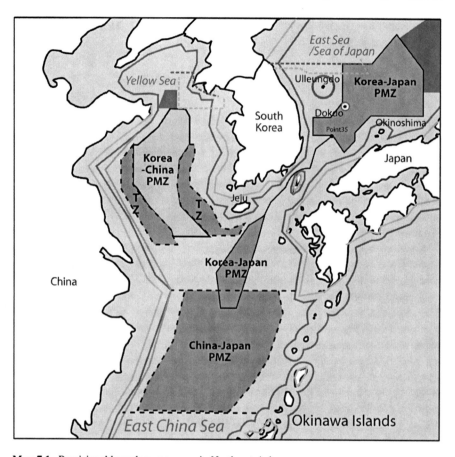

Map 7.1 Provisional boundary measures in Northeast Asia

by the Soviet Union in 1976 ignited fishery disputes between South Korea and Japan because the South Korean distant water fishing vessels that had lost their fishing ground in the Soviet zone in the Northwest Pacific began to swamp the coastal areas of Japan's Hokkaido. In response to the Soviet proclamation, Japan proclaimed its own 200 nm exclusive fishing zone in 1977. However, Japan decided not to enforce it against South Korea and China in the waters beyond the 12 nm from its coasts because of the extant fishery agreements, which allowed the freedom of fishing under the flag state jurisdiction in the area beyond 12 nm from the coasts (Park 1983a: 146–7; Kim 2007: 62).

For both parties, the stakes of maritime boundaries were high. Because the existing maritime regime in the East Sea or Sea of Japan favored it, South Korea had no intention to replace the 1965 fishery agreement. Japan's newly announced exclusive fishing zone would no longer provide South Korea with the exemptions allowed under the old maritime and fishing regime. In the 1980s, the so-called "autonomous fishing operation regulation measures" were adopted in the waters around South Korea's Jeju Island and Japan's Kyushu and Hokkaido. Yet this scheme failed to completely keep bilateral fishery disputes at by, partly because some of the South Korean fishing vessels did not faithfully comply with the autonomous fishing operation regulations. Therefore, the local fishermen and some *susanzoku* politicians in Japan took the initiative for the abolishment of the 1965 agreement and establishment of a new fishery agreement with South Korea. In August 1996, the two countries opened negotiations aimed at drawing EEZ delimitation lines, but the negotiation process was rocky at best. The Japanese officials proposed separating EEZ delimitation from the revision of the fishery agreement in order to promptly conclude the latter. Also, they suggested setting up a temporary joint fishing zone around Dokdo and shelving the sensitive problem of delimiting each other's EEZs around the islands. After hard negotiations, the two parties reached a new fishery agreement in September 1998 on the basis of modified 35 nm exclusive fishing zones of each country and establishment of joint fishing zones outside the exclusive fishing zones (Bong 2002: 101–2; Kim 2004:251–3; Kim 2007: 62–3).

Article 9 of the new fishery agreement does not clearly mention the two joint fishing zones, leaving their official names undecided. The South Korean government favors the term "middle zones" or "intermediate zone," whereas the Japanese government prefers the term "provisional zones" probably in order to highlight the fact that the related area is in dispute. An important consideration in shaping the joint fishing zones was the equitable principle. Yet a more important implication of establishing a joint fishing zone in the East Sea/Sea of Japan is whether this provisional arrangement can be considered as a precedent where Dokdo is not used as a base point for either party. An immediate answer to this question appears to favor South Korea's position. As illustrated in Map 7.1, some part of the median line between Ulleungdo and Dokdo, which could have been argued by Japan in the delimitation negotiation is located to the west of the joint fishing zone, i.e., in South Korea's EEZ, whereas the median line between Dokdo and Japan's Okinoshima is well within the joint fishing zone (Kim 2004:254–7).

In sum, the new fishery agreement substantially altered the maritime order in the East Sea/Sea of Japan. First, both governments agreed to apply the "coastal state" principle to illegal fishing within their respective EEZs. Concerning the width of the EEZ, South Korea accepted the Japanese delineation of 35 nm from the baseline of territorial waters. To resolve the problem of overlapping EEZs, both South Korea and Japan agreed to provisionally delimit their overlapping EEZs based upon the 1974 maritime boundary agreement. In particular, both sides agreed to set up two joint fishing zones: one in the East Sea/Sea of Japan around Dokdo and the other in the East China Sea near Jeju. Yet the solution to the Dokdo problem left ample room for confusion and diverse interpretations because the legal status of the joint fishing zone around Dokdo was not clearly defined.

7.4.2   *Provisional Measures between Japan and China*

In the East China Sea, China argues that the boundary with Japan should be set at the natural prolongation of the continental shelf – that is, along the outer edge of the continental shelf on the northern side of the Okinawa Trough.[8] China prefers the application of proportionality in relation to Japan because it has a much longer coastal line in the East China Sea. The substantial part of the Japanese coast in the area is formed not by the coasts of Japan proper but by the dispersed chain of Ryukyu Islands. Conversely, Japan argues that the maritime boundary should be determined along the equidistance line between the two states. In the absence of an agreement, Japan unilaterally declared an equidistance line despite China's protest. Japan considers all waters east of this unilaterally proclaimed line as part of Japanese territory.

Since the late 1960s the exploration of seabed hydrocarbon resources in the East China Sea has marked the thorny Sino–Japanese relations. In the wake of the second island flare-up in 1978, Deng Xiaoping proposed that China and Japan jointly explore the oil and gas deposits near the disputed Senkaku Islands without touching the sovereignty issue. As discussed in Chapter 5, however, national pride, yearning for energy supply, and ultranationalist public pressures all pushed both the Chinese and Japanese governments to depart from such a conciliatory approach.

Much of the recent tension in the East China Sea dispute between the two countries has revolved around Beijing's decision to explore oil and gas in the Chunxiao field, which is located only 4 km inside the Chinese side of the EEZ boundary claimed by Japan. Japan argues that the Chinese exploration will siphon off natural gas resources that might straddle the equidistance line.[9] Although lying slightly to the north of the maritime area affected by the sovereignty dispute, the Chunxiao issue is closely associated with the Senkaku dispute. Indeed, if Beijing agrees to a

---

[8]The East China Sea is relatively shallow, with water depths of less than 200 meters except in the Okinawa Trough along the Japanese coast. The seabed slopes gently from the Chinese coast until it drops abruptly into the Okinawa Trough whose depth reaches 2,716 meters at its deepest. China holds that the Okinawa Trough, which does not follow the Japanese coast closely, proves that the continental shelves of China and Japan are not connected, and that the Trough serves as the boundary between them ("East China Sea" and "Okinawa Trough" in Wikipedia, http://en.wikipedia.org/wiki/East_China_Sea; http://en.wikipedia.org/ wiki/Okinawa_Trough, Accessed 10 February 2009).

[9]Despite the absence of a mutually agreed delimitation line, China began explorations in the 1980s with a view to develop natural gas in the Xihu Trough, a region slightly under 200 nm from the nearest point of the China coast baseline. The development of the Chunxiao gas field, which is the flag ship in the group of seven under development in the Xihu Trough, began in August 2003. The Chinese National Offshore Oil Corporation (CNOOC) and the China National Petroleum Corporation (CNPC) entered into a joint venture agreement in 2003 with America's Unocal and Royal Dutch/Shell for oil development. Although these foreign companies suddenly withdrew in 2004 presumably due to Japanese protests, the Chinese went ahead with drilling on their own, beginning in early 2005 ("Xihu Trough" in Wikipedia, http://en.wikipedia.or g/wiki/Xihu_Trough, Accessed 10 February 2009).

maritime boundary over the Chunxiao area that is anything other than the natural prolongation of its continental shelf, it is likely to jeopardize its claim to the disputed islands.[10]

On top of gas and oil exploration, the fishery issue in the East China Sea has further complicated the delimitation of the maritime space. At the turn of the 1990s, Japan began to openly defend its sovereignty claim to the islands, while continuing to express a desire to separate the territorial issue from bilateral negotiations over fishery accord and EEZ delimitation. As detailed in Chapter 5, the year 1996 was a difficult period for the Sino–Japanese relationship, as the ultranationalist elements in Japanese politics undermined the previous consensus on good-neighbor diplomacy with China. In 1997, however, the two countries managed to prevent political activities from igniting antagonism on the other side. The immediate payoff was a new bilateral fishery agreement signed in November 1997. The new fishery agreement between China and Japan is a provisional agreement for regulating fishery relations on the basis of an exclusive fishing regime pending the ultimate resolution of the sovereignty issue as well as the delimitation of EEZ. As illustrated in Map 7.1, the two countries agreed on establishing a jointly controlled provisional sea zone in the East China Sea, between 30° 40′ and 27° north latitude excluding areas up to 52 nm from both countries' shores, while continuing talks to establish their respective 200 nm EEZs. The two sides also agreed to mutually set fishing quotas in their future EEZs and apply the coastal-country principle to control illegal fishing. Yet it was not until February 2000 that the two countries reached an agreement on fishing quotas and fishing conditions in each other's EEZ, and on the fishing order in the waters to the north of the provisional sea zone (Bong 2002: 60–6, 90–1; Kim 2004: 273–6; Zou 2005: 99–100).[11]

Because the provisional measure zone (PMZ) has implications for the delimitation of the EEZs, it became the toughest issue in the negotiation of the fishery agreement. At the beginning Japan proposed a median line as a provisional fishery line, but China opposed it. In early 1997, Japan proposed the establishment of a PMZ and it was accepted by China. The size of the PMZ became a focal difference between the two sides. Japan preferred a PMZ with as small a size as possible,

---

[10]On the one hand, the Chinese position seems to find support in the ICJ's ruling in the case concerning the continental shelf (Libya vs. Malta): "If there exists a fundamental discontinuity between the [continental] shelf area adjacent to one Party and the [continental] shelf area adjacent to the other," the Court said, "the boundary should lie along the general line of the fundamental discontinuity" (ICJ Judgment of 3 June 1985; Quoted in Hsiung 2005). On the other hand, the case of the maritime boundary based on a natural prolongation argument seems increasingly untenable and controversial. While boundaries based on seabed geomorphology were in vogue during the 1960s and 1970s, the ICJ has ruled out geomorphology as a relevant factor in boundary delimitation between coasts that are less than 400 nm apart. Thus, it appears that Japan may have the stronger case (Donaldson and Williams 2005: 148–9).

[11]In comparison with the 1975 Sino–Japanese fishery agreement, which applied only to the water areas along the Chinese coast and within the *de facto* Chinese EEZ, the new agreement applies to the EEZs of both sides (Zou 2005: 101).

while China preferred a larger PMZ. Japan proposed that the distance from the PMZ to each other's coast should be no less than 100 nm, but China wanted to reduce it to 24 nm. As a compromise, the distance of 52 nm was determined (Zou 2005: 104).[12]

7.4.3 Provisional Measures between South Korea and China

There is no prominent dispute over islands between South Korea and China. However, it would not be at all easy for South Korea and China to agree on each other's valid base points as there are several problematic islets and submerged features situated far from the shores. As both South Korea and China proclaimed EEZs and the continental shelf in the Yellow Sea and in the East China Sea where the width between the nearest coasts of the two countries is less than 400 nm, the need for delimitation of EEZ boundaries has arisen. In 1996, the two parties launched bilateral negotiations for delimiting their EEZs and continental shelves. And the negotiation is yet to be completed. The two countries have not narrowed down their differences over the principle of delimitation. South Korea insists upon the "equidistance-special circumstances" principles for the boundaries in the Yellow Sea, whereas China argues for the application of "equitable" principles. The South Korean government has proposed that an equidistance line should be drawn first in the Yellow Sea and then adjustment and modification should be followed where appropriate. Yet China has refused such a proposal, arguing that the first step in delimiting maritime jurisdiction is to list and balance all the relevant factors and then the next step of drawing the boundaries is to be followed (Kim 2004: 206).

From South Korea's standpoint, the Chinese argument would seem a tactic for delaying the ultimate delimitation of EEZ and continental shelf in the Yellow Sea and thus for maintaining its own nationals' sometimes predatory fishing practices as long as possible. Interestingly, China does not always stick to the equitable principles, as illustrated by its adoption of equidistance lines for delimitation in the Bay of Korea with North Korea and in the Gulf of Tonkin with Vietnam. Ironically, South Korea would still have some difficulty in consistently endorsing the equidistance principle because it might undermine its national interest in the East China Sea

---

[12]When compared to the common fishing zone in the Gulf of Tonkin agreed between China and Vietnam in 2000, the Sino–Japanese common fishing zone is unique in that: (1) the latter is provisional whereas the former is permanent; and (2) the Sino–Japanese fishery agreement chose to shelve the thorny sovereignty and EEZ issues, while the areas near the disputed islands became subject to tight and carefully coordinated common fishing zone. In contrast, the former is connected to the maritime boundary delimitation and the fishery issue was one of the critical considerations during the delimitation negotiation (Zou 2005: 104).

where it competes for maritime jurisdiction with China and Japan (Park 1983d: 114–6; Kim 2004: 208).[13]

South Korea and China agreed to bring a new fishery agreement into force in June 2001. It shares some key properties with the new South Korea–Japan fishery agreement: (1) both agreements are consistent with the exclusive fishing regime as defined by the UNCLOS; and (2) both are provisional fishery agreements pending the ultimate delimitation of EEZ and continental shelf boundaries. As shown in Map 7.1, there is no EEZ boundary drawn between South Korea and China and joint fishing zones were established under two different nomenclatures: the one is called the PMZ and the other Transitional Zones (TZ) (Kim 2004:266–7).

7.4.4 Delimitation between China and Vietnam

After the adoption of UNCLOS, the dispute over the Gulf of Tonkin became more intensive and complicated between China and Vietnam. Currently, the control of the maritime space is mainly for the control of natural resources. In particular, the fishing ground in the Gulf has traditionally been important for both countries. The first fishery agreement between China and North Vietnam was signed in 1957, leaving the fishing grounds in the middle of the Gulf open to fishermen from both countries. Due to the deterioration of the Sino–Vietnamese relationship in the 1970s, the fishery agreement was not amended until the end of 2000 (Zou 2005: 109–10).

With the normalization of their relations, the two countries began negotiating the delimitation of the Gulf of Tonkin in the early 1990s. China wanted a package deal including joint fishery management and maritime boundary delimitation of the Gulf. In the early stage of the negotiations, Vietnam refused China's proposal, urging that the boundary delimitation must be resolved first before conservation and utilization of the fisheries can be discussed at the table. It was not until 1998 that Vietnam agreed to discuss the fishery issue in connection with the boundary delimitation in the Gulf. But then Vietnam was assertive about the principle of natural prolongation to claim its continental shelf in the Gulf. Much to Vietnam's disappointment, this argument was hardly persuasive because China also shares the continental shelf in the Gulf with Vietnam. As a result, the boundary line for the EEZ and the continental shelf was drawn in light of the equidistance principle, although special circumstances existing in history and in law were considered so as to make some adjustments where appropriate (Zou 2005: 78–80, 111–2).

---

[13]South Korea's reliance on the equitable principles in the East China Sea is derived from its position that the underwater natural prolongation of the Korean peninsula extends to the Okinawa Trough which is situated about 280 nm from South Korea's southernmost island of Marado, and that Japan's natural prolongation underneath the sea ends at the Okinawa Trough which is only about 100 nm from the Japanese Ryukyu Islands. China also upholds the natural prolongation theory for the delimitation of boundaries in the East China Sea relying on the presence of the Okinawa Trough (Park 1983d: 106–13).

In December 2000, China and Vietnam officially signed the agreement on fishery cooperation – together with the agreement on maritime boundary delimitation – in the Gulf of Tonkin. The agreement applies both to parts of the EEZs and to parts of the adjacent territorial seas of the two countries in the Gulf. However, the cooperation does not affect the sovereignty of the two countries over their respective territorial seas and other rights and interests enjoyed by them in their respective EEZs. In order to avoid fishery disputes arising from small boats mistakenly entering each other's territorial waters, both parties agreed to establish a buffer zone. As illustrated in Map 7.2, the two countries have established a common fishing zone where both parties would undertake long-term fishery cooperation in the spirit of mutual benefit, and jointly take measures in relation to preservation, management, and sustainable utilization of the living and nonliving resources. This common zone is the first such zone between China and Vietnam and indicates that the fishery cooperation between the two long-time rivals has entered a new era. With respect to the area near Bach Long Vi Island, the two countries agreed to

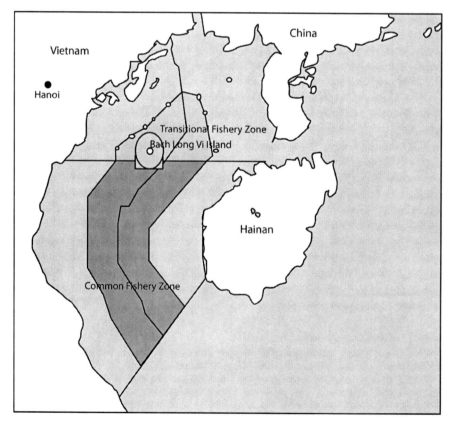

Map 7.2 Delimitation lines and joint fishing zones in the Gulf of Tonkin

establish a transitional fishing zone considering the sensitivity of the island as a base point for delimiting maritime jurisdiction (Sloreby 2002: 5; Tønnesson 2003; Zou 2005: 111–5).

7.5   The Future of Maritime Regime Building in East Asia

The delimitation of maritime space has evolved as a bilateral bargaining game in East Asia since the adoption of UNCLOS in 1982. The fishery relationship has served as a catalyst in fostering regional cooperation in maritime East Asia. It is remarkable that, at a time before the legal regime of maritime zones was established, many East Asian countries were able to reach an agreement on fishery management in the 1950s and 1960s. Yet an uncoordinated web of bilateral agreements on fisheries cooperation can adversely affect third parties and, more broadly, the region as a whole. For instance, as the joint fishing zone agreed between Japan and China overlaps with the one between South Korea and Japan in the East China Sea, there arises a need to address this problem not only at the bilateral level but also at the trilateral one. At the same time, a regional fishing organization is needed to regulate overfishing problem that has plagued the region over the past decades.

In East Asia, the delimitation of EEZ and the continental shelf boundaries is much more complicated than fisheries negotiations: (1) it is more than a twosome game; there are territorial disputes over offshore islands; (2) there are disputes on the baselines and base points; (3) the concerned coastal states do not have common positions on the applicable principles on the delimitation, whether "equitable" or "equidistant"; and (4) the relationship between the boundaries of EEZ and those of continental shelf are ambiguously defined at best.[14]

As a result, there is a growing need to move beyond bilateralism, which seems to be a dominant strategy at the moment. This does not mean that third-party arbitration is recommended. Rather, it calls for multilateral regionalism. In order for the maritime boundaries to be completed, a common understanding has to be shared across the region. The adoption of a code of conduct as seen in the South China Sea can be a good start to promote mutual understanding, while maintaining the *status quo*.[15] The next step for the littoral states would be to multilaterally negotiate the principle

---

[14] The UNCLOS provides for dispute settlement procedures in Articles 73(2) and 83(2). The identical paragraphs provide that if no agreement can be reached within a reasonable period of time, the concerned parties shall resort to the procedures provided for in Part XV (Settlement of Dispute). Yet it is unlikely that East Asian countries would ask for third-party arbitration to resolve the delimitation issues.

[15] According to UNCLOS Articles 74(3) and 83(3), states are legally obliged not to jeopardize or hamper the reaching of a final agreement on delimitation; instead, they are expected to maintain the *status quo* as to issues of final delimitation in accordance with the principle of good faith (Kim 2004: 57).

of base points and their effects, and then provisional lines and zones can be marked on the map. From there, further negotiations can be conducted for modifying the provisional lines and zones as required by special circumstances existing in history and in law. As Kim (2004) suggests, in light of designing a new regional maritime order, the intermediate option to suspend without prejudice each side's claims in favor of joint development is conceivable, albeit unlikely in the immediate future. Any settlement of the dispute would have to depend on the prior resolution of the disputants' conflicting territorial claims.

Regional maritime regime building has been successful in Europe as seen in reasonably successful and comprehensive multilateral institutions for the Baltic, the North, and the Mediterranean Sea. In sharp contrast, no comprehensive, multilateral maritime regime has been initiated in the East Asian Seas. Compared to Europe, the process of regional maritime dialogue in East Asia is indeed very young. Nevertheless, multilateral maritime regimes are on the verge of forming due to the lowering of political tension in the region, which is in turn allowing increased communication and connectivity between and among maritime officials and actors. Since the 1990s, the pace of network building, official and unofficial, formal and informal, and bilateral and minilateral, has grown substantially in the area of maritime environment (Valencia 2001: 141–2).

To conclude, there cannot be an effective maritime regime in East Asia without the full participation of all the major countries discussed in this study: China, Japan, South Korea, and Vietnam. As for China, it has successfully avoided appearing too dominant or assertive for the past decade. Yet it still has to make additional efforts to alleviate the concerns of its neighbors with respect to its irredentist ambition. As for Japan, it simply lacks the political will and credibility to serve as a leading goose in forming a multilateral maritime regime. South Korea and Vietnam (and ASEAN countries more broadly) could assume a key role, perhaps by offering a bridge role between the two regional giants. In East Asia, the perfect storm of opportunity for more effective regional cooperation in the East Asian Seas may have not arrived yet, but winds of consensus are slowly but steadily blowing that promotion of stronger regional maritime cooperation is vital to common prosperity of the region.

References

Aggarwal VK (1998) Reconciling multiple institutions: Bargaining, linkages, and nesting. In: Aggarwal VK (ed) Institutional designs for a complex world: Bargaining, linkages, and nesting. Cornell University Press, Ithaca

Andresen S (1989) The environmental North Sea regime: A successful regional approach? In: Borgese EM, Ginsburg N, Morgan JA (eds) Ocean yearbook, 8. University of Chicago Press, Chicago

Bong YD (2002) Flashpoints at sea? Legitimization strategy and East Asian island disputes. PhD Dissertation in Political Science, University of Pennsylvania, Philadelphia

Chircop A (1989) Participation in marine regionalism: An appraisal in a Mediterranean context. In: Borgese EM, Ginsburg N, Morgan JA (eds) Ocean yearbook, 8. University of Chicago Press, Chicago

Donaldson J, Williams A (2005) Understanding maritime jurisdictional disputes: The East China Sea and beyond. Journal of International Affairs 59(1):135–156

Groves H (2005) Offshore oil and gas resource: Economics, politics and the rule of law in the Nigeria-Sao Tome E Principe joint development zone. Journal of International Affairs 59(1):81–96

Haas PM (1992) Save the seas: UNEP's regional seas program and the coordination of regional pollution control efforts. In: Borgese EM, Ginsburg N, Morgan JA (eds) Ocean yearbook, 8. University of Chicago Press, Chicago

Haas PM (2000) Prospects for effective marine governance in the NW Pacific region. Marine Policy 24(4):341–348

Hsiung JC (2005) Sea power, law of the sea, and China–Japan: East China Sea resource war. A paper presented at the forum on China and the Sea Institute of Sustainable Development, Macao University of Science and Technology, Macao, October 9–11

Kajimura H (1997) The question of Takeshima/Tokdo. Korea Observer 28(3):423–475

Kim SP (2004) Maritime delimitation and interim arrangements in Northeast Asia. Martinus Nijhoff Publishers, The Hague/London/New York

Kim Y (2007) A study of international legal issues affecting maritime delimitation in the sea areas surrounding Dokdo. Korea Maritime Institute (in Korean), Seoul

Miyoshi M (1999) The joint development of offshore oil and gas in relation to maritime boundary delimitation. Maritime Briefing 2(5), International Boundaries Research Unit, Durham

Oxman BH (1994/1995) International maritime boundaries: Political, strategic, and historical considerations. University of Miami Inter-American Law Review 26(2):243–295

Park C (1983a) South Korea and the law of the sea. In: Park C (ed) East Asia and the law of the sea. Seoul National University Press, Seoul

Park C (1983b) Fishing under troubled waters: The Northeast Asia fisheries controversy. In: Park C (ed) East Asia and the law of the sea. Seoul National University Press, Seoul

Park C (1983c) Joint development of mineral resources in disputed waters: The case of Japan and South Korea in the East China Sea. In: Park C (ed) East Asia and the law of the sea. Seoul National University Press, Seoul

Park C (1983d) The Sino-Japanese-Korean sea resources controversy and the hypothesis of a 200-mile economic zone. In: Park C (ed) East Asia and the law of the sea. Seoul National University Press, Seoul

Saunders P (2001) Maritime regional cooperation: Theory and principles. In: Valencia MJ (ed) Maritime regime building: Lessons learned and their relevance for Northeast Asia. Martinus Nijhoff Publishers, The Hague/London/New York

Sloreby SJ (2002) Explaining improvement of bilateral relations: The case of Vietnam's relations with China, 1985–2001. Mater's Thesis in Political Science, University of Oslo, Oslo

Tønnesson S (2003) Sino-Vietnamese rapprochement and the South China Sea irritant. Security Dialogue 34(1):55–70

Valencia MJ (2001) Relevance of lessons learned to Northeast Asia. In: Valencia MJ (ed) Maritime regime building: Lessons learned and their relevance for Northeast Asia. Martinus Nijhoff Publishers, The Hague/London/New York

Vander Zwaag D, Johnston DM (1998) Toward the management of the Gulf of Thailand: Charting the course of cooperation. In: Johnston DM (ed) SEAPOL integrated studies of the Gulf of Thailand, vol 1. SEAPOL, Bangkok

Zou K (2005) Law of the sea in East Asia: Issues and prospects. Routledge, London and New York

Chapter 8
Conclusion and Implications

8.1 The Puzzle Revisited

Few countries in East Asia are free from territorial disputes with their neighbors. As is the case elsewhere in the world, the territories in dispute need not cover the entire soil of a particular government in order to serve as the most persistent bone of contention. Even small, barely habitable offshore islands and rocks are capable of that role, as the energy hungry littoral states in the region all eye the potentials of oil and gas deposits in their vicinities. Most of these countries also rely on these contested areas to provide a large portion of their marine diets. As has been reported widely, the danger of conflict escalation looms particularly large during a global shortage of energy and marine resources.

Aside from traditional territorial rights, islands that can sustain human habitation or economic life of their own can have EEZs and continental shelves under the UNCLOS. The problem is that the UNCLOS formulations have proliferated overlapping maritime claims around the barren islands and rocks. To make matters even more complicated, marine resources, be they oil and gas deposits or fisheries, are not subject to artificial, man-made boundaries, as exploration and exploitation of resources in one's EEZ and/or continental shelf can negatively affect their availability in the other's.

In dealing with contested territorial and maritime issues, disputant countries in East Asia have engaged in varied patterns of diplomatic and military behaviors. In some island disputes, one can find examples of the aggressive use of military force and intransigent bargaining strategies, while in other cases military inaction and accommodative diplomacy are equally evident. When and why do disputants pursue conflictual policies? Conversely, why do they at other times seek the containment, if not the resolution, of territorial disputes by shelving thorny sovereignty issues? What factors can explain patterns of dispute escalation and de-escalation in a consistent and systematic fashion? What sort of regional mechanism can be devised to manage and regulate the maritime boundaries and maritime zones, as well as the living and nonliving resources therein? These are the critical questions that motivated my efforts at theory building and empirical testing in this book.

M.G. Koo, *Island Disputes and Maritime Regime Building in East Asia,*
The Political Economy of the Asia Pacific,
DOI 10.1007/978-0-387-89670-0_8, © Springer Science+Business Media, LLC 2009

I explored the three most prominent island disputes, all of which clearly illustrate a puzzling pattern of continuity and mutual restraint: the Dokdo dispute between South Korea and Japan; the Senkaku dispute between Japan and China; and the Paracel and Spratly dispute between China and Vietnam. From the beginning, the fishery issues in the East Sea/Sea of Japan have served as a surrogate battlefield for the Dokdo dispute. The tangible value of the numerous islands in the East and South China Sea had been limited to fishing recourses until high potentials of oil and gas deposits were discovered at the end of the 1960s. The global trend to adopt the UNCLOS further heightened the tangible value of these barren islands as well as the critical sea-lanes, territorial seas, EEZs, and continental shelves in the semi-enclosed seas.

More importantly, material concerns are hardly the sole drivers of these island disputes, as contested areas raise questions of national identity and pride. Despite the frequent resort to the past to justify contemporary claims to the disputed islands, these disputes originated from the colonial times in the late nineteenth and early twentieth centuries, often exacerbated by the arbitrary map-making of colonial powers and exploited by post-colonial nationalists. The centrality of territory in national identity formation suggests that conflicts over territory should be highly salient for the victims of Western and Japanese colonialism, basically non-negotiable, and much more likely to result in the use of force.

In East Asia, the delimitation of maritime space has evolved as a bilateral bargaining game. Yet there is a growing need to move beyond bilateralism because the nature and scope of maritime issues are increasingly becoming multilateral, rather than purely bilateral. In order for the maritime boundaries in the region to be completed, a common understanding has to be shared across the region. Although the process of regional maritime dialogue in East Asia is very young, multilateral maritime regimes are on the verge of forming in the region due to the lowering of political tension, which is in turn allowing increased communication and connectivity between and among maritime officials and various other actors.

In what follows, I summarize the major findings of my quantitative and qualitative studies, and then draw implications of these findings for future research on territorial and maritime disputes in East Asia. I conclude by presenting key policy implications.

8.2 Summary of the Findings

A number of existing studies on the aforementioned island disputes tend to treat each dispute as a discrete and unique event. They have examined individual disputes in depth, but rarely compare one dispute to the others or to the broader international relations literature on territorial disputes. Hence, I used a territorial bargaining game framework to analyze the various stages of initiation, challenge the status-quo, military escalation, and de-escalation of each dispute in a more systematic and comparative manner.

I started from an assumption that territory involves mixed motive games, which can be characterized as having elements of partnership, competition, and conflict. At the very micro level, a person feels uncomfortable when other people are in his/

her personal space. The notion of human territoriality, or personal space, refers to a type of human nature to affect, influence, and control access to people and resources by delimiting and asserting control over a defined space. The same is true of interstate relations. Human territoriality makes states highly sensitive to any threat to their physical and/or symbolic space, thereby giving rise to conflict over the control of territory, be it a large land mass or a small offshore island. I approached this issue both quantitatively and qualitatively.

In Chapter 3, I examined each of the three island disputes, using regression techniques. Quantitative evidence of the pacific benefits of economic interdependence is mixed. The coefficients relating the trade dependence score of a target country to the intensity and the likelihood of dispute are statistically significant, indicating that economic interdependence measured in terms of trade dependence scores has a major explanatory effect on the process of the three island disputes. Aside from the lagged dependent variable, the other control variables vary considerably in their magnitudes and statistical significance, but there is evidence that both joint democracy and joint accession to the UNCLOS have a statistically significant influence on the likelihood of dispute occurrence.

Yet, as with any kind of regression analysis with a relatively small N, these statistical findings require a cautionary interpretation. Also, given the complexity surrounding these island disputes, there remain stories to be uncovered in a qualitative manner. Hence, I turned to in-depth, qualitative analyses in Chapters 4–6. Table 8.1 summarizes how the key components of a territorial bargaining game have affected the outcomes in each island dispute.

8.2.1   Initial Impetus

A territorial bargaining game approach begins by identifying an initial impetus – either international or domestic – for a territorial change from the prevailing *status quo* over territorial issues. I found that the sovereignty problems of the three islands arose, directly and indirectly, as a consequence of U.S. Cold War policy in East Asia, which was codified in the San Francisco Peace Treaty of 1951, as leaving the location of sovereignty over these islands under-defined and contested. Also, all the three island disputes have revolved around the introduction of UNCLOS, the discussion of which began in the late 1950s and came into force in 1994. Finally, ultranationalist activities – especially in Japan and China – have provided an additional boost to the initial impetuses for the island disputes.

8.2.2   Value of Territory

The initial impetuses often create some types of externalities that affect the value of the territory. Knowledge of the nature of the territory concerned gives us a first cut into understanding the type of problems that the actors face and their incentives.

Table 8.1 Summary of the findings

	Initial impetus	Types of goods	Geopolitical context	Domestic politics	Influence of individual bargaining situations on the dispute containment[a] Economic interdependence
Dokdo	First round (1952–65): SF Peace Treaty; Rhee Line Second (1977–78) and third (1996–98) rounds: UNCLOS Fourth round (2004–06): postage stamps; "Takeshima Day"; maritime survey	Territorial rights: private goods (intangible; non-negotiable; indivisible) Maritime rights (e.g., fisheries; oil and gas): private / CPRs (tangible; negotiable; divisible)	Positive: balancing role of the U.S.; common security threat from North Korea (and possibly China) Negative: quasi-alliance between South Korea and Japan; fluctuating U.S. defense commitment	Positive: strong political regime Negative: weak political regime; ultranationalist activities; democratization of South Korea	Rapid expansion after the 1965 normalization treaty Positive: South Korea's trade dependence on Japan
Senkakus	First round (1968–71): ECAFE report; Okinawa Reversion Agreement Second round (1978): first lighthouse; PFT negotiations Third round (1990–91): authorization of the first lighthouse Fourth round (1996–97): second lighthouse; UNCLOS Fifth round (2004–06): landing accident; oil and gas exploration		Positive: strategic triangle of the U.S.–China–Japan during the Cold War period Negative: shifting regional balance of capabilities in the post-Cold War period	Positive: strong political regime Negative: weak political regime; ultranationalist activities (e.g., *Nihon Seinensha* and the *Protect the Diaoyutai Movement*)	Rapid expansion after the 1978 peace treaty Positive: China's trade dependence on Japan (qualitative evidence only) Negative: Japan's trade dependence on China "Cold Politics and Hot Economics"

| Paracels and Spratlys | First round (1974): South Vietnam's administrative decision; U.S. withdrawal Second round (1978–79): unification of Vietnam; Sino-Vietnam rift Third round (1987–88): UNESCO IOC decision on the Fiery Cross Reef installation; imminent collapse of the Soviet Union Mutual restraints after the 1991 Normalization | Positive: Cold War bipolarity Negative: U.S. withdrawal from Indochina; the post-Cold War multipolarity | Positive: strong political regime Negative: weak political regime; China's maritimists and irredentists | Expansion after the 1991 normalization treaty Positive: China's trade dependence on Vietnam; Vietnam's trade dependence on China (qualitative evidence only) |

[a]Among the bargaining game components, IGO membership was found to have no clear impact on the dispute processes of the three island disputes

All the disputed islands in East Asia have both tangible and intangible values. In theory, a wide range of possible options has been proposed to jointly develop the tangible, material resources in disputed areas. Yet, in practice, intangible symbolic attachment of territory to national identity and pride makes those island disputes all the more intractable and difficult to resolve.

South Korea's claim to Dokdo has emotional content far beyond material significance, because giving way on the island issue to Japan would be considered as compromising the sovereignty over the whole peninsula again. For Japan, "Takeshima" may lack the same degree of strategic and economic values and emotional appeal as the other two territorial disputes that Japan has – namely the Northern Territories and the Senkaku Islands. Nevertheless, the legal, political, economic, and symbolic issues surrounding the East Sea/Sea of Japan are far from trivial, because any concessions made to South Korea could possibly jeopardize Japan's claims to the other two islands..

In a similar vein, the process of the Senkaku and the Paracel and Spratly disputes are closely related to the rise of territorial nationalism following the end of ideology. With the collapse of Communism in particular and ideology in general, nationalism seems to have returned with gusto. To the Chinese, the disputes over "Diaoyutai" and the Paracels and Spratlys all represent persistent attempts by their regional nemeses – Japan and Vietnam, respectively – to keep from the Chinese what had been stolen from China during half a century of Western and Japanese invasion and occupation. Conversely, for both Japan and Vietnam, their claims to the disputed islands have emotional contents, reflecting their long-time concerns that giving way on the sovereignty over the disputed islands to China would enhance Chinese irredentism at the expense of Japanese and Vietnamese national interests.

In sum, the examination of the value of the territory involved in these island disputes indicates that they are most likely to continue to be contested in the foreseeable future because the disputed areas have not only tangible but also intangible values. Yet the analysis of the value of territory alone falls short of uncovering the causal links behind the dual nature of continuity and mutual restraint in these island disputes. Hence, I turned to individual bargaining situations to investigate the various ways in which countries respond to initial impetuses and subsequent changes in the value of territory.

8.2.3 Individual Bargaining Situation

Countries' individual bargaining situations consist of their: (1) geopolitical postures; (2) domestic power dynamics; (3) regional and global context of intergovernmental organizations; and (4) complex economic interdependence. Consistent with conventional wisdom, I discovered that the combination of resource competition, fluid geopolitics, and unstable domestic power dynamics has regularly brought about the initiation and escalation of island disputes. Yet, I found little evidence that supports the mitigating influence of intergovernmental organizations on these island disputes. Finally, and most importantly, I found that the pacific influence of economic interdependence has repeatedly prevented the sovereignty disputes from escalating into a full-scale diplomatic and/or military crisis.

8.2.3.1   Geopolitical Context

The three island disputes have involved the U.S. as an architect of the post war international system and as a hegemonic broker between the territorial disputants. On the one hand, the U.S. has officially remained neutral on sovereignty matters, but its hegemonic position has ensured that enduring tensions exist within certain confines. On the other hand, the balance-of-power politics involving the U.S. and the Soviet Union from the Cold War era fluctuated widely over time, thereby exacerbating local conflicts occasionally, if not frequently. I found that East Asian countries are more likely to initiate and escalate territorial disputes when the U.S. security commitment to the region declines.

First, the common threat from North Korea (and a rising China) has consolidated the security triangle among the U.S., South Korea, and Japan. Yet, the occurrence of all the four rounds of the Dokdo dispute has coincided with the rift in the security triangle. Particularly in the post-Cold War and post-9-11 era, the rapidly shifting security environment has made the three allies scramble in search of an alternative security mechanism. The role of the U.S. as an ultimate pacifier is increasingly eroding, although a complete U.S. withdrawal from the region is highly unlikely in the foreseeable future.

Second, at the height of the Cold War, the U.S., China, and Japan formed a *de facto* strategic alliance against the Soviet Union, and the Senkaku island issue could be contained for the sake of common security interests. Yet, the geopolitical vacuum left by the Soviet-U.S. *détente* in the 1970s was exploited by regional powers to advance their own interests, leading to the two rounds of Senkaku clashes in the same decade. In the post-Cold War era, the biggest source of uncertainty and change in regional balance of power has been China. The emerging perception of a China threat makes Japan as well as the U.S. scramble to balance against the possible dangers. To be sure, terms in favor of Japanese (and American) strategic interests alone are not acceptable to China. Therefore, the Senkaku incident has the potential to inflict substantial damage not only on Sino-Japanese relations, but also on the fragile balance of power in East Asia.

Finally, the advent of territorial disputes between China and Vietnam has coincided with the shift in the strategic landscape in Indochina. The 1974 Sino-Vietnamese battle for the Paracel Islands was preceded by the geopolitical vacuum in Indochina left by the Sino-American rapprochement, and the subsequent U.S. decision to withdraw from Vietnam. After the Vietnamese unification, deepening ties between Hanoi and Moscow and their hegemonic ambition in Indochina greatly frustrated China, thereby motivating it to initiate and escalate the 1978 island dispute and the 1979 Sino-Vietnamese border war. In the wake of the collapse of the

Soviet bloc, China once again made a preemptive move to forcefully occupy several reefs in the Spratly chain in 1988, clearly demonstrating its growing assertiveness and ambition in the South China Sea.

8.2.3.2 Domestic Power Dynamics

While geopolitical factors set the outer boundary conditions for the process of a territorial dispute, it is domestic power dynamics that translate the initial impetuses for a territorial change into an actual conflict. In general, the state elites' desire to remain in office allows domestic coalitions and electoral politics to influence their decisions on conflict behavior. In contemporary East Asia, the twin challenges of responding to nationalist sentiments and maintaining political legitimacy are major constraining factors that often grow more important as liberalization takes greater hold across the region.

In the case of the Dokdo dispute, the combination of competitive domestic politics and enduring rivalry between South Korea and Japan has repeatedly undermined their bilateral relations. To be sure, a return to the territorial *status quo* that has left the sovereignty issue of the Dokdo Islands undefined is satisfactory neither to South Korean nor to Japanese nationalisms. Conservative politicians and nationalist groups on both sides have exerted considerable pressures on their respective governments for more assertive territorial policies. With the arrival of the Internet and information technology, it is becoming increasingly easier for them to mobilize the public against foreign countries and/or their own governments, as demonstrated by the cyber wars conducted during the 2004–05 flare-up. The Dokdo dispute might not immediately trigger any major conflicts between South Korea and Japan. Yet, the accumulation of grievances and underlying nationalist sentiments could escalate minor quarrels, such as those involving fishing rights near the islands, into major conflicts, particularly when the political leaders on either side experience legitimacy deficits.

In a similar vein, I found that the Senkaku dispute is more likely to be initiated and escalated when the overall regime strength of either the Chinese or the Japanese government is weak. Most notably, the activities of ultranationalist groups have been fundamental to the way in which the Senkaku dispute has manifested itself. In Japan, these groups – such as the *Seirankai* in the 1970s and 1980s and the *Nihon Seinensha* since the 1990s – have been central in driving the island dispute beyond political leaders' control. Beijing has also used nationalist activities – such as the *Protect the Diaoyutai Movement* – to mobilize political support for their regime, while attempting to avoid the political backfire of those nationalist activities. The ultranationalist activities in Japan and China alike may be a minor political force, but they strongly indicate the rise of a more assertive nationalism following the end of ideology.

Finally, there is evidence that the weaker the ruling executives are, the more likely either China or Vietnam is to initiate and escalate the Paracel and/or Spratly dispute. All the three rounds of the Sino-Vietnamese clash in the South China Sea took place when the leadership in Saigon (before 1975), Hanoi (after 1975), and/or Beijing underwent a legitimacy crisis in some way .

8.2.3.3 Intergovernmental Organizations

I found that intergovernmental organizations have had little impact on the process of the Dokdo and the Senkaku disputes. This may not be surprising given the traditional organization gap in Northeast Asia. By contrast, the findings of my qualitative analysis indicate that the stabilizing role of ASEAN is becoming increasingly salient in the South China Sea island disputes. The main reason why China has, seemingly, stopped pursuing its sovereignty claims more aggressively in the South China Sea is probably that it wishes to avoid a head-on conflict with ASEAN countries as a whole, when its eyes are fixed on bigger goals, such as continued economic growth, access to the world's major export markets, and reunification with Taiwan.

8.2.3.4 Economic Interdependence

Consistent with a liberal claim that economic interdependence will foster peaceful relations by giving states an economic incentive to avoid costly disputes, I found that increasing economic interaction between territorial disputants has played a role in containing, if not resolving, the intractable island disputes in East Asia. The point is not that economic ties can prevent costly disputes for sure, but that, variations in these economic ties have had an observable impact on the de-escalation of these island disputes.

There is compelling evidence that greater common economic interests have moved the Dokdo and the Senkaku disputes to the periphery of overall diplomatic relationships since South Korea–Japan and Japan–China began to forge close economic ties in the 1960s and 1970s. In spite of the fact that the island disputes remain unresolved, all the disputant governments – particularly the foreign policy experts therein – have found it a convenient strategy to continually shelve final resolution attempts in favor of getting on with more pressing economic affairs. Certainly the relationship between territorial dispute and economic interdependence could be explosive, if the latter takes on highly asymmetric characteristics. Nevertheless, as long as profitable economic opportunities continue, it can be concluded that a system of control and restraint has become a salient feature of the disputes over the Dokdo and the Senkaku Islands.

During the Cold War period, a series of violent clashes between China and Vietnam, over the Paracel and Spratly Islands may not be surprising, given that the two countries had lacked substantial economic ties. Unlike its relatively mild responses to Japan with respect to the Senkaku dispute, China had responded aggressively to Vietnam's territorial claims to the Paracel and the Spratly Islands. Yet, more recently, lucrative trade and investment opportunities in Vietnam, as well as in other Southeast Asian countries, began to mitigate China's assertiveness in the South China Sea.

8.3   Theoretical and Policy Implications

The major theme running throughout this book was a concern for the continuity and mutual restraint that has featured in the island disputes in East Asia. The analysis of this theme bears directly upon the peace and stability in the region. The lessons in this book run the gamut from empirical findings about the processes of East Asian island disputes to theoretical and policy implications for the future study of territorial disputes on the one hand and maritime regime building on the other.

From a realist perspective, the struggle over territory gives rise to a struggle for power rather than *vice versa*. Hence, the struggle for power with its danger of conflict escalation, never disappears as long as human tendency for territoriality persists. Conversely, the non-realist territorial explanation of interstate conflict maintains that states that settle their differences over territory can be expected to have peaceful relations even if other salient nonterritorial disputes arise. Yet, neither realist nor non-realist accounts can simultaneously capture the dual aspect of continuity and mutual restraint frequently observed in the island disputes in East Asia.

Set against this puzzling backdrop, the starting point of my theory building is to think broadly about the causal pathways that are associated with the presence or absence of diplomatic/military conflict between states, and the continued stalemate or settlement of territorial disputes. In contrast to conventional explanations that do not identify specific outcomes for measurement, my quantitative approach offers a more fine-tuned operationalization of the varying degrees of the island disputes as well as a plausible, if not the only possible, prediction about the likelihood of dispute occurrence and escalation. In addition, my qualitative approach allowed me to examine East Asia's prominent island disputes across time and space, thereby producing more generalizable knowledge.

The arguments in this book are ingrained in international relations theory as well as in more general literature on territorial disputes. Many of the components of my territorial bargaining game are not novel. Yet, the innovation here is that an adept combination of key analytical components has allowed me to consider varying effects of causal factors on the different stages of a territorial dispute process. Also, economic interdependence was a new, important addition to a bargaining game approach.

Figure 8.1 illustrates the components and the process of a territorial bargaining game that pertain to the evolution of territorial disputes over time, along with some of the principal pathways leading to different diplomatic and military outcomes. This general analytical framework is broad enough to incorporate key factors that affect territorial disputes, but narrow enough in focus to generate reasonable explanations and useful predictions on the future direction of territorial disputes in East Asia.

As noted above, the disputed islands in East Asia all contain competitive elements, which have symbolic, political, economic, historical, and other kinds of significance that make them difficult for states to give up. Given the growing economic and strategic value of the disputed islands, East Asian countries would likely pursue maximal territorial demands, backed by the threat or use of force.

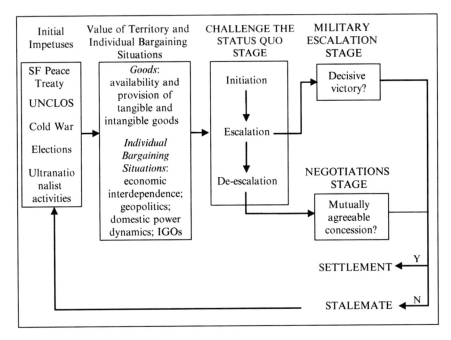

Fig. 8.1 A bargaining game approach to territorial disputes

Then, what are the challenges for political leaders in East Asia when managing island and maritime disputes in the future?

As shown in Chapter 7, East Asian maritime issues have become multilateral, rather than purely bilateral, issues, possibly making bilateral solutions contradictory and conflicting with one another. Within the theaters of existing regional forums such as the ASEAN Regional Forum, APEC, and the Council for Security Cooperation in the Asia-Pacific, there have been some formal and informal, bilateral and multilateral dialogues to contain and/or resolve the territorial and maritime issues. In order for the maritime boundaries in the region to be completed, a common understanding has to be shared across the region. The adoption of a code of conduct as seen in the South China Sea can be a good start. The next step for the littoral states would be to multilaterally negotiate the principle of base points and delimitation lines. From there, further negotiations can be conducted to modify the provisional lines and zones as required by special circumstances. Despite the persistent weakness of regional forums in East Asia, positive and dynamic processes have been emerging, though with different degrees, across the region.

Not all is grim in the East Asian Seas. As strongly shown in this book, economic interdependence can mitigate the aggravating circumstances caused by contending territorial nationalisms and/or fluid geopolitics. For East Asian countries, the question now is how they institutionalize their deepening and widening economic interdependence to get more mileage out of it. The burgeoning efforts to form FTAs amongst themselves generate positive expectations in this regard. Most notably, at the heart of this newfound rush towards FTAs is the new dynamics of rivalry between Japan and China.

In view of the rising pressure of territorial nationalism and fluid geopolitics in the post-Cold War and post-9-11 era, even the mere containment of the island disputes in East Asia requires the skillful diplomacy and tireless efforts of political leaders. The best strategy to hedge against potentially disruptive behaviors is to engage more with each other by facilitating greater economic and maritime interdependence. The path to deeper and wider economic and maritime interdependence in East Asia is likely to be a bumpy one, but establishing regional mechanisms to manage and regulate economic and maritime activities may help to smooth it.

Index

LaVergne, TN USA
11 September 2009
157653LV00001B/46/P